# THE SECRET LIFE OF BIKERS

# THE SECRET LIFE OF BIKERS

### Jerry Langton

HarperCollinsPublishersLtd

HarperCollins Publishers Ltd
Bay Adelaide Centre, East Tower
22 Adelaide Street West, 41st Floor
Toronto, Ontario, Canada
M5H 4E3

*www.harpercollins.ca*

Library and Archives Canada Cataloguing in Publication
information is available upon request.

ISBN 978-1-44345-466-7

Printed and bound in the United States

LSC/H 9 8 7 6 5 4 3 2

*To my own little gang: T, D and H*

# Contents

# States and Provinces Claimed

### Hells Angels

States and provinces with Hells Angels chapters. Note the club's dominance in Canada and its absence in states controlled by the Bandidos.

### Sons of Silence

The Sons of Silence began in Colorado and expanded primarily eastward. They are considered to be among the more violent clubs, a reputation many club members relish.

### Bandidos

The Bandidos expanded quickly from Texas to other states and throughout the world. After a disastrous foray into Canada, and friction from chapters in Europe, the American Bandidos have distanced themselves from the chapters in other countries.

### Pagan's

The Pagan's are limited in their distribution but are locally very powerful. Sworn enemies of the Hells Angels, they are present in many of the same East Coast states.

**Vagos**

The Vagos started in southern California and—much to the annoyance of the Hells Angels—expanded quickly.

**Mongols**

The Mongols also started in southern California and have often fought with the Hells Angels in their expansion to other states.

**Outlaws**

The Outlaws are especially powerful in the Great Lakes region and Florida.

**Bacchus**

Bacchus is not well known outside of eastern Canada, but they have seen great success expanding in recent years.

# Introduction

**N**either of us got exactly what we wanted. I was interviewing a prominent biker over pizza when he complained about the sources I used for my books.

"Cops, lawyers and snitches," he spat out, his disgust with those groups clearly evident. "Cops, lawyers and snitches," his friend, the guy who'd set up our meeting, repeated with a sigh.

I use sources a lot more diverse than that, but I got his point.

I hadn't been too surprised when I received the call that this big-time biker wanted to meet with me. Since I had written a couple of books about bikers that were successful and surprisingly well received by the biker community itself, I had been getting repeated calls, texts, emails and even letters from people in and around motorcycle clubs, either wanting me to tell their story or hoping to contribute something to any new book ideas I might have. Word got around quickly. As one Hells Angel told me, "We don't mind you because you don't make shit up, and you don't want to be one of us."

During the interview over pizza, I couldn't stop thinking about the dilemma of trying to write the truth about a society that is sworn to secrecy and more than a touch paranoid these days.

The biker had just been through the legal system—a process that cost him months behind bars and hundreds of thousands of dollars in bail and seized property—and was now a free man. He hadn't been acquitted. The primary witness against him suddenly had a change of heart. He told the judge that after all the years that had passed, he no longer trusted his memory to be accurate enough for court. The prosecutors withdrew the charges and the biker walked. The biker's lawyer made a point of asking the recalcitrant witness if he had been intimidated in any way. He replied that he had not.

And the biker was free of the club too. Of the many bikers from his club arrested in the raid, several pleaded guilty to lesser charges in exchange for shorter sentences. That disgusted the biker I was interviewing, who pointed out that all the bikers he knew who hadn't been arrested or had been freed "were partying" and "hadn't contributed a dime" to his struggle.

He quit the club, wanted to talk and wanted my help writing a book, the story of his life. He even had a title picked out: "Last Man Standing."

But as we talked, I became less and less intrigued by his offer. In his vision of his biker career, cops, lawyers and snitches were the bad guys. So were judges, corrections officers, the media and pretty much anyone who wasn't a biker.

The bikers, least of all him, would not be accused of any wrongdoing or law-breaking whatsoever in the book.

"What about the homicide you did time for?"

"Self-defense."

"What about the time bullets from your car shot up a bus with two rival bikers on it?"

"Mistaken identity."

"How about all the cocaine you are alleged to have sold?"

"They never caught me with any."

He did, however, admit to beating many, many people up and proudly pointed out he'd never been charged in connection with any of those assaults. He also acknowledged that he knew of several women who had been sexually assaulted, even gang raped, but told me he'd never say who did what to whom.

While he no doubt had some great stories to tell, I had to turn him down. The book he wanted would be nothing but biker propaganda and, I believe, a totally inaccurate picture of what had actually happened.

But that mantra of "cops, lawyers and snitches" stuck with me. I wanted to be able to tell people the truth about outlaw motorcycle club life in an accurate and even-handed way. I wanted to get a bigger, more in-depth look at their lives, including what they would rather the public did not know, so I cast a wider net, speaking to more people, including bikers themselves.

After the books came magazine and newspaper articles, then TV and radio appearances. Not only did I need to know more about the biker world to speak with any authority, but the exposure meant that more and more bikers sought me out to talk. Over the last decade, I've talked to plenty of bikers, but it's almost always the same thing. They tell me they don't break any laws and then give me that of-course-I-really-do smirk.

But they do tell me things that shed more light on their lives, and I have also rounded up several ex-bikers—only one of whom would accurately be considered a snitch—to tell me even more. They include Dave, a Hells Angels sergeant-at-arms who turned informant and now lives under a new identity; Duane, a former Hells Angels full-patch member who left the club after a dispute and now lives in a state without any Hells Angels;

Randy, a former Outlaw full patch who quit the club after a series of arrests; Mitch, a former Bandidos prospect who left the club after it cost him his wife and job; Pete, a Hells Angels prospect whom the club expelled for being soft; Sean, who had been with an independent club but left when it patched over to the Hells Angels; and Frankie, who had been a prospect with the Outlaws but quit because he felt "abused" by the full-patch members.

I have also included in this book quotes and anecdotes from memoirs of and interviews with other bikers, like Sonny Barger, Chuck Zito, George Christie, Pat Matter, Anthony Menginie, Edward Winterhalder and others, although the books themselves are frequently self-serving, with glaring omissions.

And finally, I have included the views of law enforcement officers who have gone undercover and successfully passed themselves off as bikers. They seek me out too.

*The Secret Life of Bikers* gives readers a way to understand what it's like to belong to an outlaw motorcycle club, and what it's like to have a clubhouse, a biker bar or the bikers themselves in your community. It is, I'm confident to say, a more accurate picture than any single biker would be willing to paint.

# CHAPTER 1

# Clubs, Gangs and the Difference

A sudden and severe winter storm had dumped more than a foot of snow on Toronto in a matter of minutes. Cars and trucks were sliding dangerously all over the place, but I got into my trusty old Volkswagen and headed out to the suburbs.

I had to get to the CTV studios far away on the northeastern edge of town. It was January 2007, and because my first book, *Fallen Angel*, had turned out to be a surprise bestseller, I had been invited to be part of a panel of experts discussing how outlaw motorcycle gangs had infiltrated the tow truck industry in the Toronto area. The show was called *Goldhawk Live*. It was hosted by veteran print and TV journalist Dale Goldhawk and consisted of short interviews followed by questions from callers. It's normally a forty-five-minute drive to the studio, but, since the roads were so bad, I gave myself twice that.

The panel was supposed to consist of me, a cop I knew who specialized in biker-related crime and a guy representing the local tow-truck-industry association. But neither of the other guests showed up in time. That meant the panel was just me.

It was my first TV appearance to promote the book, so I was nervous to begin with. But as the show started rolling, and with Goldhawk's patience, I fell into a pretty confident rhythm. So, when a caller demanded that I "stop calling them gangs, they're clubs," I was prepared.

I could tell from experience that he was almost certainly a biker. The way he ordered me to do what he wanted without explanation, defending that particular concept about which name could be used to describe biker clubs, rang stunningly familiar.

Then he continued: "I should know, I was in one."

"Which one?" I asked.

"Satan's Choice, Kitchener."

"That was a gang."

LET'S GET ALL the disclaimers out of the way right from the start; I don't want there to be any confusion. This book is not about motorcyclists or even motorcycle clubs, but motorcycle gangs. All motorcycle clubs say that they exist for members to ride their bikes, hang out with friends and enjoy camaraderie. If doing that was a crime, you'd have to reserve a cell for me too.

But some clubs are gangs. In fact, some of them are at the highest levels of organized crime in the communities where they operate. They represent a minority of motorcyclists and even motorcycle clubs, and they are indeed gangs.

So, what's the difference between a club and a gang? Well, the U.S. Department of Justice will be more than happy to tell you. To be defined as a gang, they say, an organization has to fulfill two basic requirements.

The first is that the group has to have a leadership structure, identifying clothes or tattoos, and a set of rituals that members must follow. Of course, that describes organizations as divergent as the Boy Scouts and La Cosa Nostra, and the former is definitely not a gang.

It's actually the second requirement that really defines a gang. Either the majority of the organization's membership must be involved in crime, or some element of the group—more than a single person—must be serially involved in crime.

Canada's Criminal Code has similar wording and points out that to be defined as a criminal organization, a group of three or more people "has as one of its main purposes or main activities the facilitation or commission of one or more serious offences, that, if committed, would likely result in the direct or indirect receipt of a material benefit, including a financial benefit, by the group or by any one of the persons who constitute the group." So, even if motorcycle riding is a group's primary activity, if trafficking is as well, then the group members are a gang.

So, the Kitchener chapter of Satan's Choice, several members of which were convicted of homicide, assault, sexual assault, drug trafficking, drug manufacturing, weapons offenses and other crimes over its years of existence, was—by any definition—a gang. The Kitchener chapter of the Hells Angels still exists and has not been prosecuted as a criminal organization as a unit, and those members and prospects convicted of major crimes are no longer with the club.

Bikers are fond of saying that motorcycle clubs are not street gangs—you can even buy a bumper sticker online that says exactly that—and they are right, but it's only the word "street" that makes that statement true. Saying that biker clubs are not gangs because they are not street gangs is like saying that station wagons are not cars because they are not convertibles, and convertibles are cars.

The fact is that many of them have historically operated as crime organizations, although they always deny it.
Many bikers have been convicted of murder, drug trafficking,
weapons offenses or other various charges, often in conspiracy
with fellow club members. In 2012, law enforcement officers
recorded the president and former president of the Rock Hill,
South Carolina, chapter of the Hells Angels discussing the fact
that any member, prospect, hangaround or even associate of
the club engaged in illegal activity was expected to report that
activity and pay the club a portion of their proceeds or face
violent punishment. And they were hardly the first bikers to be
recorded saying something to that effect. The bikers and people
within their orbit I have spoken to tell me that that sort of
behavior is commonplace, and like to add that they're surprised
I didn't already know that.

The bikers' claim that they are not gangs relies on the concept
of plausible deniability. Despite mountains of evidence that they
operate as gangs and numerous convictions of bikers, often in
the company of their "brothers," they maintain that they are not
gang members simply because law enforcement has failed to convict every single one of them. Unconvicted bikers point to their
convicted brothers and say that they were acting on their own—
even if the bikers behind bars admit in surreptitious recordings
that they were indeed acting on behalf of the club.

It stretches credulity, but it works.

For decades, the largely agreed-upon history of biker gangs was
that, after World War II, some combat veterans found that they no
longer fit into mainstream society, which lacked the intense adrena-
line highs and feeling of brotherhood they had experienced in wartime. So they began to look for thrills on customized motorcycles,
stopped adhering to society's rules and lived as a breed apart.

While largely accepted as truth, the story is dubious, if not outright wrong. Biker gangs actually predate World War II and certainly American involvement in it. The Outlaws, then known as the McCook Outlaws, were formed in 1935, more than six full years before the attack on Pearl Harbor.

And, although some gangs were founded by ex-military, like the Bandidos in 1966, most were not. The Hells Angels, who are generally considered the definitive motorcycle gang, are widely reputed to have been formed by combat veterans but almost certainly were not. The club was formed in a garage in Fontana, California, in 1948 when several small clubs agreed to merge.

The frequently repeated story is that the original Hells Angels were elite paratroopers who had served in World War II and that one of them, Otto Friedli, came up with the name.

There are a couple of problems with that story. Friedli was not quite fourteen years old when World War II ended. And, while he did serve in the military, he was not a commando or anything like that. He had briefly served stateside as an army mechanic but was dishonorably discharged after his superiors discovered he had lied about not having a criminal record. And he was not present at the first meeting of the Hells Angels (which happened two months before his seventeenth birthday), nor did he come up with the name. In an interview, he admitted that his first exposure to the Hells Angels was in 1951, when a guy who was dating his ex-girlfriend invited him to a club party. He was then almost twenty years old. He later became a member—even serving as interim West Coast president—but left after finding religion while serving time in prison on a weapons conviction. Friedli later joined the Black Sheep, a decidedly non-gangster motorcycle club dedicated to spreading evangelical Christianity, and died in 2006. His epitaph read, "Bye bye, suckers, see you in heaven."

None of the original members of the Hells Angels had a verifiable military service record. In fact, the Bishop brothers, whose garage the meeting took place in, had moved with their parents from England to California in 1940—a time when people believed that Germany would invade Britain (and the United States was still neutral), effectively making the Bishop family refugees.

The confusion might have originated because there were actually several American combat units in World War II that called themselves "Hell's Angels," and there had been a popular 1930 movie about World War I fighter pilots named *Hell's Angels*, which seems to have kicked off the whole concept. Of course, members, friends and fans of an organization like the Hells Angels would much rather believe the romantic notion that it was founded by brave but misunderstood commandos rather than just a bunch of guys (much less a couple of war refugees), so the fiction continues. I even believed it myself—because why would they lie, right?—until I did more thorough research.

Readers often argue with me on that one point about the Hells Angels' origins, but usually with no more evidence than, as several have said, "Everyone knows it's true." The closest anyone has ever come to presenting me with an actual case for it was when a few years ago a woman sent me a link to an official document, which showed that a California prosecutor had repeated the story of Friedli and the veterans founding the Hells Angels in a high-profile case. But I tracked that down and found out that a legal assistant had merely done a copy-and-paste job from the club's history on its official website.

Veterans' rights advocacy groups and others have shown great anger at the use of the name by the motorcycle club, saying—mostly on social media—that it's wrong for the club to make it look as though their founders served in such esteemed units. Several of them point out that the name "Hell's Angels" was also widely used in World War II to refer to army nurses.

Interestingly, the club's official site, which has recently been redesigned, now makes the history very clear with a tiringly long essay called the Hells Angels Motorcycle Club Lineage Clarification that promises "No sensation No myth Just facts." It explains that there is no direct connection between the military Hell's Angels and the motorcycling Hells Angels. Seemingly written with the help of a team of lawyers, it also points out that the only person to have any involvement with both was Arvid Olson, who was a member of the Flying Tigers, a group of American volunteer pilots who fought against the Japanese invasion of China before the attack on Pearl Harbor and who had a squadron called the Hell's Angels. Although Olson knew several of the original Hells Angels, he was never a member of the club. Some sources—at least those who don't believe the Friedli story—say he came up with the name for the club, while others credit the Bishop brothers.

The root of what we now consider to be biker culture began to form as much as fifty years before the Hells Angels were established, certainly well before the United States entered World War I in 1917. Motorcycles were still a relatively new phenomenon and were undeniably dangerous. Most people considered their riders to be only the boldest, even most foolhardy, young men. And, since all motorcycles back then were single-seaters, those who rode them were often thought of as loners, outside the norm.

But motorcyclists have long sought to race and share their experiences with one another, and very early in their history, they started to band together and hold rallies. Motorcycle clubs existed in the U.S. almost from the start of commercial motorcycle production. They go way back. In 1903, two existing clubs—the

New York Motorcycle Club and the Alpha Motorcycle Club—merged to become the Federation of American Motorcyclists. Their stated goal was to improve road conditions and promote safe motorcycling.

Not long after, motorcycle clubs started meeting to race and socialize. Originally called "gypsy tours" (although they are generally called runs or rallies today), these events were usually small in attendance and regional. The oldest one still going, Laconia Bike Week in New Hampshire, began in 1916.

As these rallies grew from a few dozen attendees to tens of thousands, two distinct groups began to emerge. Those who liked to party a bit more and a bit more hedonistically than others became something of a separate entity. They recognized each other with particular outfits and patches they had begun to wear to set themselves apart.

Before long, all legal races and other major motorcycle events were organized through the American Motorcycling Association, or AMA.

A couple of years after World War II ended, and about a year before the Hells Angels were founded, one of the AMA-sponsored gypsy tours took a turn for the worse. At a 1947 Fourth of July event in the small town of Hollister, California, members of some of the rowdier clubs, like the Pissed Off Bastards of Bloomington, the Tulare Riders, the Galloping Goose and the Boozefighters, along with some unaffiliated revelers, didn't want to stop enjoying themselves after the scheduled races ended. They started to race in the street and engage in other beer-fueled shenanigans.

A reporter and photographer from the *San Francisco Chronicle* attended, and the paper ran two stories about the event—one titled "Havoc in Hollister" and a follow-up called

"Hollister's Bad Time"—that characterized the night as "pande-monium" and even "terrorism." Later that month, the influential *Life* magazine reprinted one of the *Chronicle's* pictures—that of a clearly drunk biker named Eddie Davenport sitting on a motor-cycle with a beer bottle in both hands surrounded by broken bot-tles. The lurid photo ran almost a full page.

AT THE TIME, *Life* magazine held a massive grip on the American popular consciousness, and its images and words often defined people, places and movements. The picture from Hollister sparked an outrage. By many, motorcyclists began to be seen even more as outsiders—as bad guys. The traditional story says that the AMA, desperate to preserve the image of its membership, issued a state-ment in which they claimed that all the trouble at such events was caused by 1 percent of their membership. But, like most biker history and lore, it's apocryphal. In 2009, after conducting an extensive internal investigation, the AMA announced that it had never issued such a statement.

Still, the name stuck. And bikers who wanted to promote an image of living outside mainstream society, even outside the law, started calling themselves "1-percenters."

The *Life* magazine picture inspired actor and Guggenheim Award–winning author Frank Rooney to write a short story called "Cyclists' Raid," which was published in *Harper's Magazine* in 1951. It portrayed the bikers as an invading force, hell-bent on bringing chaos, mayhem and violence to a sleepy, law-abiding town. Prominent Hollywood movie producer Stanley Kramer read the story and made it into a wildly popular 1953 melodramatic movie called *The Wild One* starring Marlon Brando and Lee Marvin.

The characters' behavior and, more important, their outfits came to define biker culture for decades. They set a style—leather jackets or denim vests with club-identifying patches, worn with jeans—that lasts to this day. While the star of the movie was heartthrob Brando, many bikers preferred the look established by Marvin's psychotically violent character, Chino, and 1-percenters even today universally wear his sleeveless vest as their identifying totem.

Suddenly, the number of motorcycle clubs whose members emulated what they had seen in *The Wild One* erupted. By the mid-1950s, every town in North America seemed to have at least one, especially in California and other states where year-round riding was possible. Even Quebec, with some of the continent's harshest and longest winters, had 350 separate clubs at one point.

The Hells Angels then did something that would establish themselves as the leaders in the field and separate themselves from the thousands of other clubs. With membership growing, some of the original Hells Angels headed off to San Francisco in 1954. Instead of starting a new club with a new identity, they established a second group of Hells Angels. To make sure they did not do anything to embarrass the guys in the original club, they took with them a document called a charter that laid out the club's rules. Many Hells Angels still use the word "charter" to refer to individual chapters, but I prefer to use "chapter" to prevent confusing the group of people with the document, and because it's the accepted standard with other clubs, law enforcement and the media.

The original group of Hells Angels called themselves the San Bernardino chapter (Fontana is a small suburb of the much larger city of San Bernardino, and both are in San Bernardino County), which they later shortened to Berdoo. The chapter in San Francisco was called Frisco.

Something clicked. The name, the death's-head logo and the group's reputation as partiers and brawlers made lots and lots of

Californians want to become Hells Angels. The club continued to expand in California and added its first chapter outside the state—all the way in Auckland, New Zealand—in 1961. The New Zealanders operated with near autonomy, rarely making any contact with the California clubs. Known for decades as "the lost chapter," they and other international chapters enjoyed much closer relations with the rest of the club a generation or so later as communication technology improved.

Expansion for the Hells Angels didn't always go as planned. Because the Hells Angels name and logo were so popular, more than a few clubs adopted them without the genuine club's permission. Guys would just put on the patch and dare anyone to take it off them. The actual Hells Angels always did their best to quash that as quickly as possible, beating up the pretenders and taking their patches and, usually, their bikes.

When the San Francisco chapter heard about a biker club in Massachusetts copying their name and logo, they prepared to ride cross-country to do something about it. But since they had been in contact with a nearby club, called the Disciples, who desperately wanted to become Hells Angels, San Francisco chapter president Ralph "Sonny" Barger made the Disciples an offer—if they could take the fake Hells Angels' patches from the Massachusetts club, they would become a bona fide Hells Angels chapter.

The Disciples proved they weren't up to the task, so, impressed by the fake Hells Angels' toughness, Barger offered them real patches. They accepted and became the Lowell, Massachusetts, chapter, the first in the U.S. outside of California. Barger later claimed that the also-ran Disciples became a chapter of the rival Outlaws.

After that, the Hells Angels quickly expanded throughout the United States. They entered the United Kingdom in 1969 and

Canada in 1977 before taking off all over the world.

And it was in 1966 that the Hells Angels set another precedent, after their concept of separate chapters was such a success: they started selling drugs. Well, that's not entirely true. Members of the Hells Angels had admitted to and been convicted of selling drugs before that. But in 1966, four members were on trial for raping two girls, fourteen and fifteen years old, and they needed money for bail and legal representation. At the club's next weekly meeting (bikers call such meetings "church"), it was moved, debated and finally voted that members would sell methamphetamine to cover the defendants' legal costs.

That would have turned the club into an organized crime syndicate, at least by today's definition in both Canada and the U.S. Back then, such anti-gangster laws did not exist. The Hells Angels have since backed off from and frequently denied the concept of selling drugs as a group, instead saying they do so merely as individuals.

And, like lots of other things the Hells Angels did, the other big clubs followed suit. There was plenty of money to be made selling drugs—or by committing other crimes—and that appealed to many members within the Hells Angels and other clubs. Since the biker life is not cheap—the parties, the bikes and the rallies all cost money—and fewer and fewer serious bikers could find legitimate work to fit around their schedules and lifestyles, more and more of them turned to crime. Several clubs, especially in big cities, developed strong and lucrative relationships with mafia families and other crime organizations.

When anti-racketeering laws were enacted in the U.S. and Canada, club leaders made it clear to their members that if any were caught engaging in illegal activity, it was the member's responsibility, not the club's, and the club would always deny any knowledge of their crimes. And, when the Hells Angels were brought up on charges of being a crime organization in the early 1970s, Barger successfully argued that even though he sold heroin, he did it for his own gain, not the club's. He was in the club to ride; he sold drugs to make money. That separation might be a legal fine point, but it worked. The prosecution could not prove without a shadow of a doubt that the club existed to facilitate crime, no matter how much crime was associated with it. The Hells Angels avoided being named a crime organization. Since then, many 1-percenters have been convicted of racketeering, but never has the racket proven to involve an entire club or even chapter, which allows the clubs to operate as motorcycle-enthusiast organizations.

Of course, not every member of every motorcycle club is a criminal. Far from it. Not even every member of a club that represents itself as a 1-percenter club.

But there are seven major clubs in the United States that the U.S. Justice Department has labeled large-scale crime organizations: the Hells Angels, the Bandidos, the Outlaws, the Mongols, the Pagan's, the Sons of Silence and the Vagos (although only one, the Hells Angels, has been declared a criminal organization in court, and only in Ontario). And I'd like to add one more Canadian-based club—Bacchus—because they have many members, control a large area, have expanded from a small base and sometimes find themselves at odds with other clubs, in addition to sharing several more characteristics with the Big Seven clubs. As well, many of their members have been convicted of the same serious crimes that we associate with the Big Seven. But they have not been declared a criminal organization in any court.

Of course, there are plenty of other regional 1-percenter clubs, like the Galloping Goose and the Warlocks, but they don't hold the sway of the Big Seven or Bacchus. And there are many clubs that are more widespread, like the Black Pistons and the Red Devils, but they are what law enforcement calls "puppet clubs," which take their orders from bigger clubs. The big clubs call them "support clubs."

That difference represents another sticking point with bikers. One prominent biker recently posted on Facebook that the name "puppet club" is incorrect, because "who calls their friends puppets?" He has a point, but so does law enforcement, who counter that because of the strict hierarchy of biker life, support clubs by their very definition exist merely to support the big clubs. Their members must carry out orders from the big club without question or complaint; they are little more than servants. That's not how I treat my friends.

While all the big clubs share many similarities, they all have their own history, traditions, allies and enemies, and culture. Here's a rough guide.

## HELLS ANGELS

**Founded:** 1948, Fontana (San Bernardino/Berdoo), California
**Distribution:** 425 chapters in 50 countries, with 82 in 23 American states (primarily on the East and West Coasts and in the Great Lakes region) and 38 in 7 Canadian provinces
**Colors:** Red and white
**Motto:** Angels Forever, Forever Angels (AFFA)
**Support clubs:** Red Devils, primarily; also Alky Haulers, Desperado's, Demon Knights, Devils Choice, Few Good Men, Merciless Souls, Mortal Skulls, Rebel Rousers, Road Reapers, Unforgiven, Valhalla and others
**Allies:** Few, because the Hells Angels have a reputation among other 1-percenter groups for being violently unwilling to share space; but

they do have some cooperation from Bacchus, El Forastero, Galloping Goose and other regional powers

**Enemies:** Mongols, Outlaws, Sons of Silence, Vagos and many others

Any discussion about 1-percenter clubs almost has to begin with the Hells Angels. Although not the oldest of the clubs, they defined the look, the organization and much of the behavior of all biker gangs. The subject of countless books and several feature films, the Hells Angels are, by a huge margin, the best-known biker gang in the world. With a name, logo and brand and enviable name recognition, the Hells Angels have success-fully expanded throughout the world.

However, recent expansion by rival gangs in the U.S.—particu-larly in the Hells Angels' ancestral home of southern California—has forced them out of much of the country, often through violence, as shootouts with clubs like the Mongols and Pagan's have prompted Hells Angels to abandon certain communities.

Their logo is a winged skull (known as the "death's head" or "death head") and they are very protective of it, allowing only full-patch members to wear it or the club's name in any form. The Hells Angels frequently make the news when they sue for copyright infringement, having seen their name or logo or too close a fac-simile of either in movies or TV. Note that they do not use a posses-sive apostrophe in "Hells." One explanation I have been offered is that the word is plural "because there are many hells." If that were so, it should be written as Hells' Angels, but it would appear proper punctuation is not high on the club's list of priorities.

Supporters usually refer to the Hells Angels as 81 (because *H* is the eighth letter of the alphabet and *A* is the first) or the Big Red Machine, while opponents call them "featherheads," "candy canes" or "pinks."

While the Hells Angels have one national president in every other country they occupy, in the United States, they have two—one for the east, usually in New York City, and one for the west in California, often Oakland. They're of more or less equal importance, although individual charisma can give one an edge.

## BANDIDOS
**Founded:** 1966, San Leon, Texas, near Houston
**Distribution:** In the United States, mainly mountain and plains states, radiating out from Texas and ranging from Washington to Alabama; none in Canada (Bandidos chapters also exist in 30 other countries, but they are a separate, dubiously allied entity)
**Colors:** Red and yellow (which they call gold)
**Motto:** We Are The People Our Parents Warned Us About
**Support clubs:** Amigos, Companeros, Desperados, Destralos, Hermanos, Hombres, Pistoleros and others
**Allies:** Mongols and, outside of the U.S., Satudarah
**Enemies:** Hells Angels and their allies throughout the world; Night Wolves in Russia

Unlike the Hells Angels, the Bandidos actually were founded by a veteran. Donald "Mother" Chambers served as a U.S. Marine in Vietnam in the early 1960s before large-scale hostilities there, and when he returned to Texas's Gulf Shore, he was disappointed to find no Hells Angels chapter nearby. Instead, he formed his own club, which rapidly attracted members.

In 1972, Chambers and two other Bandidos murdered Marley Leon and Preston LeRay Tarver because they had sold the club baking soda, which they had misrepresented as methamphetamine. While the loss of Chambers to a life sentence in prison was a significant blow, the Bandidos were already well established by that point. Ronald "Stepmother" Hodge took the reins and presided over the club's expansion.

The name "Bandidos," the club says, came from an innocent bystander in a Mexican restaurant Chambers and his friends frequented. When he asked who the tough-looking guys were, the waitress answered, "the American *bandidos*." *Bandido*, of course, is Spanish for bandit or outlaw. They are frequently called the Banditos in books and the media, even in the memoir of well-known Hells Angel Ralph "Sonny" Barger, but that's the Italian word for bandit and even Bandidos in Italy don't use it.

For years, the club had a penchant for often-fractured Spanish, using titles like "el Presidente" for president and "sargento de armas" for sergeant-at-arms, but that has largely died out. Members are referred to as "Bandido" and then their nickname. For example, Carlton "Pervert" Bare would be referred to as "Bandido Pervert" by others in the club and Bare himself.

They originally differed from the Hells Angels in accepting Hispanic members and quickly set up new chapters in Texas and surrounding states. After that came expansion to Australia in 1983 and Europe, beginning in Marseille, France, in 1989. The European Bandidos became particularly strong, especially in Scandinavia, where they fought what most in the media called the Great Nordic Biker War against the Hells Angels from 1993 to 1997. Violence has flared from time to time since then.

In 2000, the Bandidos patched over the Rock Machine, a Canadian club fighting its own war with the Hells Angels in Canada. After the 2006 Shedden Massacre—in which several Canadian Bandidos killed eight of their own—the club left the country, vowing never to return.

In 2007, the American Bandidos broke with the chapters in the rest of the world, posting on their website, "Though we share a common name and a similar patch, we are no longer associated with Bandidos MC in Europe, Asia and Australia." Sources have told me that ongoing tensions and violence between Bandidos and Hells Angels and their allies in Europe and Australia prompted the split. (Bandidos and Hells Angels are generally more tolerant of each other in the United States, as long as they don't challenge established territorial claims.) There is also a persistent rumor that many non-U.S. chapters will accept members without motorcycles—a move that could lead to convictions under anti-gang legislation.

In 2011, the American Bandidos redesigned their logo to reflect the difference. The old Bandidos patch depicts a cartoon caricature of a stereotypical Mexican bandit wielding a machete and pistol. He is lovingly referred to as "the Fat Mexican." The new U.S.-only patch is similar but is more detailed and less cartoonish, with a small Texas flag on the bandit's arm.

Counted as a single entity, the Bandidos are almost certainly the second-biggest 1-percenter club in the world. The American Bandidos are the second-biggest club in the United States.

## OUTLAWS

**Founded:** 1935, McCook (Chicago), Illinois; the "mother chapter," or headquarters, has since moved to Detroit
**Distribution:** 284 chapters in 22 countries, including 116 chapters in 26 states, primarily in the Midwest and the Southeast; 10 in 2 provinces in Canada
**Colors:** Black and white
**Motto:** God Forgives, Outlaws Don't
**Support clubs:** Officially, the Black Pistons, but there are others

**Allies:** Mongols
**Enemies:** Hells Angels and their allies; Warlocks in Florida

Despite predating them by a long margin, the Outlaws have spent most of their existence in the shadow of the Hells Angels, and have even been eclipsed in importance by the Bandidos. As a biker cop once said to me, "They don't make movies about the Outlaws, do they?"

Originally dressing in cowboy gear with piped shirts and pointy boots, the Outlaws switched over to the leather look in the middle 1950s, after the Hells Angels adopted it from *The Wild One.* Not long after, they changed their logo from a winged motorcycle to a skull—affectionately known as Charlie— over crossed pistons (although the club's corporate entity, the American Outlaw Association, or AOA, features a hand with an upstretched middle finger as its logo).

Relations with the Hells Angels have always been tense, and that has resulted in small wars from time to time. The first is said to have arisen from a 1969 rape of the wife of a Hells Angel by an Outlaw, but most have been over territorial disputes. Lingering animosity has kept the two clubs at odds, and the Outlaws have adopted an alternate motto, "Angels Die in Outlaw States," which is often displayed as "ADIOS" on a patch or tattoo.

In many countries—notably Canada, Australia, Denmark and Norway—Outlaws have been known to work in correlation with the Bandidos and other clubs to try to curb the Hells Angels' expansion, with varying levels of success.

# PAGAN'S

**Founded:** 1959, in an unincorporated part of Prince George's County, Maryland (near Washington, D.C.), although some sources have told me the club was actually formed in nearby Vienna, Virginia; the headquarters have since moved to Delaware County, Pennsylvania, just outside Philadelphia
**Distribution:** About 40 chapters on the East Coast of the United States, from Pennsylvania to North Carolina and Florida; there are frequent rumors of Pagan's chapters in other countries, but they are almost certainly unfounded
**Colors:** Blue, white and red
**Motto:** Live and Die
**Support clubs:** The Sons of Satan, named after "Satan" Marron
**Allies:** Mongols
**Enemies:** Hells Angels and their allies; in 2002, a brief war with the Hells Angels forced the big club to abandon their Philadelphia chapter, leaving the city to the Pagan's

Founded by Lou Dobkin, an ex–Navy medic turned biochemist for the National Institutes of Health in Washington, the Pagan's were originally just a bunch of small-time toughs looking for a good time. After Dobkin was replaced as president by John "Satan" Marron, the club is said to have forged ties with the Philadelphia Mafia and moved on to a much higher level of criminal activity.

The Pagan's don't look like most other 1-percenter clubs. While other clubs prefer leather vests, the Pagan's invariably wear denim ones. They also don't wear bottom rockers, the patches that identify a bike club's territory. Sources tell me that is because they don't want law enforcement or other bikers to know their numbers or territorial claims.

Their logo is a cartoon image of Surtr, a fire giant from Norse mythology who plays a major role in Ragnarök, the ultimate destruction of the world. They took the logo directly from a Jack Kirby–illustrated Thor comic book.

Interestingly, the Pagan's have an apostrophe in their name where they shouldn't, and the Hells Angels don't have one where they should.

The Pagan's—who emerged from a more ethnically diverse area—appear more likely, from my own observation and in the opinion of law enforcement officers I have spoken to, than other clubs to wear Nazi, white supremacist or Confederate regalia.

## MONGOLS

**Founded:** 1969, in Montebello (Los Angeles), California

**Distribution:** There are two problems with trying to determine where Mongols are and aren't. The first is that they like to tease law enforcement and other 1-percenter clubs by claiming they have chapters where they don't. The other is that many Mongols chapters overseas have been established without the blessing of, or even communication with, American management and have been repeatedly accused of patch selling (allowing candidates to buy their way into the club) and even recruiting members without motorcycles. They are not acknowledged by the club and are considered Mongols in name only. Genuine Mongols are, however, present in 14 American states, mainly in the west; Alberta; Mexico; and several European countries, especially Germany and Switzerland

**Colors:** Black and white

**Motto:** The Best of the Best

**Support clubs:** Officially, the Raiders, and others

**Allies:** Bandidos, Outlaws, Pagan's, Sons of Silence and Vagos (essentially, any club at odds with the Hells Angels)

**Enemies:** Hells Angels and their allies

When their attempts to join the Hells Angels were rebuffed, a group of disgruntled southern California bikers formed their own club: the Mongols. Most, but not all of them, had been turned down by the Hells Angels because of their Hispanic heritage. The new gang expanded rapidly (they are said to have recruited directly from the California Men's Colony prison in San Luis Obispo) and developed ties with local street gangs and Mexican organized crime, many of which preferred to deal with them rather than the Hells Angels.

The consequent tension between the Mongols and the Hells Angels led to many violent encounters, which often came out in the Mongols' favor. Eventually, a peace deal was hammered out: the Mongols could claim southern California as their own, except for scattered pockets around existing Hells Angels clubhouses, including the mother chapter in San Bernardino. Even so, Mongols and Hells Angels consider one another enemies, and violent clashes still erupt from time to time.

Their patch is a cartoonish Mongol warrior (some say it's Genghis Khan) they call "the Raider," riding what appears to be a Harley. In 2008, a federal court issued an injunction that prevented the Mongols from using their name and logo on clothing. It was a demand by the Department of Justice in a plea deal after 110 Mongols were arrested for murder, drug trafficking, robbery, extortion and money laundering. But in 2011, the injunction was overturned in civil court as a violation of the members' First Amendment rights.

Rivals, particularly Hells Angels, call the Mongols "girls."

# SONS OF SILENCE

**Founded:** 1966, in Niwot (Boulder), Colorado
**Distribution:** Midwestern and mountain states and Germany
**Colors:** Blue, red and white
**Motto:** *Donec mors non separat* (Latin for "Until Death Separates Us")
**Support clubs:** American Iron, Silent, Silent Few, Silent Rebels, Silent Thunder, Southern Steel
**Allies:** Mongols
**Enemies:** Hells Angels, Outlaws

Bruce "The Dude" Richardson returned to his family's cattle farm in 1960 after a short stint in the U.S. Navy, serving briefly on the aircraft carrier U.S.S. *Shangri-La*. He liked to ride and party, and he formed the Sons of Silence in 1966. The club quickly expanded, first to Iowa, and is now spread throughout the Midwest and to Germany as well. Richardson left the club in 1974 after a large conflict with law enforcement led to his constant surveillance.

The Sons of Silence have had violent clashes with both the Outlaws and Hells Angels.

Their logo, a standing bald eagle, is taken directly from the Anheuser-Busch corporate logo.

Both law enforcement and Sons of Silence themselves like to talk about how the Sons of Silence are more heavily armed and likely to use violence than other clubs. Many people inside and outside of the club refer to themselves as the Sons of Violence.

# VAGOS

**Founded:** 1966, in Redlands (San Bernardino), California
**Distribution:** 46 chapters worldwide, including 24 in 11 U.S. states
(primarily in the Southwest), 1 in Canada and 15 in Mexico
**Colors:** Green and red
**Motto:** We Give What We Get
**Support clubs:** None major
**Allies:** Mongols
**Enemies:** Sons of Silence, Hells Angels and the Galloping Goose

Southern California, particularly the Inland Empire region, was teeming with motorcycle clubs in the middle 1960s. One of the major ones was a multi-ethnic gang called the Psychos. However, inner dissension over the use of injectable drugs by members led to a split. About half the club, led by Rudy "Puro" Esparza, left to establish their own club, the Vagos.

"Vago" means gypsy or vagabond in Spanish, but it also connotes someone with rare wisdom or inside knowledge. The club's logo is a cartoon image of the Norse god Loki over a winged motorcycle wheel. They are more likely to wear denim vests than leather, but it varies by region.

The club expanded through southern California very quickly, then into Mexico and surrounding American states and overseas. An attempt to establish the club in Ontario failed—that particular group of bikers essentially went from being Annihilators to Loners to Rock Machine to Bandidos to Vagos to Outlaws in less than twenty years—but the club appears to have had better success in Alberta.

A close relationship with crime organizations in Mexico has allowed the Vagos to prosper.

Friends and rivals alike call Vagos "greenies," while members and supporters refer to them as the "Green Nation."

# BACCHUS

**Founded:** 1972, Edgetts Landing (Moncton), New Brunswick
**Distribution:** 11 chapters in 5 eastern Canadian provinces
**Colors:** Black and gold
**Motto:** Black and Gold Will Never Fold
**Support clubs:** None
**Allies:** Hells Angels
**Enemies:** Outlaws

Bacchus started as a small club in New Brunswick, but after repeated failed attempts by the Hells Angels and Outlaws to establish themselves in Atlantic Canada, they rapidly expanded to become the dominant club there.

Frequently portrayed in mainstream media as a Hells Angels puppet club, Bacchus has long had a working relationship with the Hells Angels but has remained independent of them. A patch-over had been seriously discussed, but two sources, including an ex–Hells Angels sergeant-at-arms, have told me that the Hells Angels declined to take over Bacchus because of their members' propensity to be arrested on minor charges.

Recent years, however, have seen friction between the two clubs. When the Red Devils—Canada's oldest club, established in 1948—were forced by the Hells Angels to change their name in 2014 to make room for a Hells Angels support club of the same name, they patched over their three Ontario chapters to Bacchus. The Hells Angels opened a chapter in New Brunswick in 2016, and the Outlaws established themselves in Newfoundland the same year, adding to the tension.

The club is named after Bacchus, a Greek god better known as Dionysius. Although the club says that he is the god of "wine, women and song," historians say that he is the god of the grape harvest, winemaking, wine, ritual madness, fertility, theater and religious ecstasy. The club's logo is a bizarre skull-like caricature of his face.

FOR THE PURPOSES of this book, the terms *biker* and *1-percenter* will refer to members of these groups, their allies and those like them. And, because of the enormous number of convictions for conspiracy, trafficking and murder, I have to agree with the U.S. Department of Justice in calling the clubs they belong to gangs. I have changed some of the names throughout.

## CHAPTER 2

# So You Want To Be a Biker

After moving to a new town for construction work, Mitch went to a gym to work out. On his first visit, he was approached by a "large, tattooed guy"—it should be noted that Mitch is also a large, tattooed guy—who offered to spot for him. The two started working out together and, after about six weeks, the guy, Ben, invited him to a bar he hung out at.

Mitch was delighted to see a lineup of Harleys outside as he too liked riding. Inside, he was even more impressed. Ben and his friends never paid for any drinks and always seemed to be having a great time. They were all friendly to him, patting him on the back, shaking his hand, laughing at his jokes and making sure he always had a full beer.

"I didn't even know they were Bandidos then," he told me. He thought they were "just guys who liked to have a good time."

He enjoyed himself so much that he ended up returning to the bar week after week. He found out the guys were Bandidos, but it didn't bother him. "I thought they were cool," he said. "And I never saw them break any laws or anything—just little stuff, like anyone would do."

Before long, there was talk of Mitch riding with the Bandidos. He went on a couple of runs with them, riding in the back. They teased him about his Kawasaki and said he'd have to trade it for a Harley if he ever wanted to get serious.

He admired them, and he didn't see much difference between the way they lived and how he wanted to live. He was, however, "creeped out" by how much they knew about him—like his parents' names and what school he went to.

It was only after weeks of partying and riding with the Bandidos that Ben told him he could become a hangaround, conditional on his changing his motorcycle. While that title meant that the club recognized him as an acceptable candidate for potential membership and that the individual members of the club would back him up in a fight, it also meant that the club owed him nothing else, that he was not a representative of the club and that he could not speak for, or even of, the club to others. It also meant that he was forbidden to associate with any other club without the Bandidos' approval.

Mitch agreed and started shopping for a used Harley.

YOU CAN'T JUST apply to be a 1-percenter biker. The official statement from the Hells Angels is "If you have to ask, you probably will not understand the answer." Though awkwardly worded, its meaning is clear—you can't just join a biker club. And all the other big clubs say basically the same thing.

It's an understatement to say that the clubs are extremely picky about who they accept for membership. The official word is that the clubs are looking for just the right kind of people without much more in the way of specifics, while law enforcement says that because such clubs are involved in so much illegal activity, they live in constant fear that sensitive information will be leaked and want only those candidates who won't spill their secrets.

No successful 1-percenter club has ever accepted candidates who approached them for membership. But new bikers have to come from somewhere, of course, so clubs actively recruit men they think check all of their boxes.

Often, that means clubs will lean heavily on relatives and old friends, but they also reach out into the community for new recruits. Three criteria stand out in an ideal recruit: the ability to take care of himself in a fight, the ability to make himself, or the club, money and the ability to keep his mouth shut.

Typically, clubs will go to gyms, especially those that feature mixed martial arts, to find guys they know can fight. Similarly, they might look at bodybuilders, wrestlers, men recently discharged from the military, doormen and bouncers from nightclubs and strip joints, and men with careers in personal security and experience serving as bodyguards. Those are all guys who are usually valuable to have around in a scrap.

Jail can be a fertile recruiting ground, as imprisoned bikers frequently make connections and alliances behind bars. And it's very easy to assess a man's fighting ability, or his reputation as a fighter at least, in prison.

Clubs also prize guys who have successful businesses, especially if they deal in cash or provide a service considered valuable to the club. That means that clubs go out of their way to recruit tattoo artists, gun shop owners and employees, strip joint and nightclub owners, talent agents (especially those who handle strippers), importers and exporters, motorcycle mechanics and people who work with leather. Cash-intensive businesses, of course, provide an excellent way to launder money. And they'd never admit it, but the big clubs also target pimps, drug dealers, marijuana growers and meth cooks.

The best way to become a biker, I have been told repeatedly, is simply to hang out where bikers do and act like one. If you're good at it and show an aptitude for the values they hold, they will eventually approach you. Several bikers have told me that the best way to become a 1-percenter is to put on a vest with a 1-percenter patch and fight anyone who tries to take it off you.

Of course, it's also important that the candidate own and ride a motorcycle. The bikers themselves say that their clubs really are organizations dedicated to riding, while their critics contend that that's a convenient fiction they maintain to prevent them from being busted up by anti-gangster laws. Either way, you can't be a biker unless you own and operate a bike.

At least in theory. There have been many instances of that rule being fudged. When the Hells Angels created their Niagara Falls chapter, they had to teach several members—including president Gerald "Skinny" Ward—how to ride, and the Quebec Biker War was kicked off when the Hells Angels wrote a note to the leadership of the Rock Machine asking them to stop calling themselves a motorcycle club because (and they were right) only a few of them actually owned motorcycles. Even now, many overseas chapters of the big clubs infuriate domestic leadership by accepting members who ride small motorcycles, even scooters, if they even ride at all.

Although it varies from club to club and nation to nation, most 1-percenter organizations limit their members to Harley-Davidson or, at least, American-made motorcycles. That also includes Indian, a smaller-output manufacturer owned by Polaris Industries, and Victory, which was also owned by Polaris and was discontinued in 2017. That's been a bit of a problem for many bikers, as all but the most jingoistic motorcycle enthusiasts will agree that all Japanese and some European bikes represent better quality, performance and, especially, value for dollar than Harleys. In 2017, *Consumer Reports* wrote that over a span of four years, the average failure rate for Harley-Davidson products was more than double that of Yamaha, Suzuki and Honda and nearly double that of Kawasaki. "It's always been important for Hells Angels to ride American-made machines," wrote Sonny Barger in his memoir. "In terms of pure workmanship, personally I don't like Harleys. I ride them because I'm in the club, and that's the image, but if I could, I would seriously consider riding a Honda ST1100 or a BMW. We really missed the boat not switching over to the Japanese models when they began building bigger bikes. I'll usually say, fuck Harley-Davidson." Barger later switched from a Harley-Davidson to a Victory for his primary ride.

In the case of heavily customized motorcycles, some clubs will specify that at least the engine has to have been manufactured in the U.S.

Some overseas chapters of the big clubs allow their members to ride Triumphs—British bikes that were popular with American bikers in the 1950s and early 1960s and were the type ridden by Marlon Brando in *The Wild One*—or BMWs.

Japanese and Korean bikes, despite their reputation for durability and performance, are frowned upon by 1-percenters around the world and derisively called "rice," "rice burners" or "rice rockets."

Most clubs have a minimum size limit for bikes, measured by their engine displacement. The Outlaws constitution says that they will take bikes with engines as small as 605 cubic centimeters, while Bandidos cut off at 750, the Warlocks at 883 and the Pagan's at 900. These rules originated in the 1970s when the Harley-Davidson brand hit its lowest point. AMF, a bowling alley operator, bought the company in 1969. After slashing the number of workers, AMF outsourced component manufacturing to low bidders, resulting in very poor-quality bikes. Steadily losing revenue and market share to the Japanese, the company had acquired a significant stake in an Italian airplane and bike manufacturer, Aermacchi, and started putting the Harley-Davidson name on their little two-stroke bikes, some as small as 50 cc. The short and dreary existence of these "spaghetti hoglets," as they were called, prompted the minimum-size bylaws in 1-percenter clubs. Current Harleys—AMF sold the company in 1981 to a group of private investors, including Willie G. Davidson, grandson of one of the company's founders—range from 492 to 1,868 cc, with just a single entry-level model under 605.

The candidate also has to be male. You might see women in cut-off denim vests with patches riding Harleys, but they are not members of the major clubs.

In the 1970s, a few women tried to sue the Hells Angels for denying them membership, but they didn't get far. Since the Hells Angels are a private club, receive no funding from any government and aren't officially an employer, they can use any criteria they want to accept or deny members. Even if they had been legally compelled to accept women, Hells Angels leader Ralph "Sonny" Barger was quoted as saying, "We wouldn't do it anyway."

And the candidate, not surprisingly, has to be an adult. According to the Pagan's Motorcycle Club constitution, candidates must be eighteen, while other big clubs specify they must be twenty-one. But those numbers are just the bare minimum and are not put to the test very often. Because clubs are looking for candidates they know they can trust and who can potentially help the club in a fight or, and this is increasingly important, financially, they aren't looking for kids as members. Certainly, they wouldn't want someone who is not old enough to drink legally. Serving alcohol to minors is exactly the kind of legal problem clubs want to avoid. Law enforcement can frequently build bigger cases out of small infractions, and evidence of underage drinking in a clubhouse or member's home could easily lead to a search warrant.

Although not expressly worded in their constitutions, the major 1-percenter clubs do not admit openly gay men as members. There have been several cases of covertly gay men in these clubs—like Dany Kane and Aimé Simard, members of the Rockers support club and contract killers for two different Hells Angels members—whose orientation has come out after their arrest or death.

After a 1968 murder in the clubhouse of the Satan's Angels— a Vancouver club that would later become Hells Angels—local police wiretapped their phone. One remark they heard—"We got a new butler"—caused them some alarm. After some investigation, police learned that the "butler" in question was a young man who had been kidnapped by members of the Satan's Angels and sodomized and tortured for no reason other than they found it entertaining.

As the LGBT community has gained more widespread acceptance and has become more visible, bikers have distanced themselves from it. Most 1-percenters display animosity toward the LGBT community, and some have even taken to disrupting pride marches and other events.

Interestingly, before LGBT rights became a major cultural issue, bikers (and there are records of both Hells Angels and Outlaws doing this) used to have a habit of passionately tongue-kissing each other for "shock value" and to "express brotherhood." In his 1965 book *Hells Angels: A Strange and Terrible Saga*, Hunter S. Thompson wrote that such kissing "is a guaranteed square-jolter, and the Angels are gleefully aware of the reaction it gets. The sight of a photographer invariably whips the Angels into a kissing frenzy."

Some years later, things had changed. Chuck Zito wrote in his memoir that he had been part of a group that in 1985 had the authority to set up a chapter in Japan, but he called it off because he saw two men on a street corner holding hands. "In Japanese culture, we were told, that sort of display of affection is perfectly normal, acceptable behavior and is not seen as a reflection on one's sexuality," he wrote. "Well, that may be, but I have to tell you: there is no way that any Hells Angel is ever going to prance hand-in-hand with another guy. Call it homophobic; call it narrow-minded, call it whatever the hell you want to call it. It simply is not going to happen. Case closed. End of story."

And then there's the race question, which is a huge deal in the biker community. Over the years, readers have told me that I'm wrong to say that there are no black members of the big 1-percenter clubs, even including the Hells Angels. But if there have been any, I have found no solid evidence of them, just rumors. There have been, however, several notable Americans and Canadians of African descent in the 1-percenter orbit, but never as members of big clubs.

Sometimes, existing clubs with black members will have to expel them when patching over to a bigger club. That happened in 1977 in Hamilton, Ontario. The dominant club at the time was Satan's Choice, which had three black members, and it frequently referred to itself, tongue in cheek, as the Good-Looking Guys Club. One of the conditions of the patch-over to the Outlaws was that they get rid of those three guys. The expelled bikers started their own club, the Not-So-Good-Looking Guys Club, but it ended when they were convicted of disposing bodies for the local Cosa Nostra boss. Later incarnations of Satan's Choice were all white, and they patched over to the Hells Angels.

On other occasions, black bikers are simply barred from being members, no matter how qualified. Haitian-born Greg "Picasso" Wooley beat guys up, allegedly killed people and sold drugs for the Montreal Hells Angels over the years and was a close friend of Maurice "Mom" Boucher—a Hells Angel sometimes referred to as Canada's Pablo Escobar—but was never a Hells Angel himself. Barred from wearing the winged skull because of his skin color, Wooley instead wore the patch of the Rockers, a support club.

Legend has it that one of the founding members of El Forastero was black—indeed, he is referred to in several recountings of the club's early days only as "Nigger Sam." However, there is no other corroborating evidence of his existence, or even a last name that I can track down. And when Tom Fugle gave a eulogy for Dave Mann in 2004, he recounted the story of how they and Harlan "Tiny" Brower had founded the club, making no mention of Sam. In fact, he said in his speech that Brower convinced him to customize his "dresser" (a stock touring bike) into a chopper because "the only ones who rode dressers were niggers and old men." It reportedly drew a big laugh. Sam was, I think it's safe to say, fictional.

The reality is that the major 1-percenter clubs do not accept black members. In fact, the Hells Angels issued a bylaw in 1986 that simply states, "No niggers in the club," and the Outlaws constitution also puts it plainly: "All members must be white." Undercover U.S. Bureau of Alcohol, Tobacco, Firearms and Explosives (ATF) agent Jay Dobyns noted in his memoir many instances of racial bias by the Hells Angels, some as petty as members being greatly offended that the ringtone on his cell phone was a Nelly song.

You might be tempted to think that the Mongols—a club formed in part by men who were rejected by the Hells Angels because of their ethnicity—would be more progressive when it comes to race relations, but the Southern Poverty Law Center would hasten to disagree. The leading civil rights group maintains an exhaustive file on the club that includes incidents of African-Americans being threatened or assaulted by Mongols for entering the wrong bar or restaurant and even more cases of women close to the club being beaten after it was witnessed, or alleged, that they had spoken with an African-American man.

Don't get me wrong; there are black 1-percenters, but they are in their own clubs. The East Bay Dragons of Oakland, California, for example, look like a 1-percenter club, even partying with the Hells Angels from time to time, and just happen to have an all-black membership. "They have their clubs, and we have ours," said Randy, a former Outlaw. "They like it like that, and we like it like that."

While the number of black clubs is dwarfed by the number of white clubs, the number of black-and-white clubs is positively tiny and makes almost no blip on the biker radar screen. One, the Chosen Few of Los Angeles, claims that it was the first integrated club. The barrier was broken in 1960, members say, when the all-black club accepted "White Boy Art" and then "White Boy Tom" as members.

Although the major 1-percenter clubs will work and even party with all-black clubs, some—like the Pagan's and Sons of Silence—will draw the line at clubs with both black and white members. Being black, apparently, is not as egregious to them as mixing races within a club.

40

The acceptance of other ethnicities in the big clubs varies from chapter to chapter and club to club. Older clubs like the Hells Angels and Outlaws were formed specifically by, and for, men of northwestern European descent, but they are hardly immune to demographic and cultural changes. They eventually started to accept people of Mediterranean descent, like Greeks and Italians—"as long as they don't act Italian," Randy told me.

Clubs like the Mongols and Vagos were formed, in no small part, by men of Hispanic descent who had been barred from the big clubs. But other clubs eased up on that rule, and many Hells Angels and Outlaws chapters, particularly in big cities, have Hispanic members. Indeed, Mark "Papa Frisco" Guardado was president of the Hells Angels San Francisco chapter until he was murdered by Christopher "Stoney" Ablett, a full-patch Mongol, in 2008. Ablett was convicted and received a life sentence.

Members of East Asian descent started showing up in big clubs beginning in the 1970s, but only in large, ethnically diverse cities like New York, Boston and Toronto, and they are still very few in number. There have been a handful of people of South and West Asian heritage associated with clubs—the Hells Angels Downtown Toronto chapter had an Iranian Shia Muslim prospect for a while—but that has become even rarer since the 9/11 attacks in 2001 stoked anti-Muslim sentiment in much of North America. Some members might go under assumed names to appease the rules of the mother club.

Several clubs allow indigenous Americans and Canadians to join, particularly in western states and provinces. Traditionally, these members wear a patch with the number nine on it ("I" is the ninth letter of the alphabet and denotes "Indian").

Jews have shown up in the big clubs, but they are exceedingly rare in a culture that has a long history of embracing Nazi memorabilia. One, Jamie "Goldberg" Flanz, was a full-patch Bandido in Canada until he was murdered in the 2006 Shedden Massacre. Wayne "Wiener" Kellestine, architect of the killings and an avid collector of Nazi memorabilia, told him, "I'm saving you for last because you're Jewish."

Of course, that sort of diversity would never fly in, say, Oklahoma or Arkansas. The general rule of thumb there is that the major 1-percenter clubs are all white, with a few other ethnicities thrown into the chapters in big, diverse cities, but no blacks. Those members, prospects and associates who aren't of northwestern European background can expect a lot of ribbing and stereotyping at their expense, and a nickname like—and I have run into all of these—Goldberg, Mike the Wop, Chinese Dave or Sean the Paki.

Okay, let's say you are male and of age; can fight; know how to make money; own, operate and maintain a Harley-Davidson of sufficient size; and possess an ethnic background that the chapter deems acceptable. Now can you join? Not so fast. They will let you know.

There are ways, however, to signal to the clubs that you are interested in joining. The easiest is to become a supporter. All clubs make money selling T-shirts, hoodies and other branded items. These items feature text or symbols associated with the club. Since the Hells Angels forbid non-members from wearing their name or logo, they use names like the Big Red Machine or 81 instead. You can find plenty of items with the Hells Angels name and the death's-head logo online, but they are counterfeit, and wearing them is a quick way to get a ride to a hospital.

Often, support gear will feature sayings associated with a particular club, like "Three can keep a secret if two are dead" for the Hells Angels or "Snitches are a dying breed" for the Outlaws. Also popular are acronyms like SYLB, for "Support your local

Bandidos." The Outlaws started that one years ago with SYLO, but pretty well all the big clubs except the Hells Angels use some version of it.

Anyone—women, cops, members of other clubs—can buy and wear support gear, and it does not constitute any formal relationship with the club. However, wearing support gear can be a good way to catch the eye of a biker who might be interested in getting to know you better. There is sort of an unwritten rule that if you are male and not a cop and you are wearing support gear when a brawl breaks out, you are expected to intervene on behalf of the club.

The other solid way to get bikers to know you is to do business with them. Open a tattoo parlor, leather store, motorcycle repair shop or any one of a number of businesses related to their lifestyle, and the local bikers will find you before long.

The first step in becoming a 1-percenter is usually to be invited to become a hangaround. Some clubs use the name "comearound," some differentiate hangarounds as potential members and comearounds as friends or associates who have no hope of becoming members, and the Outlaws don't use any specific title for the status. As a hangaround, the candidate has few privileges with the club and usually has to perform specific and often minor services like cleaning, chauffeuring and bartending.

Hangarounds are usually issued a vest (or cut, as most bikers call them, because the vest is created by cutting the sleeves off a jacket). Some vests, like those of the Pagan's, are without patches; the Bandidos and Sons of Silence prefer small, round patches—called cookies—on the front of the vest; and the Hells Angels and Mongols have small, rectangular patches on the back, called license plates.

It's as a hangaround that the candidate gets his nickname —what the clubs call his riding name, road name or roader.

There's no set criteria for nicknames; they often just arise from the candidate's name or personality or something he's been remembered for. Some clubs have a guy who makes up all the nicknames, while others prefer the hangaround's nickname to be generated naturally. Nicknames can be mundane, like Petey for a guy named Peter, or they can be more arcane, like Nubz, Tomato Pie or Quack Quack. They can be derived from incidents, like Wrongway, or from the candidate's appearance, like Bug-Eye. Some nicknames are common to the point of being tiresome; for example, it's rare to find a chapter without a guy called Taz. Hangarounds, prospects and members are forbidden to call one another by anything but their nickname, especially in front of citizens.

When riding with the club, hangarounds are careful to stay behind all members and prospects.

Hangarounds are treated cordially and are frequently hugged and given words of encouragement, which helps foster a feeling of loyalty to the club and individual members. Several law enforcement officers have told me that they find the hangaround process very similar to how candidates are treated by religious cults.

During the hangaround period, the candidate will be watched very closely. Everything he says and does will be noted. The club is looking for signs of weakness, untrustworthiness or an inability to stay subordinate under stress, any of which would result in his immediate ouster.

Should the hangaround prove himself worthy, a full-patch member can sponsor him for membership. He is then elevated to a prospect, also known as a probate (the Sons of Silence use both titles, with prospects becoming probates after six months) or a striker.

A prospect is often given his bottom rocker—that's the bottom component, usually arced, of the three-piece patch that indicates

44

which territory he represents. Some clubs will also give the candidate the top rocker (which identifies the club) but never the center patch, which features the club's logo. The Bandidos give a prospect only a top rocker that reads "prospect," instead of the club's name.

Things change for the candidate rapidly after his elevation from hangaround. Prospects are the primary workforce for the club and are expected to clean the clubhouse, serve as cooks and bartenders at club events, provide personal security for full-patch members and perform any other necessary jobs, like arranging catering for events.

A prospect must perform any task his sponsor instructs him to do without question or excuse, from mundanities like getting a six-pack from the store to more important jobs like providing security for the member's wife or children. He also has to do whatever any full-patch member tells him to, as long as it's reasonable and for the good of the club.

Prospects are required to carry a prospect kit with them at all times. Inside are items that the sponsor might need, including breath mints, condoms, a sewing kit and other personal items. If the sponsor wants drugs, it's the prospect's job to carry them (sometimes even acquire them) and take the subsequent risk of getting caught.

Many clubs have an unwritten rule that prospects can't be asked to do anything illegal, but it's frequently broken and does not include acts of violence (which many bikers do not consider "illegal" in their code). Prospects are frequently ordered to knock cold those who have offended a full-patch member. Failure to do so results in a gang beating and expulsion from the club.

Some sponsors make an attempt to be reasonable, but many do not. Prospects are on call twenty-four hours a day, seven days a week, and must perform their duties quickly, completely and without complaint. Every single biker I have spoken to about his prospect days has his own set of horror stories of members freaking out over minor details (like getting a hamburger with the wrong kind of cheese on it), giving impossible orders (like "drop my wife off at the airport at 3:15 and pick up my kids from school at 3:30") or bleeding the prospect dry (like going on a mandatory run without any money, expecting the prospect to pay for gas, food and lodging on the way and beer and entertainment once they get there). With only one exception, every biker I have ever spoken with about his prospect period has told me a variation on the theme of being invited by his sponsor to meet at an expensive restaurant. Certain he was going to have a nice meal, perhaps even at his sponsor's expense, he arrives to find the sponsor surrounded by a large group of his family and/or friends. The prospect is told to stand guard outside the restaurant while the group eats. When they are finished, he is presented with the bill. Ah, brotherhood.

Failure to carry out any task can be hazardous to the prospect's health. When Thomas "Schnozz" Burke—a prospect for the Breed, a fiercely independent club from New Jersey and Pennsylvania—failed to deliver a package of meth on time, he was summoned to the home of his boss, John "Junior" Napoli, president of the Bristol, Pennsylvania, chapter. As punishment, Napoli took an electric screwdriver and drove a screw into Burke's right bicep, then beat him into unconsciousness. Napoli was preparing to set him on fire when another full patch, Christopher "Slam" Quattrocchi, pointed out that might not be a great idea in his own house. Napoli and Quattrocchi were later convicted of a passel of crimes, including the assault on Burke.

No matter how benevolent the sponsor, prospects are pressed hard, both for time and for money. Since they can be called in to serve at any time and for any length of time, for most, maintaining a traditional job is impossible. Recently, law enforcement officers in many jurisdictions have taken it upon themselves to inform employers of prospects' involvement with 1-percenter clubs, making it even more difficult for prospects to stay legally employed.

And since catering to sponsors' whims can be very expensive, many prospects who were not already involved in a criminal enterprise start finding ways to make money. Often, the only choice is trafficking illegal drugs. "I never thought about selling drugs before I was a Hells Angel," said Dave, a former Hells Angels sergeant-at-arms. "But I couldn't work outside the club anymore, so I just kind of fell into it." Two other members of his chapter supplied him with cocaine.

Prospects can expect to forget the cordial camaraderie they enjoyed as hangarounds. Members make the life of a prospect intentionally tough to test how well he handles stress and maintains his respect for their authority when they are abusing him. That concept is best exemplified by an activity called a mud check, during which a full-patch member assaults a prospect. The prospect is expected to fight back but never, ever to win. There are rules—like no weapons and no kicking a man when he's down— but the truth is that a prospect can be brutally beaten by a man he just bought dinner for. According to Blake "Bo" Boteler, an ATF agent who infiltrated the Sons of Silence, becoming a full-patch member, the club is particularly rough on prospects. "They like to punch their prospects in the mouth, head butt 'em, kick 'em, do those kind of things," he said, pointing out that full patches would sometimes drag prospects behind their motorcycles on grassy fields.

"Whatever you're told to do, you have to do," said Sons of Silence full-patch member Big Larry to interviewers on an episode of the television show *Gangland*. "If it's fucking pick up a dog turd off the floor and eat the fucker, you got to do it."

At any time, and for any reason (or no reason at all, as the sponsor need not explain why), the prospect can have his status taken from him and be expelled from the club.

All candidates must fill out a detailed questionnaire about their lives and pay a fee—traditionally $250 to $500—before they can become prospects. That money is used to hire a private investigator to look into the prospect's past and usually also to pay for a polygraph (lie detector) test to verify the claims he made on his written application. More than one law enforcement officer has told me than an operation was saved by the fact that the sponsor simply pocketed the prospect's money instead of hiring a professional to thoroughly check an undercover agent's claims.

Other tests are administered. Contacts—usually girlfriends or wives—who work in financial institutions or government offices check official records to see if the prospect is who he says he is. If he has ever even applied for a law enforcement or corrections officer job, if he's ever been accused of certain crimes (often involving children), if he uses certain drugs or if he has a gambling problem, he's out. Drug addicts and habitual gamblers are looked down upon because of the widespread belief that men who owe money are malleable and can be persuaded by their creditors to do anything, including betray the club.

Some clubs go to great pains to make sure prospects are exactly who they say they are. One common test is to get the prospect to introduce his parents to his sponsor. In cases where a parent is deceased, sponsors have been known to insist on seeing the grave.

Other requirements vary from club to club, but they are usually trivial. The Mongols, for example, won't allow a prospect to graduate to full membership until he learns every word of their drinking song, "We Are the Mongols."

Should the prospect pass all the tests after a specific period of time (which varies by club and out of necessity but which is usually six months to a year), his membership is put to a vote. Only a unanimous return will allow him to pass into membership. Any member who votes against a prospect's advancing to full patch is expected to explain his opposition. Two bikers have told me that many members test the tenor of the room before voting on prospects, and raise their hands slowly.

If the prospect advances, he is given the center, and final, piece of his patch—which explains the term "full patch." The patch ceremony is often a surprise to prospects, although they generally have an idea when their time is due, and several times I have heard of the prospect being fooled into believing he is being called into a disciplinary meeting when he is, in fact, receiving his patch. Most clubs just hand the new member a patch; others have his sponsor or the president ceremoniously put his new cut on him. The Sons of Silence, however, take the prospect into a field and force him to fight for his patch.

No matter how he gets his patch, there will be a huge party afterward.

Chapters can have several different prospects at any one time, and they are not always newcomers to the 1-percenter life. Some might be patching over from other clubs, while others are full-patch members who were busted down to prospect after a serious rule infraction. Patch-overs from rival clubs—like Outlaws to Hells Angels—are becoming increasingly rare, though, as the big clubs usually have distinct geographical dividing lines and turncoats have a reputation for being prone to becoming informants; that they were already disloyal to one club makes them more likely to betray another. Far more common are patch-overs from support clubs who have already earned a reputation for loyalty.

The prospecting period can be a harrowing existence, and many candidates fall by the wayside. "I hated every second of it," said Frankie, an Outlaws prospect who quit before he could be voted in or out. "After the abuse they all poured on me, there was no way I could call those men my 'brothers.'"

Depending on the reason, those who fail their prospect period might be bumped back down to hangaround or chased off. Most big clubs make a prospect sign over the ownership documents of his motorcycle to the club. While he's with the club, it is as though it is still his own, but if he fails to become a member, the bike then becomes club property and is usually sold to whichever member bids the most for it. Sponsoring someone who fails his prospect period can also lead to a member being bumped back down to prospect.

The benefits of membership are immense, though. Once you're a full patch, it's unlikely anyone other than law enforcement will ever give you trouble again. Your drinks are usually free, and you always have a seat. Making money becomes easy, as long as you're careful, and, after a while, you can get your own prospect to wait on you hand and foot. Boteler, the undercover ATF agent who became a Sons of Silence full-patch member, said in his memoir that once he became a member, "I no longer had to justify why I wanted to buy a gun, or why I wanted to buy meth; you are immediately confirmed as part of a criminal element."

In most communities, bikers rarely wear their colors, saving them for special occasions, get-togethers and, occasionally, shows of force. But many want to have the club tied to them in a permanent way. Getting the club's name or logo tattooed on your body is called earning your skin patch. In most clubs, it is only available to veteran members, usually those who have been in the club at least ten years, although some clubs allow any member to do so. These tattoos normally have a date, reflecting the day the wearer became a member. If a member with a skin patch leaves the club in good standing, as in a retirement due to health concerns, he is expected to add his exit date to the tattoo. If he should leave the club in bad standing, his tattoo will be removed forcibly. "You better hope to God we don't find you," said the Sons of Silence full patch Big Larry, "because we will cut the fucker off you . . . with a knife, with a razor, whatever, we will take it off."

No club likes the idea of former members, and most consider membership to be lifelong, unless there is an infraction. Those expelled from the club are said to be "out in bad standing" or simply "out bad." Not only do they not have any club rights or privileges, but members, prospects and hangarounds are expected to "mess with them" and assault them if possible, every time they see them.

A good example of that concept occurred in northeastern Massachusetts in 2012. Stan and Kyle, two members of the Revere chapter of the Red Devils—a support club that answers to the Salem chapter of the Hells Angels—attended a Sweet Sixteen birthday party for the daughter of Stan's girlfriend. The party was held at the Elks Lodge in Revere and attracted many guests. One of them was a problem.

Ferdinand "Freddy" Parrott had been ejected from the Salem Hells Angels after having left a fellow Hells Angel stranded in Pagan's territory when his bike broke down on a trip. The chapter let all surrounding chapters know that Parrott was out in bad standing.

That meant that, as Red Devils, it was the sworn duty of Stan and Kyle to assault Parrott on sight. But, in the interest of not interfering with the girl's night, they let him come and go without laying a finger on him. They both hoped the Hells Angels would not find out.

According to the federal indictment against them, they did. The day after the party, one of the Hells Angels called Kyle and told him that Stan had "fucked up" by "not taking care of business" and that the club now considered him no better than a snitch.

The next day, Stan went to work at a construction site, and as soon as he got there, he was approached by Sean Barr, vice-president of the Salem Hells Angels. He told Stan to quit his job. Stan complied immediately.

A little more than two weeks later, Kyle told Stan the Hells Angels wanted to talk with him. There was a rumor that he had been seen meeting with a couple of Outlaws at a doughnut shop near Boston.

Eager to dispel that rumor, Stan agreed to meet with the club, as long as it was at the Red Devils' clubhouse, not the Hells Angels'.

When he arrived, he saw that every member of both clubs was in the clubhouse. Barr, carrying a ball-peen hammer, told Stan to "pick a hand."

Confused, Stan stammered.

"You don't mind giving me your bike, right?" Barr continued, then turned to some other bikers and told them to "take the damn bike."

Just as Stan was about to object, he felt a crashing blow to the back of his head and fell unconscious.

When he woke, Barr pointed at Stan and the blood on the floor and told him he was going to need stitches. Then he asked, "Hand or knee?"

After spending a few agonizing moments deciding, Stan placed a shaking right hand on a bar stool. The hammer slammed down twice on the man's hand, breaking four bones and leaving him forever disabled.

While Stan was out cold, two Hells Angels had driven to Stan's house to get his motorcycle. It was behind a fence, so they dragged the fence down using a pickup's tow hitch and a chain. Then they took the motorcycle over the protests of Stan's girlfriend and her children.

Stan staggered home, and his girlfriend took him to the hospital for treatment for his head wound and broken hand. Not wanting to get in any more trouble with the Hells Angels, he told the hospital staff that an engine block had accidentally fallen on his hand.

The following day, Kyle got another call from the Hells Angels. They offered to sell him Stan's Harley. Kyle knew it would be unwise to refuse, but he told them he didn't have anywhere near enough money.

A few weeks later, the Hells Angels found a buyer for the Harley and called Stan, telling him to bring the bike's ownership papers to the clubhouse in Salem. No longer considering himself part of their world, Stan refused. The calls kept coming until finally, five months after the hammer to the hand incident, he was given an ultimatum: bring the papers to the clubhouse by one o'clock the following afternoon or be held down to watch as the Hells Angels raped his girlfriend and beat her children before killing him.

Chilled, Stan hung up. His adherence to the biker code was the primary reason he had not called the police and had lied about his injuries in the hospital. But that same code was allowing these guys to permanently disable him (costing him his career), steal his bike and threaten to assault innocent children, rape his girlfriend and kill him, simply because he hadn't destroyed a girl's party by beating up someone they didn't like. He realized that—in his experience at least—the biker code wasn't about brotherhood and freedom, but about one group of guys enforcing their own set of self-serving rules, with patently unjust penalties for anyone who didn't adhere to them. At that point, Stan believed he owed the Hells Angels and Red Devils nothing. So he called the police.

Sean Barr was arrested along with Hells Angels Marc Eliason and Robert Defronzo and Red Devil Brian Weymouth. They made their own deal with the prosecution: they would plead guilty to racketeering, effectively admitting they were part of a criminal organization, in exchange for having charges of aggravated assault and extortion withdrawn. Barr and Eliason were sentenced to eighty-seven months, while Defronzo and Weymouth were given fifty-seven months. All four were also sentenced to five years of supervised release upon their exit from prison.

Even those who have made it through the prospecting period say that it can be a harrowing experience. Duane was a full-patch California Hells Angel who was accused by another club member of stealing some firearms the accuser was allegedly planning on smuggling into Mexico. A quasi–civil war between drug cartels and the government has played out in Mexico for years, and with just one legal gun store in the whole country, demand for firearms is intense. Biker clubs are among the cartels' top suppliers.

An undercover cop Duane and I both knew introduced us because they were sure that Duane's story would make a great book, a cautionary tale for anyone who wanted to join a biker club.

At their next meeting after he was accused, the club voted Duane out and immediately started beating him. According to Duane, under the direction of the chapter president, he was stripped and restrained while one member of the club used a tattoo gun to obscure all of his club-related tattoos.

He was then thrown in the back of a truck and taken to his home. Under threat of death, he signed over the ownership of his Harley. His former "brothers" then ransacked his house looking for club-related paraphernalia, which they took, as well as—just because they could—his television. As a parting shot he was warned that if he spoke to police about what had happened, the club would cut off his head.

The guns were later found and Duane exonerated, but he had had enough of the club by then. He moved to another state—one without a Hells Angels chapter—and put that part of his life behind him. Duane approached me, through a cop we both knew, in hopes of co-writing a book about his experiences.

Indeed, a whole club can be considered out in bad standing by another club, as the Outlaws consider the Tennessee Henchmen, many of whom are former Outlaws or Black Pistons. Dannie Leroy "Sawgrass" Decker was a veteran Outlaw who was arrested on previous warrants in a 2010 raid of their clubhouse in Cleveland, Tennessee. Facing a number of charges, he pleaded guilty to unlawful possession of a handgun. When it became known to the club that the language in his plea deal included a phrase in which he agreed to cooperate in the investigation and that "the defendant further agrees not to protect anyone who was truly involved and not to falsely implicate anyone who was not truly involved in the commission of criminal offenses," he was summarily expelled from the club.

But he, like many others in his position, wanted back into the biker world. Unwanted by any other club, he started his own. After his release in 2012, he established the Henchmen MC with some friends, several of them also previous members of the Outlaws and their official support club, the Black Pistons. (The Tennessee Henchmen are not affiliated with other clubs in California, Nevada, Manitoba and elsewhere that have the same name.)

That, of course, does not sit well with the Outlaws. A widely reported incident of that feeling occurred at the Easyriders motorcycle show in Nashville on February 1, 2014. According to an official report filed to police by the show's security staff, two Henchmen, who were not wearing their colors and were escorted by their wives and children, were set upon by ten to fifteen Outlaws, who began to assault them. Eyewitnesses reported that one of the Henchmen was beaten to a bloody pulp, a woman associated with the club was "body slammed," and one of the Outlaws had his ear bitten off. The official report also notes that an unaffiliated woman had her purse stolen during the altercation. There were no subsequent arrests.

A word of advice to any Tennessee Henchmen who might be reading: you might want to travel in numbers greater than two.

# CHAPTER 3

# What Does a Biker Look Like?

I look pretty normal, don't I?" Sean, a biker who quit his club after it patched over to the Hells Angels and now rides as an independent without a bottom rocker, asked me. "Like a regular businessman."

I told him that I supposed he did. His hairstyle was out of date and not really appropriate for a man his age, and he wore a long earring, but the rest checked out. He was clean-shaven, wearing a branded navy-blue golf shirt over a long-sleeve white T-shirt with jeans and a brown leather belt along with the standard New Balance sneakers that are so common among middle-aged men. He looked like a blue-collar dad trying to stay current. That's probably because that's what he is. He has two kids and was recently hired as a forklift driver at a warehouse after being between jobs for a few months.

I also told him that I noticed he had driven to the coffee shop where we met and asked him if he looked the same way when he was riding.

He grinned and told me he wore a helmet, a leather vest, sunglasses and protective gloves, but other than that, he was the same guy.

I knew he wanted me to be surprised by that, but I couldn't be. I'd met and seen too many bikers to believe that many fit the long-haired, beer-bellied stereotype. Some of the old guys still look like that, but these days, bikers are mostly bodybuilder types, with the huge, wide frames of professional wrestlers, or look like regular dads.

Picture a biker. Like a real 1-percenter outlaw biker. You're probably imagining a guy with a long scruffy beard, a leather jacket or vest with patches on it, maybe a bandana, jeans and big boots.

Although a bit outdated and something of a caricature, there is some truth behind that stereotype. *The Wild One*, of course, made the blueprint for the traditional biker look, but the costumes for that movie were inspired by fact. The movie must have had some effect, though; in the pictures of the Hollister event that kicked off the 1-percenter movement, six years before the film, the bikers are mostly clean-shaven, and all wear canvas windbreakers, not denim or leather jackets, let alone vests.

To understand how bikers' appearance evolved, non-bikers need to know that riding a motorcycle is not like driving or being a passenger in a car at all. Bikers are not surrounded by thousands of pounds of metal and safety glass—they call cars and trucks "cages"—nor do they have impact-absorbing fenders, seat belts, airbags or even, usually, windshields. Riding a motorcycle might make some people feel free and excited, but it can also be dangerous, tiring and difficult.

If you haven't stuck your hand out of a car window at highway speed, try it. Now imagine that flood of air rushing at your face. That's what motorcyclists feel when they're riding. It's a bit of a rush, sure, but it can get old pretty quickly when you're on your bike and you're constantly being peppered by flying insects, airborne particulate and debris thrown up by passing vehicles.

And that continuous wind can freeze facial muscles even in quite mild weather.

Because of all those factors, serious motorcyclists make every effort to protect their faces and necks. Bikers tend to prefer to use things like bandanas, oversized sunglasses and thick beards. They also help keep the biker warm in the face of constant airflow. The popular belief that those items can also make a rider look rebellious or intimidating is just a bonus.

Unlike cars and trucks, which have become increasingly and exponentially safer because of innovations like seat belts and airbags, not to mention backup cameras, lane-change sensors and other devices, motorcycles have not. The leaps in technology for motorcycles have made them lighter and more powerful but not really any safer. And bikers generally ride customized bikes. But by changing component parts, customizing fiddles with balances and geometries that have been rigorously and carefully honed by the original manufacturers. The use of inferior parts—either out of a desire to go old-school or to save money—can further and significantly degrade the bike's dynamic capabilities, making it harder to handle and, thus, more prone to collisions.

Stock motorcycles are faster than they have ever been and can still throw a rider over the handlebars even in the most minor of collisions. And collisions happen far more frequently than they do with cars. Motorcycles are significantly smaller than cars and cast a far smaller image than cars and trucks do from directly in front or behind or anything but right beside. And, since motorcycles are so much rarer than cars, many drivers aren't looking for them, miss them or just don't know how much space to give them on the road, particularly when changing lanes. According to the Hurt Report, a 1981 study of motorcycle accidents in California, "The failure of motorists to detect and recognize motorcycles in traffic is the predominating cause of motorcycle accidents." By far, the most common type of collision experienced by motor-cyclists occurs when drivers of cars or trucks don't notice them turning left on a green light and plow right into them.

Making conditions even worse for motorcyclists is the fact that they are also liable to crash when presented with obstacles like ice patches, railway tracks and road debris that car and truck drivers wouldn't give a second thought to. Even worse can be the wind currents. At highway speeds, tractor-trailers can generate gusts big enough to blow a motorcycle off course and can send smaller ones off the road entirely.

According to the U.S. National Traffic Highway Safety Administration, the death rate of motorcycle riders in the United States is about thirty-five times that of people in cars and trucks, per mile traveled. And the motorcyclist death rate is rising (particularly among bikers over the age of forty and riders of bikes with engines 1,400 cc or bigger, which describes many bikers), while the death rate for drivers and passengers of cars and trucks is steadily dropping.

When a motorcyclist is involved in a collision, he or she is normally thrown from the bike and can hit the road, other vehicles, roadside signs or other surfaces at high speeds, causing major injuries or death. Once thrown, he or she also faces a strong chance of being struck again by motorists who might be unable to stop their vehicles in time.

There's not a heck of a lot riders can do about it. The fact is that if you ride a motorcycle in traffic, there's a pretty strong chance you're going over the handlebars or getting plowed into by an inattentive driver. But motorcyclists can protect themselves to some extent with modern-day versions of armor. Over decades of motorcycle use and subsequent collisions, the best solution for rider-protective armor has proven to be leather. It's afford-able, it's durable, it keeps riders warm but usually not too hot, it's comfortable, and it offers some protection against injury in a crash, especially against the abrasions that come with the almost inevitable sliding after being thrown from a bike. As a bonus for bikers who find themselves in harm's way, leather clothes can also shield against bladed weapons in a fight and can slow if not quite stop some bullets, mitigating injury.

Many serious motorcyclists, especially racers, prefer what they call full leathers, meaning a complete suit consisting of boots, pants, jackets and gloves. You might be surprised to learn that the gloves are considered perhaps the most important arti-cles because of the innate human reaction of reaching out in times of danger. And, as anyone who has ridden a motorcycle at any speed will tell you, knuckles can go numb and become almost useless from prolonged airflow, even if temperatures feel comfortable when you're not on the road.

Few 1-percenters will use full leathers, except while racing, instead relying upon gloves, boots and a vest, which offers little help to the very vulnerable elbow and shoulder joints. Leather pants and chaps were once popular with bikers but are rare now.

There's a funny section in *Role Models*, a memoir by renowned filmmaker and raconteur John Waters, in which the author describes how the Hells Angels he knew would shop at the same stores as many gay men of the same age and compete for the same items, avoiding eye contact the whole time. In fact, for a very long time, the outlaw biker look was very popular among a certain section of the LGBT community. Recognizing that real-ity, impresarios Jacques Morali and Henri Belolo made sure that there has always been a character in the pioneering band The Village People who is alternately referred to as the "Biker" or the

"Leatherman." Played primarily by Glenn Hughes—who was an almost fanatical Harley-Davidson aficionado offstage, but not a member of any club—he always appeared in head-to-toe studded leather and sported an outsized handlebar mustache.

Some clubs, particularly the Pagan's, eschew leather (except for boots and gloves), preferring to go with far less protective denim.

Ironically, while the leather look sprang from bikers' desire to stay safe and warm, the same thinking did not extend to the protection offered by helmets.

While most studies—especially the wide-ranging and meticulous "Motorcycle Accidents In-Depth Study" (MAIDS) of 2000—show conclusive evidence that helmets, particularly full-face helmets, reduce the likelihood and severity of head and neck injuries, 1-percenters tend not to like them.

The idea of seeing a 1-percenter in a full-face helmet borders on ridiculous, unless he's mandated to wear one while racing. In states with no or relaxed helmet laws, bikers rarely wear them at all, and in states and provinces with helmet laws, bikers will only grudgingly wear them. One biker I spoke with in Ontario told me he believes that helmets actually make riding more dangerous because he can't hear as well with one on.

The disdain for helmets stems from the fact that they were the first item to be mandated for motorcyclists by law. That, of course, clashes with the outsider, outlaw image biker gangs like to maintain and promote.

Many bikers are members of American Bikers Aimed Toward Education (ABATE), which lobbies against helmet laws. Of course, many of ABATE's members are not 1-percenters. On July 3, 2017, a Harley rider named Philip A. Contos (relatives say he's not a member of a club) was attending an anti-helmet-law protest in Syracuse, New York (where helmets are required for all riders), when he hit his brakes suddenly to avoid colliding with another Harley. They didn't make contact, but the sudden stop sent Contos over his handlebars and he hit the pavement with his head, breaking his neck. He died later that day in a nearby hospital. "The medical expert we discussed the case with who pronounced him deceased stated that he would've no doubt survived the accident had he been wearing a helmet," said a representative of the New York State Police.

So much do bikers hold helmet laws in contempt that some of them have been known to wear novelty helmets and even to go so far as to put fake "DOT-approved" stickers on them. That essentially means that they are wearing a helmet, but one that will offer no protection in the event of a crash, and that they even took the extra effort to try to make law enforcement think it's real—an absurd length to go to avoid complying with the law.

In states and provinces that do have helmet laws, 1-percenters will often flout them, riding helmetless at events like rallies and funerals. Members of law enforcement I have spoken with say they would never issue a ticket for that because it has the potential to look like undue harassment, which bikers frequently claim is the case, and it also gives them an excellent opportunity to photograph individual members' faces.

The same irony about safety applies to the motorcycles themselves. Bikers prefer large bikes (which are statistically more dangerous) and the retro-cruiser style (ditto). They also frequently customize their rides, replacing meticulously engineered and rigorously tested components with items of their own devising. These mods—like ridiculously low seats, correspondingly high handlebars, tiny headlights, rear suspensions without springs and fat back tires—are designed to look more dangerous, and generally are.

Probably the most common customization to bikers' rides is the addition of straight pipes, which are exhaust pipes that eliminate restrictive curves or baffles. That can make an already loud stock Harley-Davidson positively thunderous.

While there can be minor performance benefits, supporters of straight pipes claim that the excessive noise they make are actually a safety precaution. There's a campaign called Loud Pipes Save Lives (you can even buy bumper stickers or T-shirts with sayings like "You won't watch, so I'll make you listen" on their websites and social media pages).

Opponents of straight pipes point out that there have been no scientific studies that support the claim and that, in real-life situations, they don't help at all because drivers can't immediately pick up where the sound is coming from.

But the practice continues. The pipes almost universally contravene noise ordinances, but these are rarely enforced. That's because in most of North America, noise complaints from the public are not enforced by law enforcement unless the person complaining has already given the noisemaker fair warning, and who wants to go warn a biker that they're going to call the cops on them? And police rarely cite bikers for loud pipes of their own initiative because they don't want to look as though they are harassing bikers unnecessarily.

The loud pipes issue was lampooned in an episode of the popular animated comedy show *South Park* called "The F Word." In it, the show's main characters—four preteen boys—discover that the word "fag" actually means "a contemptible person" and has only recently been used to insult gay men. Since they have no problem with the LGBT people they know, the boys decide that the most annoying element of their community is made up of Harley owners with loud pipes and they should be called fags. Much to the dismay of the bikers, the boys succeed in having the "official" dictionary definition of the word fag changed to "(1) An extremely annoying, inconsiderate person, most commonly associated with Harley riders. (2) A loud and obnoxious person who owns or frequently rides a Harley." I would expect that *South Park* show runners Matt Stone and Trey Parker weren't exactly welcome at 1-percenter clubhouses or events after that.

It's just a coincidence that one of the few shows to narrowly beat "The F Word" in the ratings when it aired in the first week of November 2009 was "Fa Guan," an episode of *Sons of Anarchy*, a drama about bikers that has featured appearances by several actual Hells Angels, including Sonny Barger.

Since straight pipes can also cause bikes to fail government-mandated emission standards tests, an illegal cottage industry has emerged in many areas that allows owners of such bikes, and modified cars, to pay to have such tests faked.

But a biker's appearance isn't really about safety when he's in his colors. It's about being recognized as a full-patch member of the club. Bikers call it respect; law enforcement calls it intimidation. Because certain jurisdictions have determined that wearing 1-percenter gear can be intimidating and can even be considered a weapon in extortion cases, bikers have been known to take off their gear—not just cuts, but belt buckles and even rings—in situations that could become heated. Many nightclubs and restaurants also post signs telling patrons that gang colors are not allowed inside, and that applies to bikers' insignia. That has led to brawls and individual fights throughout North America, as bikers prize little if anything more than their right to wear their colors.

It has also led to some misunderstandings, especially in the South and when corners have been cut. When the owner of the

Knothole Saloon & Eatery in Lake Wylie, South Carolina, grew concerned after hearing that the Hells Angels in the area were flexing on and frequently assaulting other bikers, he put up a sign, but he left out the word "gang," so it read "No colors allowed." An Asian-American woman who identified herself only as Jane mistook the sign for racist and complained to the NAACP and the local TV station, News Channel 36. "At first, looking at it, I was offended, and then after that I got kind of angry," she said on the TV news report. "Whether you are white, black, Asian, Hispanic—it doesn't matter what race you are, just reading that sign you should be offended by it." When asked about the sign by reporters, Knothole owner Bo Legg said it didn't apply to skin color, but to gang colors. He also explained that a representative from the NAACP had been in contact with him and was more than happy with his explanation of the sign. My guess is that Jane, like many if not most North Americans, was serenely unaware of the gang activity in her community but very aware of the pervasive racism that still exists in many places.

The cut, or vest, is by far the most important part of their gear when it comes to biker culture. Bikers are serious to the point of mania about them. They are never supposed to allow anyone to touch their cuts, and losing one—especially by force—is an offense that will be punished and may lead to expulsion from the club.

It's also a serious violation to wear any garment over the cut, like a raincoat, a parka or a knapsack. If the biker feels he needs something like that, he's required to try to fit it under the vest.

The backs of the vests adhere to an almost universal pattern, with some variation. Although they are commonly referred to as the "three-piece patch," there are usually five, sometimes four, distinct patches that form a single unit.

Traditionally, the top patch is an arced rectangle containing the club's name in the club's colors. For example, the Hells Angels' reads "Hells Angels" in red letters on a white background. Support clubs will frequently reverse that pattern, as with the Head Hunters, who have their name in white letters on a red background.

Similarly, at the bottom is an arced rectangle that describes the territory that the club claims, not—as many believe—the wearer's chapter. For example, the Hells Angels have seven individual chapters in South Carolina, but they all wear a bottom rocker that reads "South Carolina." The Hells Angels in California used to have bottom rockers that used their chapters' names— like Berdoo (San Bernardino), Frisco (San Francisco) and R'Side (Riverside)—but have discontinued that. Most other clubs do the same thing with their bottom rockers, while the Pagan's don't wear bottom rockers.

In between the two rockers is the logo of the club, given only to full members, which is why they are described as full patches.

Somewhere on the back, there will always be a patch that reads MC or MCC. That, of course, stands for motorcycle club. It's considered a necessary part of the patch.

The final back patch is one that reads 1 percent or 1-percenter, usually in a diamond shape. Although many clubs and members take great pride in these patches, others do not, claiming that they are too commonplace and have lost their meaning and weight.

The front of the vest is different. Although there are some mandatory patches, the rest is up to the wearer, allowing them to get creative. In most cases, the front left of the vest has an arced patch that denotes the wearer's home chapter. Many chapters go by nicknames. In Ontario, for example, Hamilton is known as Hammertown (the members there reputedly like to use hammers as weapons, a habit most likely developed after the name), and Oshawa is the Asylum Crew because their clubhouse is near a hospital that specializes in treating mental illness.

Sometimes you'll see a 1-percenter with a similar side rocker on the right side of his vest with the name of another chapter. That occurs when a biker wins the respect or affection of another chapter. In those cases, they will give him such a rocker, indicating that he's always welcome in their clubhouse.

On the upper left side of the vest, over the heart, is often a small version of the logo, and on the upper right is the wearer's nickname. The upper right is also where various other patches tend to congregate.

Most bikers have some form of their club motto, like AFFA (Angels Forever, Forever Angels), ADIOS (Angels Die in Outlaw States) or SYLB (Support Your Local Bandidos).

Various other patches adorn the front. Of all of them, the one I am most frequently asked about by readers is the one that says "Filthy Few." Over the years it has been around, many in law enforcement have told media, including me, that it was reserved for members who had killed for the club. But given the sheer number of Filthy Few patches I've seen, that would mean that there should be piles of bodies in every city with a Hells Angels chapter. Other sources say that the patch is for those who have shed blood, or even just fought for the club. In his memoir, Barger says it's reserved for the club's hardest partiers. And Pat Matter, founder and president of the Hells Angels Minnesota chapter, writes in his book that they were handed out essentially to any member who wanted one. Although it's probably the least satisfying to readers, I believe Matter's explanation is the most accurate, as he's the only one who doesn't stand to gain anything by promoting his explanation.

Occasionally, you'll see bikers with a 666 patch, referring to the biblical "Number of the Beast" that has seeped its way into popular culture through horror movies and heavy metal songs. Not only is that part and parcel of the whole "shock value" thing they always talk about, but it also stands for something else in their world. Again using their familiar code of each number standing for a letter, 666 stands for FFF. For the Hells Angels, that means "Filthy Few forever." But for opposing clubs like the Outlaws and Mongols, it translates to "Fuck the Filthy Few."

Other clubs, like the Sons of Satan, award a patch that says ITCOB. That stands for "I took care of business," and it means that the wearer has undergone hardship on the club's behalf.

Other patches in the shock-value drawer include swastikas, iron crosses (the logo of the Ching-a-Lings used to feature a swastika, but they have since changed it to an iron cross), SS lightning bolts, Confederate flags and even one that I have to admit is kind of clever—styled after the Salvation Army's logo, it reads "the Satanic Army."

And then there are the wings. Just as pilots are granted wings after graduating from flight school, some bikers are given wing-shaped patches for certain achievements. According to both sides of the biker divide, they are awarded for sex (usually said to be oral sex, but not always), with various partners or positions, that has been witnessed by at least one other member. The wings are said to represent different things, based on their color.

**Black:** a partner of African descent
**Yellow:** a partner of East Asian descent
**Red:** a menstruating partner
**Green:** a partner with a sexually transmitted disease

**Brown:** anilingus
**Blue:** a partner who works in law enforcement
**Purple:** a partner who's dead
**Gold:** a partner who was subject to gang rape

Many clubs have abandoned the wings, but the Vagos, in particular, and some Mongols appear to still seem quite enthusiastic about them.

Some patches are aimed directly at intimidating law enforcement. You'll sometimes see a biker with a patch that reads "ACAB," which stands for "All cops are bastards." The phrase started with skinheads in England (a group that has many common traits with bikers) and slowly made its way around the English-speaking world. A patch with the word "dequallo" is said to indicate that its owner has assaulted a police officer. Barger denies that in his memoir but offers no alternative explanation. No matter what its meaning, the dequallo patch does get on the nerves of law enforcement officers I have spoken with.

There are few achievements as prized by the big clubs as when a member steals a cop's badge, and those who have been able to do so wear a patch that looks like a police badge. It's worn upside-down to show a lack of respect.

Other patches might just reflect the owner's personality or history. A patch that reads "22"—for BB, "behind bars" or "bye bye"—can indicate its owner has been to prison, although some clubs prefer to use the number eight or the image of an eight ball. "DFFL" stands for "Dope forever, forever loaded," indicating that its wearer likes to get high. Similarly, "FTW" means "Fuck the world" and "DILLIGAF" stands for "Do I look like I give a fuck?" There are others, like "Nunya," which is short for none of your business, that adhere to the same attitudes.

Because of the importance bikers put on their colors, stealing an enemy's cut is a genuinely valued achievement. Traditionally, any opponents' cuts were displayed in the clubhouse, always hung upside-down, and would frequently become the target of darts, spit, garbage or other signs of disrespect.

Some clubs, the Outlaws in particular, like to take photos of their girlfriends wearing the captured cuts of rivals.

Similarly, the rise of social media has allowed members and supporters to post photos or videos of themselves setting rival vests on fire, running over them with their motorcycles or committing other such indignities.

That has helped fuel a cottage industry for counterfeit patches and other gear, particularly that of the Hells Angels. These items are available online from companies in China and Indonesia, usually cost about $100 or so and look startlingly realistic.

Wearing them in front of a real Hells Angel or even supporter is a pretty sure way to wind up in a hospital, but only if they catch you. Lots of people wear them in Southeast Asia, particularly Indonesia, and rival gang members love few things more than circulating pictures of eighty-year-old Sumatran women proudly wearing official-looking death's-head T-shirts.

# CHAPTER 4

# Setting Up a Club

"Our club was set up like any other," Sean, the now-independent, told me. "There's a standard way of doing these things, the way it's set up, the officers, the organization and all that—there's rules."

I asked him if he had helped set up the structure of the club, but he told me it was already in place when he'd joined.

"They're all basically the same, though," he continued. "They say the Hells Angels came up with it, but who knows?"

IF YOU WANT to be an outlaw biker, you can always start your own club. It's not hard, really. Just register as an organization for motorcycle enthusiasts. You can register as a nonprofit or even a charitable organization, but you'll fall under much more scrutiny from your federal government, so it's probably not a great idea. Still, after convictions put away their top leaders in 2016, the Bandidos registered as a nonprofit organization under the name USARG Inc. "It was announced at the presidents' meeting on January 28, 2017, that a nonprofit corporation would be set up and that all chapters would be entering into licensing agreements in order to continue to be Bandidos chapters," read the affidavit the club used to support their change of status. They were successful. Of course, since the American Bandidos have severed their relations with the chapters overseas, their new status affects the U.S. chapters only.

For informational purposes, let's propose that your new club is set up in the fashion that the big clubs have been for decades.

First, you'll have to write a charter, which serves as a constitution and set of bylaws that the club will operate under. The rules should mandate who can join, how they must behave, what they have to pay as dues and how they will be punished, if necessary. Keep in mind that what the document says is not always how the club operates, and no mention of violence or other crimes should make it into the document. To stay under legal protection, it will have to be an actual motorcycle enthusiast club, so it's important that much of your charter be devoted to motorcycle ownership and riding.

Then, you'll need a leadership group. At the top of every club and chapter is a president. The president is elected by all full-patch members of the club by a show of hands. Depending on the club, elections are held either every year or every six months.

The president's job, primarily, is to preside over "church." All of the club's official business goes through him, and he determines which issues go to a vote, determining the solution to the other issues by himself. The president weighs every issue with regard to the charter and can work to get the club to amend existing bylaws or add new ones as the need arises.

It's also his job to settle disputes and conflicts within the club. Should Biker A claim that Biker B owes him because of a deal gone wrong, the president will determine what Biker A is owed, if anything, and whether Biker B deserves any punishment for his actions.

The president, often referred to simply as "P," is also the face of the club. He represents the interests of the club to the outside world. In clubs that have multiple chapters, the president speaks for his chapter and casts his chapter's vote. In those clubs, he often reports to the national or regional president.

Depending on the club, the chapter and his own charisma, the treatment of ex-presidents varies. Some are revered, while most simply revert to their status as full-patch members. When the Breed's Bristol, Pennsylvania, chapter president John "Junior" Napoli became convinced that former president James Graber had stolen loose change from an illegal slot machine in the clubhouse, he called a secret meeting with the other officers of the chapter. They decided to punish Graber. Later that week, Christopher "Slam" Quattrocchi lifted Graber up from behind and threw him to the floor of the chapter's clubhouse. William "Tattoo Billy" Johnson then stomped on his chest, which he said collapsed "like an accordion." Then Napoli began to kick him and beat him with a pool cue. Graber was in such bad shape that Napoli eventually called prospect Eric "Kicker" Loebsack, who had some medical training, to come and treat him. Loebsack took Graber to a nearby hospital where he spent four days in intensive care with multiple injuries to his head, back, spleen and liver. Following biker code, Graber did not report the attack to police and lied about how he had sustained his injuries to the people who treated them. The details of his punishment came out as testimony in the 2006 trial of Napoli, Quattrocchi and three other Breed members—William "Tattoo Billy" Johnson, Thomas "Fuzzy" Heilman and Frederick "Panhead Fred" Freehoff—on trafficking, extortion, racketeering and weapons offenses. Freehoff, Quattrocchi and Loebsack pleaded guilty to trafficking methamphetamine and to assault. While a jury convicted Napoli—who was surreptitiously recorded threatening his investigators' lives during the trial—and Johnson of trafficking, assault, extortion and weapons charges, Heilman was convicted of trafficking.

Being president is, of course, a prestigious title, but it can also be a dangerous one. Biker tradition dictates that the president always rides in front of the formation when the club travels and is never to be passed. That, of course, is the position most likely to get into a collision.

Far more dangerous, however, is his legal position. Even if he himself is not directly participating in, or gaining from, any illegal activities of club members, a president can be liable for conviction under "tacit approval" laws, meaning that if he knew about criminal enterprises by members and did not stop them or kick them out of the club, he was giving his blessing and is just as responsible as those who actually handled the goods or cash.

And presidents are targets. Nothing makes a rival gang or law enforcement happier than being able to say they brought down or beat up or otherwise humiliated a rival chapter's president (and a national president is even better).

Many presidents wear a patch denoting their status on the front right of their cut, but others—aware that they are a target of both rival clubs and law enforcement—prefer not to advertise their rank.

If his performance is not up to snuff, a chapter president can be removed from office. In those cases, the other members of the chapter hold a secret meeting and vote on the issue of removing him from office. If they elect to remove him, the process might be cordial or violent, depending on the president's personality and the nature of the grievances against him. Similarly, the problems that led to his removal from office can mean that his status afterward can range from ordinary full-patch status all the way to forced expulsion. In the major clubs, chapter presidents can also be removed from office by the national president. That order is given to the full-patch member the national president has earmarked to take over the chapter, and it is his duty to carry it out, after gathering support from other members. A chapter that fails to remove its president after a direct order from the national president will be expelled from the club and have its patches forcibly removed.

Since presidents are prone to a variety of incapacitating events, the position of vice-president is usually filled by a member who is held in a similarly high level of esteem, as it's his sworn duty to fill in for the president as necessary. It's his responsibility to keep the president informed of any pressing issues that might come up in church. He also is expected to attend any presidents' meetings with his president.

Many clubs also require the vice-president to carry large sums of cash, especially on runs, to cover unforeseen expenses, like bail, medical expenses and motorcycle repair costs. Any club money used in such an incident is considered loaned to the biker who needed it and is expected to be repaid quickly, and with an interest rate set by the club. Stiff penalties, ranging from a beating to expulsion, are levied against those who don't pay their debt to the club on time.

The vice-president is elected after the president, in the same way. His removal is up to the president, who can do so unilaterally, but usually after he's presented with grievances by a member or group of members.

There's usually no special position for the vice-president in the road formation as long as he stays among the full-patch members, but he is often right behind the president.

After them in the order of authority is the sergeant-at-arms. Some clubs elect a sergeant-at-arms, while others allow the president to select one. Generally considered the toughest guy in the chapter—or at least the best fighter—it's the sergeant-at-arms' responsibility to keep the peace within the club and to enforce any of the president's decisions. It's also his duty to ensure all dues and fines are paid on time and in full, and to mete out punishments as directed by the president.

If a member is expelled from the club, it's the duty of the sergeant-at-arms to collect club property from him. That includes his cut and any other club-sanctioned items. In most clubs, it also means his motorcycle. Many clubs expect members or even prospects to sign their motorcycle's ownership over to the club. As long as they are in good standing, the bike is for their use only, but if they are expelled, the club keeps the bike.

In times of war, the sergeant-at-arms becomes the chapter's top general, making strategic plans and reporting directly to the president. Depending on the scale of the conflict, the sergeant-at-arms can also serve as a personal bodyguard for the president.

In some cases, especially on long runs through territories held by adversarial clubs, the sergeant-at-arms will have an assistant, usually called the enforcer, who will take on similar duties. While the sergeant-at-arms is sometimes an elected position, the enforcer can be appointed by the president or the sergeant-at-arms himself.

In most cases, the sergeant-at-arms rides at the back of the group of full patches, just ahead of the prospects. If the club uses an enforcer, he rides at the very back of the group, behind even the hangarounds, while the sergeant-at-arms rides up front with the president, being careful never to pass him.

Once the sergeant-at-arms position is filled, most clubs require a secretary and a treasurer. Although those two titles come with very disparate responsibilities, almost all chapters and clubs combine the two positions, with one person serving as secretary-treasurer.

The secretary's job is primarily to maintain the club's records and history. He takes minutes at church and looks after the club's archives. It's also the secretary's job to maintain a complete and up-to-date dossier on all the chapter's members and prospects, including recent photos and contact information. Similarly, he also has a file on former members of the club—including those in both good and bad standing, members who are serving time behind bars and known informants. He acquires pictures and bios of the law enforcement officers in the area who might be involved in investigations of the club. In times of war, he collects as much of the same type of information as he can on the rival club's membership and known associates. He also communicates with the mother chapter, if the club has one, to keep up to date on any new bylaws or events.

Because the secretary has the responsibility to keep the chapter's historical records and items intact, he is usually a long-serving member with an encyclopedic knowledge of the club's past.

The treasurer, as the name implies, handles the books for the club. He records all incoming and outgoing assets, signs checks, pays bills, keeps receipts and files monthly reports pertaining to the chapter's finances. This, of course, is limited to legal transactions, as anything illegal is not recorded in the club's official books. Revenues come in the form of member's dues, prospect application fees, licensing, parties and other events and the sale of support merchandise.

Being reliable and good with numbers are important qualities clubs look for in a treasurer, and clubs frequently try to find a candidate who has a close relationship with the sergeant-at-arms, who collects debts on his behalf. Stealing from the club is considered a particularly grievous offense, so the treasurer is carefully selected and under great scrutiny for his entire term.

Because these two jobs are both difficult and time consuming, and often go largely unappreciated by other members, it can be hard to get good candidates to run for the office or offices. In some cases, the secretary-treasurer can be appointed by the president.

The secretary-treasurer has no predetermined spot in the riding formation but must stay with the full patches.

Finally, clubs have a position called road captain. It's his job to organize any trips or runs the club goes on and to be in charge of bike maintenance. For runs, he plans the route and sets up food, gas and overnight stops. It's his responsibility to keep the chapter out of, or at least aware of, any trips through territories claimed by rival clubs.

It's also his job to inspect every motorcycle headed out on the run and to decide what happens in the event of a breakdown. Should a bike break down, it's unlikely its rider would hitch a ride with another biker. Sitting on the back of a motorcycle is called "riding bitch" and is reserved for women except in cases of absolute necessity. While not an offense, riding bitch is considered a blow to the biker's masculinity, and it can garner years of mockery and even hinder the rider's ability to advance in the club.

Bikers on the run may change position in formation at will, as long as they stay with their group and don't pass any of the members who can't be passed. Any other types of position changes or requests to stop must have the road captain's consent. The road captain rides at the front of the formation, beside and just behind the president. Large groups might designate an assistant road captain, who rides at the back, behind the hangarounds.

The road captain also usually organizes the "crash wagon," a truck that drives some distance ahead of or behind the club. Driven by a non-member or a member too old to ride long distances comfortably, the crash wagon (some clubs use the term "crash truck") carries tools and spare parts in case one of the bikes breaks down. Crash wagons can also carry medical or party supplies and, as many in law enforcement have told me, contraband like guns and other weapons. The driver—or passenger, if there is one—stays in contact with the road captain.

The road captain is rarely elected, instead usually being appointed by the president, and is sometimes not even truly considered among the chapter's officers.

The officers as a group have several duties, but none is more important than conducting trials. When a member is accused of breaking a club or chapter rule he will appear before the officers, who will decide whether he requires punishment and what his punishment will be, in accordance with the club's charter and any chapter bylaws.

Okay, now you've got your club and your officers. You'll need a name. Most 1-percenter clubs like to choose names that involve biblical hell—often in possessive form, like Devil's this or Satan's that—or some kind of warrior, like the Mongols, the many different sets of Cossacks and others. Still more have names reflecting their self-declared outsider status, like the Outlaws, the Vagos and many different clubs called the Loners. Some are kind of silly, like the Galloping Goose, which was named after a founder's racing bike, and the Alky Haulers. And some just lack imagination. There probably wasn't a huge amount of stimulating conversation about names when the Americans MC was formed.

And you'll need a logo. Skulls are popular, as are flames, bikes, devils, vampires and characters from Norse legends:

anything that would look at home on a junior high school bully's binder will do. Tastefulness and subtlety are anything but prerequisites. And don't worry too much about copyright violations, either. While the Hells Angels' winged skull concept had been around for a while before the club adopted it, and has no clear originator, the Pagan's logo has been frequently said to bear a stunning resemblance to an image directly from a Marvel Thor comic book, and the Sons of Silence appear to have outright copied the Anheuser-Busch logo. Sons of Silence founder Bruce "The Dude" Richardson admitted in a TV interview that "We was drinking Budweiser beer, and I seen the emblem and I said hey, that'd make a good one." Neither club has yet been the target of legal action. Be careful, however, to ensure that your logo does not look too much like an existing club's. That, of course, would be inviting trouble.

Above the logo usually goes your top rocker, which announces your club's name. And below goes the bottom rocker, which stakes your claim to a territory. That, of course, is the most contentious part of forming a club. If you form a club that claims the territory of an existing club, you had better be prepared to fight to keep your rocker. If a member of a club sees a biker from a different patch claiming the same territory, it's his sworn duty to remove the offending biker's cut, forcibly if necessary.

A good example of that mentality happened in Spokane, Washington. When the Hells Angels formed a chapter there, they let the established 1-percenter club in the city, the Ghost Riders, know immediately. A group of them stormed the Ghost Riders' clubhouse, viciously assaulted the only person in there, club president Kenneth "Maggot" Fisette, and took his cut as a trophy.

Two years later, on December 9, 2010, a Hells Angel named Timothy Gail Myers showed up at the Comet Restaurant and

Bar—a hangout for local bikers that was owned by a Spokane city councilman who got into trouble with health officials for refusing to stock toilet paper in the tavern's restrooms because "thieves" kept taking it (he was forced to restock or face a fine)—in his colors.

According to witnesses, Fisette's wife, Yolanda, said something contentious to Myers's girlfriend, and the two started fighting. Soon, almost everyone in the bar joined in. "It was a mess in here," said Lori Johnson, a bartender at The Comet. "Bar stools were flying, fists were swinging, teeth, hair, everything."

Myers, Spokane's sergeant-at-arms at the time, was down and getting kicked by several people. A Ghost Rider, Sean Kilgallen, pulled Myers's cut off him and threw it to Kenneth Fisette, although his pass was intercepted by Yolanda. The couple fled with the vest.

As the brawl raged on—Ghost Rider Gary Fisette, Kenneth's nephew, had one of his eyes gouged out in the melee—the sound of gunshots rang out. By the time police got there, two men were on the ground with gunshot wounds—Myers and Kilgallen. Kilgallen would die in a nearby hospital that night, while Myers recovered.

Myers was arrested and charged with manslaughter. Although he admitted in court that he had fired the bullet that killed Kilgallen, he was acquitted, as his defense attorneys successfully argued that he was in mortal danger at the time. Kenneth Fisette testified he had lied to police because he didn't know that he was legally bound to tell them the truth.

The day after the brawl, Yolanda Fisette returned Myers's cut to the Hells Angels through go-betweens. She testified that if she hadn't, she believed there would be a war.

In fact, if you are forming a motorcycle club—1-percenter or not, bottom rocker or not—it's considered proper etiquette to ask the permission of the dominant club in the area what you can call your club, what you can put on your bottom rocker and even if you can form a club at all. Failure to comply with any of their decisions would almost certainly be an invitation to violence.

If you intend to wear a 1-percenter patch, do so with the knowledge that you will be treated differently by members of other clubs. Other 1-percenter clubs will likely test your mettle, either by partying with you or by fighting you, or both. Two different bikers have told me that the true definition of a 1-percenter is someone who puts on a 1-percent patch and can defend it from anyone who tries to take it.

Non-1-percenter motorcycle clubs will likely steer clear of you—there's a reason they don't accept that title themselves—and make space for you at motorcycle shows and other events that draw people who are aware of the 1-percenter lifestyle.

And, of course, law enforcement will treat you differently. If you wear a 1-percenter patch or have a 1-percent sticker on your bike or car, be prepared to be stopped by police frequently. Have your license, ownership and proof of insurance ready at all times.

Most civilians don't attach any special importance to the 1-percenter patch—to them, everyone who fits the standard description of biker is dangerous—but those in the know of the biker subculture might give you a little more respect or a little more room.

The most important patch you absolutely must have, however, is the one that says MC or MCC. Remember, if you want to exist as a motorcycle club, your members have to own and ride motorcycles. Some clubs will even mandate the minimum number of miles a member must ride to maintain his membership.

The reasoning behind that is simple. In recent years, law enforcement has become increasingly aware of the large number of 1-percenter bikers involved in organized crime. If they are able to prove that members of the club do not own or operate motorcycles, it helps them set up a case that the club exists for reasons other than the enthusiasm of riding. Should members be charged with felonies, the club or chapter could then be charged under RICO (Racketeer Influenced and Corrupt Organizations Act, a law targeting organized crime in the United States) or other anti-gangster statutes.

Now you have members, officers, a name, a set of colors and your bikes, so you'll need someplace to meet. Traditionally, bikers buy clubhouses to stay away from prying eyes and ears, although those without the financial capability will sometimes meet at bars or restaurants—prospects ensuring that others keep their distance—until they can afford a place of their own.

Although clubhouses can be set up in personal homes, strip malls and other buildings, former restaurants are preferred for reasons that will become evident.

Unlike traditional buyers, bikers prefer their real estate to be in run-down, high-crime areas. Not only does that keep the price down, but it often surrounds them with people who fear, disrespect or have open contempt for law enforcement and who are far less likely to call the police or even speak with them when they see or hear about crimes being committed.

The primary concern when setting up a clubhouse is usually security. Ideally, a clubhouse should be a free-standing structure, making it more difficult for anyone to listen through or burst through adjoining walls undetected.

Biker clubhouses are usually stocked with video cameras, motion sensors, floodlights and sometimes listening devices to monitor the area around the building.

Many clubs place bollards, cement barriers that prevent

vehicles from running into the clubhouse, around the property. Sometimes they disguise them as decorative planters.

Windows are often covered over or made opaque and are usually barred. Even if they aren't, all windows and doors will be hooked up to an alarm system.

The front door will be secure, and usually it is all metal and able to be opened from the inside only. It will be manned 24/7, and anyone wanting in or out, even during parties with civilians in the clubhouse, must ask permission from the biker manning it. The doors are so effective in keeping outsiders at bay that police now often choose to pull down or blast holes in exterior walls to gain entry into clubhouses.

Inside the clubhouse are essentially two sections: one guests see and the other they don't.

In the part guests can see, the clubhouse is essentially like a nightclub. There is usually a bar (or two), a dance floor, a DJ booth and/or a place for bands to play. There are often pool tables, occasionally foosball tables, pinball machines, video games, slot machines and other diversions.

The walls are decorated with framed photographs and even cuts, as well as murals depicting the club's logos, mottos and other related images and phrases.

For years, any items captured from other clubs or law enforcement—usually cuts, flags or other branded paraphernalia—were displayed (upside-down, of course) in the clubhouse and could be targeted for spitting contests and other indignities. But the groups who were being stolen from started making concerted efforts to get their stuff back. These days, captured items are usually burned, often on camera for posting to social media.

Occasionally, clubhouses will have a drug room for members and guests. It's not a room to store drugs—no smart biker would ever store drugs at a clubhouse, endangering the whole chapter in the event of a police raid—but a place for people to use their own drugs in private. The user will bring only his or her own drugs, use them behind closed doors and take everything he or she brought into the room back out. Guests may use the drug room only if a member escorts them in and out.

Firearms generally fall into the same category as drugs when it comes to storing them in the clubhouse. In the event of a raid, the club could face serious problems if the police find a firearm in the clubhouse. If the chapter feels a need for firearms in the clubhouse, like in times of war, then they are kept in secure areas—behind the bar, usually—and any members who have been convicted of felonies are instructed to keep as far away from them as possible.

That doesn't mean there are no weapons in the clubhouse. Baseball bats, hammers and other deadly weapons that can be explained away as household items are commonplace.

Near the clubhouse's entrance, there will always be a place to store any cell phones. Members and knowledgeable guests know to keep their cell phones out of the clubhouse, but if any are brought in, they are stored securely to prevent any photos, videos or sound recordings from getting out and to keep anyone from calling law enforcement if a conflict arises. If the phone has a removable battery, it will be taken out before storage.

Next, there will always be a section devoted to the sale of support gear. Guests, especially male ones, are strongly encouraged to buy some as a show of respect and loyalty.

Some clubs have metal detectors or a rule that guests must be frisked before entering the clubhouse's main room.

Once inside, guests are allowed to enjoy the party but must abide by the club's rules. Unfortunately, those rules aren't always clear, and the punishment for just about any infraction is a beating. Here are a few pointers: Once inside, don't talk to a biker without being spoken to first, and similarly, do not offer to shake hands with a biker before he offers. Don't talk too much or about potentially contentious subjects, don't touch anything before being invited to and don't look at anyone or anything for too long. Don't ask about the club or the meanings of patches, and definitely don't call anyone "brother," "bro" or "bruh." If you don't like those rules, you won't enjoy your stay in the clubhouse.

Those rules might seem obvious, but they aren't to everyone, and some people, through inebriation or some other lack of self-control, break them.

In October 2001, several Arizona Hells Angels—full patches Michael "Mesa Mike" Kramer, Kevin Augustiniak and Richard Hyder, along with prospect Paul Eischeid—were in the Mesa clubhouse when one of the members ordered Eischeid to go pick up an attractive woman the member had seen in the neighborhood and bring her back to the clubhouse. He described her as wearing a red dress. Unable to find the woman in question, Eischeid started talking to another woman, a forty-four-year-old single mother supporting five children named Cynthia Garcia. He invited her to a party back at the clubhouse.

Not very familiar with the Hells Angels, she accepted. After Garcia arrived at the clubhouse, she had a few drinks. As they were talking, Garcia said something that the Hells Angels considered "disrespectful"—nobody will admit to exactly what it was, but I have been told that one of the Hells Angels brushed against her and she told him to watch it—so Kramer grabbed her by the hair and warned her to mind her language.

What happened next is no longer in legal dispute, but many of those who are familiar with the case maintain that it did not play out exactly as the court ruled. Kramer said that Augustiniak punched Garcia, knocking her to the ground, while Augustiniak said it was Kramer who threw her to the ground. He claims that since Kramer turned informant, the court believed Kramer's story over his own and that if he had been the one to turn snitch, it would have been his story that was legally decided to be true. Whichever is the case, what's not in doubt is that while Garcia was on the ground, Kramer, Augustiniak and Eischeid began to kick and stomp her, as is time-honored Hells Angels custom.

Barely clinging to life, Garcia was thrown into the bed of a pickup truck and driven out to a desolate part of the desert. In Kramer's version of events, Augustiniak decided that Garcia had to die. They lived in the same neighborhood, and she could easily identify his face if she went to the police. He also maintained that Eischeid agreed to help kill her because he wanted to be promoted from prospect to member. Augustiniak said it was Kramer's idea to kill her.

Either way, Garcia was stabbed forty times, and the Hells Angels made a botched attempt to behead her (Augustiniak said that Kramer wanted to put her head on a fence post).

Her body, which had been ravaged by scavengers, was found by a pair of hikers weeks later on Halloween.

After Kramer went informant, he was given five years of probation for his admitted contributions to the assault and death of Garcia. Augustiniak pleaded guilty to second-degree murder and received a twenty-three-year sentence. Eischeid fled to Argentina, where he was caught, but is still fighting extradition on the grounds that he could be eligible for the death penalty, which he is liable to face if convincted of the first-degree murder charge against him. He is being held for an indefinite period in an Argentine prison. There is a "Free Paul Eischeid" Facebook page with more than five thousand followers. A Hells Angels hangaround, Robert Tutokey, was sentenced to nine months for applying for a passport with false information. Tutokey bore a resemblance to Eischeid and obtained a passport that allowed him to flee the United States. On his passport application, Tutokey claimed his eyes were blue, like Eischeid's, when they are in reality brown.

In December 2002, Hyder, who was not charged with any crime in connection to Garcia's death, was riding his Harley on the way to a funeral for two Hells Angels killed by Mongols when the pickup truck in front of him—driven by Kramer, who was out on bail and had yet to testify and reveal himself as an inform-ant—stopped short. Helmetless, Hyder collided with the truck, went over the handlebars and died not long after. His death was ruled an accident, and no charges were laid.

In the part of the clubhouses that guests don't see are the places where the inner workings of the club happen.

There will be a conference room for church (although clubs with more limited resources sometimes use the main party room for that if they don't have much space).

Church is usually held weekly and is closed to non-members, even to prospects (they stand outside to provide security). Since discussing any illegal activities is banned from church, it's often a pretty sedate affair, with most conversation focused on running the club. Finances are discussed, status reports on prospects are announced, updates are given on any members who have found themselves behind bars or before a judge and, of course, runs and other events are planned.

The president will usually have his own office with a desk and the usual office equipment trimmings. On the room's walls will be photos and contact information for all members, prospects and, usually, hangarounds. Sometimes there will also be photos and information related to rival club members, alleged snitches and the more troublesome members of law enforcement or the media. There will be a safe for the secretary-treasurer.

The clubhouse will also have a small kitchen and some form of sleeping accommodation. Members who have traveled from other chapters and need someplace to stay, people who have had too much to drink and others are permitted to stay the night with the club's permission. While the rest of the clubhouse is usually quite clean, thanks to the prospects, the bedding areas can be quite filthy.

Then there's the security room. It has monitors for all the video cameras, usually a police radio scanner and other electronic devices like alarm monitors.

Because of the extra attention bikers have received from law enforcement in recent years, and how many convictions there have been, the assumption among them is that every one of their clubhouses is loaded with listening devices. That has prompted a nearly universal rule about not discussing any illegal business within the clubhouse. Inside many of them are signs, evocative of wartime, that warn members and guests not to say anything inside the clubhouse that they wouldn't want law enforcement to hear. Anyone who does not heed the warning—from invited guest all the way to chapter president—can be subject to a beating.

Many bikers, however, have told me that it's nearly impossible to comply with that mandate. They often get around it by speaking in code; I know of bikers who have used code words for cocaine like "girls," "dancers," "coffee," "gifts," "T-shirts" and plenty of other innocuous-sounding terms.

Bikers inside the clubhouse also communicate through the use of dry-erase markers on what are commonly called "whiteboards." Anything written on such a board can be quickly erased without leaving behind any evidence. I know of one big-volume, Vancouver-area drug dealer—not a biker, but someone who worked with plenty of them—who was released by a judge on bail with the condition he not own a whiteboard, so he bought a green one and continued his business as before.

Less frequently, bikers have been known to communicate by passing handwritten notes on paper, then destroying them afterward, usually by burning them or eating them.

If actual conversation between two bikers is required and the subject is sensitive, they will leave the clubhouse and talk in an open area that they are sure isn't bugged. Public parks are considered ideal. Some prominent bikers—most notably Montreal Hells Angels drug kingpin Maurice "Mom" Boucher—have been known to invite their lawyers to attend any contentious conversations and then claim that anything overheard could not be used as evidence against them due to attorney-client privilege.

There is a trend among some chapters to rent, instead of buy, their clubhouses. Although that, of course, can make it more difficult to add certain renovations, it makes sense in the paranoid world that biker culture has become in the last few years. Because clubhouses are routinely seized under proceeds-of-crime legislation, often costing the clubs $500,000 or more, renting means that law enforcement would have nothing to seize even if the whole chapter were convicted.

One enterprising Hells Angels chapter—Downtown Toronto —who lost their $700,000 clubhouse to police now rents a new clubhouse on the west side of town and a brick-and-mortar store to sell support gear on the east side.

There is a downside to renting, though: eviction. In Canada and Australia, Hells Angels chapters have been locked out of their rented clubhouses and asked never to return. The chapter in Hamilton was evicted over a rent dispute—the Hells Angels said they paid in full, but the former restaurant's owner, Greg Tilley, disagreed—while the Darkside chapter near Melbourne, Australia, was evicted over lease violations. Both quickly relocated to less-desirable buildings nearby.

Okay, by this point your club has got members, a leadership structure, a patch and a place to meet. You've got the right kind of bikes, and you've settled your bottom rocker issue and 1-percenter status or non-status with the existing clubs in the area. Congratulations—you've got a motorcycle club. Now it's up to you to decide whether it's an outlaw motorcycle club or just a motorcycle club.

Should you take the outlaw route and succeed, it's almost certain your startup club will be wooed by a bigger club. Relationships between clubs almost always start when a small club is invited to a bigger club's party. If they seem like the kind of guys the big club wants, and show enough deference (they say "respect," but they use that word for a lot of different things) without being overtly obsequious, they will probably be invited back or on a run. Chuck Zito, in his memoir, tells a story about when he was a Ching-a-Ling and his club was invited to a Hells Angels party. When the Hells Angels started to threaten the Ching-a-Lings, all of them but Zito left. Because he stood his ground, Zito was welcomed into the Hells Angels fold and continued to party with them. The following day, he went to the Ching-a-Lings' clubhouse and handed in his colors. They didn't, as biker code dictates, fight him, he wrote, because they knew it was a lost cause. He then began hanging out with the Hells Angels, eventually becoming a full-patch member.

The early part of the feeling-out process is easier to understand if you consider it very much as if the entire chapter is undergoing the hangaround process again. They are allowed to retain their colors, name and identity, and are treated well, if with perhaps a little condescension.

It's during this time that the big club will decide what they want to do with the small club. They can reject them entirely, usually forcing them to give up their colors and disband their club; they can anoint them as a support club; or they can make them a prospective chapter of their own club.

For decades, most clubs that became support clubs retained their names, logos and identities, but recently—as the big clubs have taken a keener interest in branding—they have been assigned new, standardized names, new colors (which correspond to the big club's) and even new mottos. It began with the Outlaws, who strongly encouraged all new support clubs, and some old ones, to take on the name Black Pistons, as well as a black-and-white color scheme with a logo featuring a pair of crossed pistons. Interestingly, their bottom rocker is the name of the country they exist in, such as "United States."

The Hells Angels have dozens of different support clubs around the globe but have made a distinct strategic move toward having all new support clubs take on the Red Devils name, a red-on-white scheme and a flaming devil's-head logo. Red Devils even call themselves 184, just as the Hells Angels call themselves 81.

The standardization of names for support clubs hasn't always been without problems. Canada's oldest club—founded in Hamilton in 1948, a few months after the Hells Angels—was called the Red Devils. But when the Hells Angels formed a new Red Devils chapter in Hamilton, the original Red Devils had no choice but to change their name. Actually, they did more than that, patching over their three chapters to Bacchus, causing friction between the previously compatible clubs and forming the first Bacchus chapters outside of Atlantic Canada.

What support clubs actually do varies, but many have been known to engage in illegal activities on behalf of the parent club. For example, according to witness testimony and surveillance transcripts, one Montreal Hells Angels support club called the Rockers existed essentially to take on violent tasks to help the big club. During the war against the Rock Machine and Dark Circle, the Rockers were divided into two groups: the Baseball Team, who assaulted enemies and debtors, and the Football Team, who killed them. That, of course, would have to be considered the extreme end of the scale.

Other members of support clubs have been convicted of taking part in illegal activities on behalf of members of the big club. Frequently, members of such support clubs are granted the right to traffic drugs or carry on other criminal enterprises if they pay a portion of their proceeds to a member or members of the big club. Others are required to perform criminal acts at the behest of a big-club member to protect him from prosecution, as was shown in several convictions of members of the Montreal Hells Angels who ordered members of the Rockers to assault and kill opponents.

Support clubs in communities that are without a big club chapter—like the Demon Knights, a Hells Angels support club on Pagan's-dominated Long Island—are expected to serve the big club's interests in their area.

And, of course, in times of war, support clubs must take an active role on behalf of the big club.

The value of being a member of a support club also varies. Many, especially the branded ones like the Black Pistons and the

Red Devils, have significant status in their communities. And, while it's unlikely that a support club, especially in a community with a chapter of the main club, will ever become a big-club chapter, individual members stand a very good chance of being promoted.

In general, members of support clubs are treated in much the same way as prospects from the big club. Although they aren't used as slavishly as prospects, support club members are expected to show deference, carry out any tasks ordered by full patches of the big club and provide essential services like security and bartending. They might even share the same clubhouse, although the support club can be ejected—temporarily or permanently—at the direction of the big club.

If the new club is not rejected nor transformed into a support club, then the big club will make it a probationary chapter of its own club. In that status, the new club's members are even more like prospects. They are required to get rid of their old colors— usually by burning them—and wear the prospect cuts of the club they are hoping to join. After a predetermined length of time, they will be invited to become a new chapter of the big club or told to get lost.

Similarly, any big clubs wishing to expand in a new region can set up a probationary chapter by either importing their own guys or recruiting locals, or they may even wish to prospect an existing club. The process of trading one club for another is called a patch-over because members essentially trade one patch for another.

Rarely, big clubs—most often, surprisingly, the Hells Angels—will waive any prospecting time and trade clubs patch-for-patch in an effort to expand into new regions or make up their numbers after members have been lost to war or mass incarceration. History has shown that has not always worked out for them in the short-term, as many new Hells Angels from those no-prospecting patch trades get arrested pretty quickly, but the strategic plan of establishing the club in a new territory and weeding out the less capable members has been remarkably successful.

Of course, there will be members of prospective clubs that aren't wanted by the big club after a patch-over. They might not fit the big club's vision, they might have a previous beef with a member of the big club, they might owe money, or the new club just might not like the way they look. Those guys are generally expelled, and many of them wind up with nearby rival clubs.

One drawback of patch-overs for big clubs is that they allow clubs much less opportunity to scrutinize incoming members than they would have with their own prospects. That has led to several successful infiltrations of big-time clubs by law enforcement. For example, ATF agent Jay "Bird" Dobyns—along with other agents and informants—created an unsanctioned Arizona chapter of the Solo Angeles, a small Mexican-based 1-percenter club with loose ties to the Hells Angels. They were quickly approached by the Hells Angels and became a prospective chapter even though the real Solo Angeles in Tijuana told the Arizona Hells Angels that Dobyns's group was not sanctioned by them; in fact, they had never even heard from them. The Hells Angels chose to believe Dobyns and patched his group over. Of course, they later regretted that rash decision.

It's like they say: It's not hard to become a 1-percenter; just sew a 1-percent patch or a bottom rocker onto your vest. Then be prepared to defend it.

# CHAPTER 5

# Women

"There's just some women who want to be with bikers," Randy, a former Outlaw, told me. "I guess you'd call it daddy issues or something; they just want a man who's a man, you know, like, a real man."

I asked him about the kind of women who like bikers, if there was any special trait they had in common.

"Nothing specific, nothing I could describe," he told me. "Just a look." He continued. "Lots of them are interested, but it takes a while before you figure out which ones are trainable."

"Trainable?"

"Yeah, not all women can fit into the life," he told me. "They have to know their place, and what's expected of them."

YOU PROBABLY KNOW Chrissie Hynde as a musician. Lead singer and songwriter for The Pretenders—in fact, the only member to have been with the band since its 1978 inception until the present—she was inducted into the Rock and Roll Hall of Fame in 2005. She is an incredibly accomplished person, certainly popular music royalty, if there is such a thing.

But in 1972, she was just a lost and idealistic kid from Akron, Ohio. It was a tumultuous time for everyone, but especially her. She was studying art at Kent State University, where she played in a band with future members of Devo. Her boyfriend had been one of the victims of the 1970 Kent State shootings, in which four people were killed after Ohio National Guardsmen opened fire on unarmed anti-war protesters. She was questioning authority and looking for things to believe in.

According to Hynde's autobiography, at a rock show in Cleveland, she and some friends were invited by some bikers, who were serving as security for the concert, to a party at their club-house. Hynde, high on Quaaludes at the time, agreed to go. The friend she was with, she would later write in her autobiography *Reckless: My Life as a Pretender*, "recoiled in horror" and left.

Although she never explicitly identified them as Hells Angels in the book or subsequent interviews, she described the bikers' patch as being a winged skull (which, of course, is an image that belongs to the Hells Angels, and they defend it vigorously). The Hells Angels established a chapter in Cleveland in 1966.

Hynde, who was a big supporter of hippie-style peace and love ideals at the time, was surprised to see that the clubhouse was filled with weapons—including whips, crossbows and swords— as well as Nazi regalia and huge swastika flags.

Noting that she was the only person in the clubhouse besides the bikers and that they were padlocking the door, Hynde quickly surmised, as she wrote in her book, "that the party was going to be hosted exclusively by yours truly."

"Get your fuckin' clothes off," ordered the biker who brought her.

She did.

Then they told her to perform various sexual acts on all of them. She hesitated, so they began to throw lit matches at her naked body. Finally, she wrote, she gave in.

The following morning, one of the bikers—whom she remembered as blond and not at all attractive—gave her a ride home. As they parted, he told her, "You ain't a half bad chick."

Hynde didn't report the event to authorities and later enraged many by saying that she blamed herself for dressing provocatively, being stoned and agreeing to go to a biker clubhouse by herself. In fact, she even started seeing the blond biker a few times afterward.

He then "loaned" her to a friend, telling her that it was a biker custom. She saw the friend a few times, but he had a habit of beating her up before sex. When she complained about it, he hit her so hard, she later recalled, that she started "seeing stars."

Desperate to get away, she was scared. She had heard that the last woman to try to break it off with one of the club's members was forced to strip nude, shot in the leg and told to call herself an ambulance. Without telling either of the bikers, Hynde moved to London and, after a few other jobs, began her musical career.

TRADITIONALLY, THE RELATIONSHIP between bikers and women has been something of a feminist nightmare. In biker culture, women are expected to be subservient, quiet, supportive and sexually available. They are also expected to perform domestic tasks like cooking, serving and cleaning, without argument or complaint.

Women's value to bikers is often based primarily on their sex appeal, and their ability to make money from it. Many of the women in the biker world who are not strippers or prostitutes are often encouraged to take up those professions.

Strippers are highly valued by bikers for strategic reasons as well. By supplying strippers to a town, the bikers are putting eyes and ears on the ground. Although very few strippers actually sell drugs, they are quickly able to learn who does, which gangs are active in the area and who the real players are.

There are different ranks of women in the biker world, generally ranked according to how the club views not their rights, but who has a right to them.

The first rank is traditionally called a sheep, a pass-around, a honey or a cutie. These are women who are typically new to the biker world and have not formed a long-lasting or exclusive relationship with any one biker. They are expected to be sexually available to any and all members of the club. If a prospect or hangaround has a relationship with a honey and a full-patch member has any interest in her, the lower-ranked member is expected to step aside.

Group sex is frequently expected of honeys. Sex with multiple partners at the same time is called a "gang bang," and sex with consecutive partners is called "pulling a train" or a "honey train" (especially by the Pagan's). In Hells Angels culture, the fist-pumping gesture—based on an old-time truck driver's pulling on an overhead cord to sound his horn—traditionally means a gang bang or honey train is about to begin.

While honeys can never wear a club patch, many wear support gear to signify their status.

If a woman has a long-term, exclusive relationship with a biker, she is referred to as his "old lady," no matter how old she actually is. That means that the other members of the club can no longer consider her sexually available.

Old ladies are welcome at events but are not allowed at church. Their opinions are not sought, and discussing club business with an old lady—or even allowing her to overhear such conversations—is considered a grave offense and can be punished with expulsion from the club.

To signify their status as a step above cuties, old ladies can wear gear specifically designed for them. In many clubs, old ladies can wear vests, often with the words "property of" and then the name of a club or a member's nickname. The Hells Angels and Sons of Silence discontinued the practice years ago, but the Mongols, Vagos and Pagan's still do it. Some women associated with the Bandidos also wear vests or T-shirts that read "Proud Bandido old lady," while those connected with the Outlaws generally wear a "property of" belt buckle.

And the clubs take the word property literally. When a member of a club is expelled, many gangs believe they have the right to seize his property, especially anything related to the club, his motorcycle and, sometimes, his old lady.

In some clubs, old ladies can graduate to wife—regardless of legal marital status—which grants no real difference in rights or privileges but elevates them above the other old ladies socially.

While cuties are strongly encouraged to become strippers or prostitutes, old ladies and wives are not, especially as they age. Many bikers, particularly in more remote areas, lean heavily on their old ladies' ability to make money, and encourage them to get steady jobs.

Members of more sophisticated chapters frequently encourage their old ladies to get jobs in banks and other financial institutions, government offices (especially licensing bureaus) and even in the civilian arms of law enforcement agencies. Typically, these jobs allow the women access to sensitive information, which they can turn over to the club. That information is frequently used to check the veracity of prospects' life stories, but it can also be used to track down enemies. In September 2000, the Montreal Hells Angels used motor vehicle registration information obtained by an old lady who worked in a licensing bureau to identify the car of reporter Michel Auger. He was shot in the back six times but survived.

Similarly, the Hells Angels used details obtained by a girlfriend who worked at a post office to track down Margo Compton, who was at the time writing a book about what it's like to be a woman involved with the Hells Angels.

Born Margo Sanford in Benicia, California, she was slim, dark-haired and pretty. As a youngster she liked to paint and draw, and she told her family that her ambition was to go to school to learn how to be a beautician and hairstylist.

But she began to run with a rough crowd, and by the age of sixteen, in 1969, she was married and working as a grocery bagger. She gave birth to twins in 1971. Her husband, Doug Compton, became involved with the Hells Angels chapter in nearby Vallejo and eventually became a full-patch member. He also began to do drugs and to beat her regularly.

By the summer of 1976, Margo had had enough, and she sought protection from another, more powerful, Vallejo Hells Angel named Odis "Buck" Garrett. Margo didn't know it, but Garrett was in the middle of a tense situation with his chapter. He had served time with two other bikers for shooting a U.S. Marine in a 1973 bar fight, but what was fueling the problem with his brothers in the Vallejo chapter was that after he was released, he had started to make hundreds of thousands of dollars selling meth, and he wouldn't cut any other members of the chapter in on his success. He had already been stripped of his rank of chapter president, and it was becoming abundantly clear that he should move on.

And he did, with Margo. Garrett patched over to the San Francisco chapter and partnered with chapter president Gordon "Flash Gordon" Grow to open a brothel in the Tenderloin District they called the Love Nest. After administering what he called "the sex test" to assess her abilities, Garrett forced Margo, then twenty-three, to work there as a prostitute.

She had already endured eight weeks at the Love Nest when a client beat and raped her. She told Garrett that she was going to quit, but he wouldn't allow her to do that. When she insisted, he told her that the only way she could leave would be to pay him $4,800, which he said she owed him for protecting her from Doug and for the meth he had given her.

Frustrated, she went to the police. Margo described how she and the other four employees operated the Love Nest and were required to give 40 percent of all revenue to Garrett and Grow. Going to the cops was a tough decision for her to make, made far worse by the fact that she also named two San Francisco police officers who were in on the scheme and had kept their mouths shut in exchange for sex and cash.

Knowing that when Garrett found out he would be enraged, Margo then fled with her twin girls—Sandra and Sylvia—to a modest house between the tiny farming villages of Gaston and Laurelwood, Oregon.

She essentially hid there, doing little outside the house but drive the kids to school while she furiously wrote her manuscript. It was Margo's new ambition to write a book that exposed how the Hells Angels treat women in hopes that other women and girls would heed her warning and stay away from them. She typed tirelessly well into the night.

She did, however, find the time to befriend her next-door neighbor, Bonnie Sleeper, and her fiancé, Gary Seslar.

Seslar was visiting Margo and the kids on August 7, 1977, when two men burst through the front door. One of the intruders shot Seslar in the head with a .22-caliber pistol. He went down in a pool of blood.

Margo ran into the front room, and the other intruder grabbed her and held her from behind. She was then dragged to the kids' room and forced to watch as the first man shot both Sandra and Sylvia—still in their pajamas and holding their teddy bears—once each in the back of the head. Then they shot and killed her.

All of the shots were in the same spot—just behind the left ear. Seven months earlier, former San Francisco chapter president Harry "The Horse" Flamburis and his much-younger girlfriend, Dannette Barrett, had been shot in the same spot with the same caliber gun. Flamburis had been resisting efforts by Grow and Garrett to get the chapter more deeply involved in prostitution and drug trafficking.

Sleeper arrived later in the day to find Margo and the girls dead and Seslar barely clinging to life. He died in a nearby hospital soon thereafter.

The brazen killing made national news. One person who saw the story on television—narcotics detective Bill Zerby of the Solano County Sheriff's Department—would later get a pretty good idea of who had done it. An informant told him that one of the Vallejo Hells Angels full-patch members had bragged to him about driving the two killers up to Oregon because "we know how to take care of people like that."

And meth dealer Henry Crabtree—who had a very close relationship with Hells Angel James "Jim-Jim" Brandes since they befriended each other as toddlers—told Zerby that Brandes, Kenneth "K.O." Owen and four other Hells Angels had paid very close attention to the media coverage of the murders. "The Margo Compton thing had been aired over the television, and they had videotaped it out of Kenny's house," Crabtree told him. "So we sat out there in his garage, listening to the playback. They were laughing and joking about it."

But Zerby couldn't put enough evidence together to indict anyone. "What makes me sick is that these scumbags are so damn arrogant," Zerby later told *Rolling Stone*. "They think they can get away with anything because they're the fucking Hells Angels." Zerby, who was staunchly anti-drugs, had a long-standing feud with the Hells Angels, who he said monopolized the drug trade in his jurisdiction, which he vowed to put to an end. He had a particular beef with Brandes, who he said once threatened his life because Brandes was offended that the sheriff's department had dared to ticket him for driving with a suspended license.

On November 3, 1977, Garrett was convicted of pimping and sent to prison. Less than two weeks later, Zerby and his partner, Richard Grundy, were watching a suspected drug house when they happened to spot Brandes, license still suspended, pass by in the driver's seat of a Lincoln Continental.

After a brief chase they managed to stop him, and they noticed a Phillips-head screwdriver on the passenger seat. A quick check of the car determined that the panel underneath the driver's door had two loose Phillips-head screws. The cops removed them and found a sandwich bag full of meth underneath the panel—enough for a trafficking charge. They also found several electronic devices, including a police radio scanner, a fake police light for the roof of the car, a bug detector and, more chillingly, a book that described how to build bombs and booby traps and a notebook listing Zerby's home address, his phone number and the license-plate number of his car.

Gary Milligan was a Hells Angels–affiliated meth dealer who kept Zerby up to date on the club in exchange for leniency on an arson charge related to setting his estranged wife's truck on fire. He told Zerby that Owen and especially Brandes had it in for him and were talking about killing him. Apparently, the last straw was when federal agents confiscated Brandes's Lincoln. He also mentioned that Brandes and Owen had spoken about the Margo Compton murders as a major accomplishment for the club, although they did not take personal responsibility.

The day after Brandes failed to show for his January 29, 1978, court date for the trafficking charge, Zerby, as had become his custom, checked all around his Mercury Montego for a bomb. Once he decided it was clear, he went to open the driver's side door and boom! A remote-controlled bomb exploded in the bushes behind him.

Zerby was thrown into the street, and a passerby called an ambulance. He survived but lost hearing completely in one ear and significantly in the other and still suffers from chronic pain in his head, neck and hands.

A subsequent raid of the Hells Angels clubhouse yielded a fugitive from another case, traces of dynamite and a picture of Zerby that had been used as a dartboard, but there was not much solid evidence to link any Hells Angels members with the bombing or the killings in Oregon.

Months later, Brandes, Owen and Douglas "Dirty Doug" Bontempi were indicted with conspiracy to murder Zerby and trafficking charges. Despite bail being set at a then-record $1 million for Brandes (about $4 million in 2018 dollars) and $500,000 for the others, it was quickly paid, and the men were set free.

When Crabtree, the star witness, failed to show, the case against the Hells Angels fell apart. Despite learning from Zerby that Brandes had hired someone to kill him because he was selling meth in Hells Angels territory without cutting any of them in, Crabtree decided not to rat on his childhood friend.

Garrett soon got out of prison for the pimping conviction and was back in on a trafficking conviction not much later.

But the Margo Compton case wouldn't go away. The brazen killing of innocent children while their mother, who had done nothing wrong other than to get involved with very bad men, was forced to watch kept many cops in both states working on it. There were very few leads until 1986, when an unlikely source came up.

It was Michael "Iron Mike" Thompson. In prison since his teens, Thompson had risen to president of the Aryan Brotherhood, the white supremacist gang, despite being partly of indigenous heritage. He had grown disenchanted with the organization, however, after he was outvoted on a decision to kill the father and wife of informant Steve Barnes. Appalled at the use of violence against innocent parties, Thompson—who already had consecutive life sentences and no hope for parole—dedicated the rest of his life to bringing the Aryan Brotherhood and their allies down. He knew about the Margo Compton killings, he told prison authorities. In fact, he told them that the Hells Angels had approached him while he was still president of his gang in an attempt to contract one of his members to make the hits. Thompson said that the Aryan Brotherhood had agreed to kill Margo but had balked at the idea of murdering the little girls. "It might sound strange," he told one reporter, "but we do have some ethics."

Later, he said, he ran into two guys who openly bragged about the killings while in prison—Garrett in Folsom and a "weird looking" guy named Robert "Bug-Eye Bob" McClure in San Quentin.

Starting with Thompson's information, investigators interviewed a huge number of prisoners who had been in contact with Garrett and McClure behind bars, mostly Hells Angels and Aryan Brotherhood members and associates. Although they came from the group of people least likely to talk to law enforcement officers, many of the men were eventually persuaded, especially after seeing pictures of the two little girls and being told they were murdered while holding their teddy bears. None of the prisoners were offered deals, but no fewer than seventy-five agreed to cooperate.

Quickly, a story came together. Back in 1977, Garrett was determined not just to kill Margo, but to force her to watch her little girls be murdered. Apparently, that was what he considered a fitting punishment for a woman who did not want to be a prostitute for him any longer. He shopped the plan around but could find no takers. Killing a woman was, apparently, no big deal among his peers; it was the children who were the sticking point. Still, he would not budge on that condition.

But Garrett had an ace in the hole. He was sponsoring a prospect, McClure, who also owed him a lot of money for meth he'd been using instead of selling. He told McClure that he'd guarantee him his full patch, he'd forgive the debt and he'd also give him two pounds of meth if he carried out the grisly task.

McClure quickly agreed and recruited hangaround Benjamin "Psycho" Silva. They drove up to the rural Oregon house, and Silva held Margo while McClure pulled the trigger. Just as McClure's odd appearance gave him his nickname, Silva's erratic and violent behavior earned him his.

In 1991, Garrett, who was in prison for another trafficking charge, and McClure were arrested and charged with the killings. Silva was not charged. He and two other Hells Angels associates were already on death row for a bizarrely brutal kidnapping of a couple in which they raped the woman, tortured the man, then killed them both (and their dog) after approaching them pretending to be undercover police officers who would help them with their flat tire. The prosecutors didn't think putting Silva on trial again would be worth the effort and expense.

Their trial itself was a media sensation, though, and was attended by a huge number of Hells Angels, including Barger, who—as he often has before and since—would tell anyone who asked that the club disavowed the criminals and that people like Garrett did not represent the Hells Angels as a whole. That is, if he was found guilty, of course.

The defense attorneys did their best to discredit the witnesses as a bunch of lowlifes, but the fact that none of them stood to gain anything took the wind out of that argument's sails.

One of the prisoners testifying, Victor Carrafa—who had murdered a police officer and was well known for his prison escapes—claimed that it was Brandes who tried to hire him to kill Margo and the kids and later bragged about getting the job done when he came back to Carrafa to try to recruit him to help him rob a Brink's armored car.

No other witnesses implicated Brandes, in jail at the time on an unrelated charge. But days after his name came up in the trial, he was found hanged in his cell. As is Hells Angels custom with members who commit suicide, not a single person from the club attended his funeral, none offered comfort or support to his survivors, and the club demanded the return of his colors and any other club-related paraphernalia.

McClure stayed quiet during the trial, not even taking the stand in his own defense. Garrett, on the other hand, was boisterous and loud, constantly maintaining his innocence, claiming he had never met Thompson or several other witnesses (or even

McClure until well after the killings) and frequently shouting "Hearsay!" at testimony.

The jury quickly returned guilty verdicts for both men. They were sentenced to spend the rest of their days behind bars.

While the Hells Angels were quick to disavow Garrett's actions, saying that he was not representative of their membership, he is still listed on their official website's Big House Crew page, which encourages supporters to send him letters at the federal prison in Lompoc, California. That indicates they still hold him in some esteem.

Of course, 1977 was a long time ago. But sources on both sides of the biker world tell me that women are still generally treated like property by members of the clubs, and some of the 1-percenters take great pride in that.

"The Mongols are very old school and treat their women as second-class citizens, their property to serve them; but the Outlaws are worse," says Charles Falco, an undercover agent who infiltrated both clubs as a full-patch member, in his memoir *Vagos, Mongols, and Outlaws: My Infiltration of America's Deadliest Biker Gangs*. "They give their old ladies, who are their slaves, black eyes and beatings."

The life of women involved with bikers or clubs is rarely a comfortable one. In 2010, a woman who had been living with and financially supporting Thomas Heath, a Ventura County, California, full-patch Hells Angel, asked him to leave her house. He refused and threatened her and her fifteen-year-old son with death if she persisted in her request. Alarmed, she called the police—a biker familiar with Heath told me he was shocked that she would do such a thing because it counted as "snitching." Even if he didn't kill her, Heath told her, he'd tell the other Hells Angels in his chapter she was a "rat" and they would kill her.

When police arrived, Heath was still in his full tirade and, in front of them, again said he was going to kill the woman and her son, adding, "I don't threaten to kill people; I just kill them."

The case was pretty open and shut, and Heath was sentenced to thirty-five years to life. That might seem harsh just for uttering death threats, but it was hardly his first conviction. In 1977, Heath walked into a Mongols-operated motorcycle repair shop with a back tire that he said he needed repaired. The guy at the counter told him to leave it in the shop and come back in a few hours. Heath did leave the tire, which had a concealed bomb inside it, and left the store. The ensuing blast killed a Mongol named Henry Jimenez and a fifteen-year-old kid named Raymond Hernandez who just happened to be in the shop. The case wasn't solved until 1994, and when Heath was charged, he was already in prison for yet another felony. He had had an argument with his wife, started beating her and capped off his side of the argument by smacking her in the head with a gun. While being dragged away by police, he threatened to kill her if she testified against him.

And that sort of brutal behavior is hardly limited to the Hells Angels. A group of Outlaws once famously nailed a naked woman to a tree because she had withheld three dollars of her prostitution earnings from them.

But there is one area in which the rights of women are improving in the biker world, and you might be surprised to learn that it's rape. Throughout much of the existence of 1-percenter clubs, rape was so commonplace that it verged on cliché.

It became part of the culture, and rapes have touched off historic events. A rape started the animosity between the Hells Angels and the Outlaws, as the lore of both clubs goes; the rape of two young girls led to the Hells Angels selling meth; and one

Canadian club I know of ceased to exist when two of its members blew themselves up trying to deliver a homemade bomb to the house of a rape victim in hopes of preventing her from testifying (the other members just didn't have the stomach for the life after that). The history of biker gangs is littered with innumerable rape allegations and convictions.

Gang rape was so frequent among biker gangs that it was almost their signature move. Called "splashes" by the bikers, gang rapes were considered both a rite of passage and a benefit of membership. The belief at the time was that a large number of assailants makes it harder for a victim to identify any of them individually. And any women who tried to testify would routinely be intimidated out of it anyway.

But times have changed, and the clubs have grudgingly adapted. Law enforcement has become much more aggressive when it comes to investigating rape allegations, and DNA and other forensic tests can more effectively link victims to assailants. At the same time, law enforcement has gotten more serious about targeting biker gangs as crime organizations.

A request for a search warrant based on a rape allegation is unlikely to be rejected, and a search warrant for a biker clubhouse is like a lottery win for cops looking for evidence, according to the law enforcement sources I have spoken with.

Because of the current environment around rape and sexual assault, many chapters—though none of the major clubs themselves—have enacted bylaws forbidding members, prospects and hangarounds from raping anyone, at least in the clubhouse or on other club property. While that might seem like a good thing, it's a chilling reminder of exactly how biker culture regards women that they feel a need to legislate such a thing. The chapters in question have simply decided that keeping the cops out of the clubhouse is more important than being allowed to commit rape. Still, lots of clubs have rules against selling drugs, and that's rampant with all the big clubs.

To my utter lack of surprise, the individual bikers I have spoken with don't like to talk about rape. "If you want to know who got splashed and when," a former Outlaws president told me, "I'm not talking."

Mitch takes a more sanguine view. "If you can't get it on your own," he told me, "at least buy it."

But I'll let Sonny Barger have the last word on how bikers view women. As he wrote in his memoir, "Can't live with them, can't use their bones for soup."

**CHAPTER 6**

# When Bikers
# Go to War

I met a couple of those guys up in Canada, the Bandidos who got killed," said Mitch, a former Bandidos prospect. "At a run."

"Yeah," I asked him. "What did you think?"

"They were okay, but they were obsessed by the Hells Angels," he told me. "It was like every other thing they said was 'fuck the Hells Angels'; it was pretty surprising."

"I'm not that surprised," I told him. "The Hells Angels are huge in Canada; they claim the whole country. That makes it hard on other clubs, and it leads to a lot of violence."

"It's not like that down here," he said. "Clubs stay in their own states."

"Not always," I said.

"Yeah, not always," he said with a grin, "and then there's trouble."

X X X

BEING A 1-PERCENTER can be dangerous business—especially when there are lucrative activities like drug trafficking going on. While all biker clubs recruit guys who know how to fight, they often have a need to augment their fists with weapons. And, because they attract so much attention from law enforcement, bikers have innovated many ways to arm themselves and conceal their weapons.

The first is a method that bikers use in a lot of touchy legal situations: plausible deniability. Bikers frequently carry objects with other, non-violent uses and employ them as weapons. That way, they can be explained away as simple and innocent implements of the biker life. And, if one is used as a weapon, a biker can say that he just grabbed the innocuous-seeming object when he felt he was in danger.

For example, many 1-percenters carry hammers with them at all times. If law enforcement asks a biker why he has a hammer with him, he simply responds by saying that he needs it to repair his bike. Of course, hammers are essentially useless for motorcycle repair—bikes aren't made of wood and nails, after all—but he'll normally get away with it. I know of at least two people who have been involved with biker gangs—both members who had run afoul of more powerful members—who were murdered by hammer and dozens who have been punished by hammer blows to the hands or knees, often causing permanent disability.

Other tools, like screwdrivers (which can be sharpened), can also be employed as devastating weapons.

It's increasingly common for bikers to carry large flashlights with three D-cell batteries. They can be explained away as being necessary in case of a breakdown in the dark but can also be used as clubs with skull-breaking force. Many bikers call them "kill-lights," and the Sons of Silence consider them to be mandatory equipment.

Have you ever seen a bandana hanging out of someone's back pocket? Almost certainly you have. But with bikers, it's more than a mere fashion statement. Both ends of the bandana are frequently tied to the U-shaped shackle on the top of a lock. When quickly removed and swung, this weapon—which is not illegal until used as a weapon—can easily knock an opponent out.

Some bikers will use knuckle dusters or gloves with finger implants to help deliver knockout blows, but most prefer to rely on rings to stay out of legal trouble. "Biker rings" are common enough even among non-bikers that they are considered a fashion accessory. But true biker rings will often have stylized imagery—often devils or goats with prominent horns, noses or chins—that are sharp, which helps cut any opponent who's being punched. One that I have seen is carved in such a way that it has the word "victim" written backward on it. When someone is punched with a fist wearing the ring, it imprints the word "victim" into their skin, perhaps permanently.

Similarly, weapons can be hidden on bikes themselves. The dipstick—a long metal strip used to check crankcase oil levels that has a handle that sticks out of the right side of a Harley-Davidson's engine block—is frequently replaced by a hidden blade with a similar-looking handle.

Guns have been known to be stored in the stock tool-box that comes with every Harley, or under the seat padding. Customization allows the bike's owner even more opportunity to put in many different types of hidden compartments.

But even more interesting are the self-made, one-shot guns that have been found hidden in tire gauges, gloves, key chains and other everyday items. In 2002, a New Jersey state trooper pulled over a member of the Pagan's on a minor traffic infringement. The officer was inspecting the bike when he found that the left handgrip on the handlebars, on the clutch side, had been modified. He called in a forensic team, who found that the handgrip had been converted into a weapon, capable of firing a .410-caliber shotgun shell behind and to the left of the handlebars. Since the right handgrip, which houses the accelerator, is much harder to modify, many law enforcement officers are now trained to approach Harleys from the right side.

Another officer, in South Dakota, came across a stationary Harley in a parking lot near Mount Rushmore that had a 12-gauge shotgun attached to the handlebars pointing forward. However, since the gun was unloaded, in plain sight and locked to the bike, it was perfectly legal in South Dakota, as it adhered to the laws regarding firearm transportation in that and many other states.

An increasingly popular weapon with bikers is what's called a "cracker" or a "get-back whip." These are short whips made of braided leather or nylon in club colors that can be purchased at motorcycle shows or online for $30 or more. They can be used in fights and even while mounted on a moving motorcycle—sometimes to get back at a driver who the biker believes did not give him enough room on the road. The whips usually have a quick-release latch on them—like the fasteners for camping equipment or like the pull-tab on a dog's leash—which is often attached to the bike's left handgrip or under the seat and can be attached to the biker's belt for when he's away from his ride.

Many whips come with small pieces of metal, called punishers, at the end of the individual leather strips, and I have seen some on sale at motorcycle shows and conventions, as well as online, that end with a one-inch steel ball.

The bikers who have them say that get-back whips are merely decorative, but many jurisdictions have outlawed them, especially those with metal tips.

Of course, laws regarding all weapons, especially firearms, vary wildly from jurisdiction to jurisdiction. In Canada, which has seen proportionately far more violence from bikers than the United States, firearms are difficult for almost anyone to acquire. All legal gun owners must first pass a safety certification course, then a security screening and then wait twenty-eight days before purchasing a firearm. All firearms were registered by the federal government from 1995 until 2012 in the entire country except Quebec, and the Supreme Court of Canada forced Quebec to end its own registry in 2015.

The security screening—administered by the RCMP, admittedly no fan of biker clubs—can be strenuous, and no member or even close associate of one of the major biker clubs can hope to pass it. In fact, gaining membership into such a club can cause the government to revoke a license.

That, subsequently, means there is a lot of money to be made illegally importing weapons into Canada, as well as into states like Massachusetts, which have similarly tough gun control laws. In recent years, running guns to Mexico—which has stricter gun ownership laws than Canada and is in the midst of an undeclared civil war between the government and several drug cartels that has taken, by most estimates, more than 100,000 lives since 2006—has become an extraordinarily lucrative business.

Of course, the nature of biker weaponry changes when two clubs are at war.

Because the country has been effectively divided and portioned out to various clubs, war between bikers is rare in the

United States and generally consists of isolated assaults or kill-ings that make a point before an equilibrium—not always status quo ante—is established.

In his memoir, *No Angel: My Harrowing Undercover Journey to the Inner Circle of the Hells Angels*, undercover agent Jay Dobyns recounts once asking Hells Angel George "Joby" Walters what he should do if he came across any Mongols in Arizona, which had become a Hells Angels state. "Kill or other-wise fuck that bitch up," Walters told him, and fellow full patch Theodore "Teddy" Toth added, "Yeah, it's your duty to kill him, and not get caught."

Essentially, all biker wars are about territory: where they can "operate." Wars erupt when the agreed-upon boundaries are crossed. While a beating or even killing might be over something as simple as riding through another club's state with your colors on, wars are begun when a severe violation—usually establish-ing a chapter in a territory already claimed or simply trying to remove an existing club so that another can move in—happens.

The Pagan's have a long history of violence against other 1-percenter clubs in the Pennsylvania and New Jersey region, par-ticularly smaller ones like the Breed, Fates Assembly and the Tri-County MC, involving guns, pipe bombs and other weapons.

Throughout much of the late 1990s and early 2000s, the Pagan's harassed Hells Angels and their allies throughout eastern Pennsylvania and southern New York, including storming a bike show armed with baseball bats and ax handles. The FBI claimed that the Pagan's were after the lucrative drug markets in the region and had established a strong relationship with the Philadelphia Mafia. They founded a chapter in South Philadelphia, an affront to the Hells Angels, whose long-established clubhouse had long been located in West Philadelphia.

Local law enforcement makes the claim that Hells Angels East Coast president John "John the Baptist" LoFranco ordered the Philadelphia chapter to get rid of the Pagan's, while federal law enforcement maintains that Pagan's national president Steve "Gorilla" Mondevergine told his guys to expel the Hells Angels. Neither has been proven in court.

In the summer of 1999, Mondevergine was shot nine times but survived. Law enforcement officers make the claim that the shooting was perpetrated by members of his own club who bristled at his authoritarian rule.

The Philly Hells Angels were mostly older guys, reinforced by several former Pagan's—led by Anthony "Mangy" Mengenie—who were among those at odds with Mondevergine.

Hells Angels chapter president James "Slim Jim" Wysong allegedly sent Mondevergine a letter proposing that the two clubs live harmoniously in the city—something that would be seen as a severe breach of biker code and was widely interpreted by both sides as a show of weakness. Two days later, he was expelled from the club.

Mengenie took over as president, and another former Pagan, Thomas "Thinker" Wood, was installed as vice-president. In 2004, Mengenie went to prison due to a parole violation, and Wood became acting president.

On the night of January 13, 2005, Wood was with a group of several other Hells Angels who wore their cuts to Cheerleaders—a popular strip joint in South Philadelphia—and rode away on Harleys. Two weeks earlier, Hells Angel Vincent "Honcho" Heinrich had been beaten by several Pagan's, so the Hells Angels started traveling in groups and wearing their cuts everywhere they went.

The next day, Wood was driving in a pickup behind another Hells Angel, whose name was not disclosed, who was riding a Harley in South Philadelphia. A white GMC Suburban stopped in front of them, and its occupants opened fire. The Hells Angel on the Harley later said that Wood "bravely" drove his truck between the shooter and his friend. One of the bullets hit Wood in the head, and as he slumped down, his pickup careened into a used car lot. When police arrived, they saw the unnamed Hells Angel attempting to perform CPR on Wood to no avail.

Tensions remained high in the area. On April 17, 2005, a Philadelphia Pagan named Peter Ciarletta received a phone call telling him that a Hells Angel was sitting at the bar at Gatto's Sports Café in Manville, New Jersey. He collected prospect William "Rodent" Martin and they headed over to the bar. It was a Sunday afternoon and the place was full, with several families and lots of children. On arrival, they approached John Grover, who was wearing a Hells Angels T-shirt, and started shouting at him. Grover vehemently denied he was a Hells Angel. Ciarletta told him that he knew he was lying because the Hells Angels don't let anyone wear their name or logo unless they are a member. Grover got up to leave and the Pagan's followed him. As Grover was exiting the building, Ciarletta pulled out a 9-mm semiautomatic pistol and emptied the magazine into him. The two Pagan's then fled in a red Jeep Wrangler.

Dozens of shocked witnesses identified the shooter, his sidekick, the car and the license plate to police when they arrived. Ciarletta later pleaded guilty to Grover's murder, while Martin pleaded guilty to weapons offenses. Ciarletta got an eight-year sentence; Martin's was twenty-eight months. Both prosecution and defense agreed that Grover had no connection with the Hells Angels, and his sister told the court that a friend had bought him the counterfeit shirt online as a joke.

In October 2005, the rest of the Philadelphia chapter was
called to a meeting at the Hells Angels' East Coast mother chapter in Manhattan. Of the twelve of them, nine were expelled from
the club. The three allowed to remain were assigned to other
chapters in Pennsylvania and New York State. The Hells Angels
closed their chapter, leaving Philadelphia to the Pagan's. "Gorilla
beat their ass and sent 'em packin'," one Pagan's associate gleefully told a reporter from Philly News.

Similarly, wearing a patch in a territory already claimed is
even more dangerous. On March 18, 2006, Anthony Benesh
and his family—his girlfriend and their nine- and eleven-year-
old sons—were just getting out of Saccone's Pizza & Subs after
having eaten dinner at the New Jersey–style family restaurant in
Austin, Texas. As they walked through the strip mall parking lot,
bustling with families and seniors, a shell from a high-powered
rifle went through Benesh's head, splattering its contents on his
sons. He was dead before he hit the ground.

Nobody saw any shooters, but police said that they suspected
the shot came from within a vehicle stopped on the U.S. 183
access road nearby.

The killing surprised the public at large (Austin is known
for its very low homicide rate) but few in local law enforcement or the 1-percenter world. For a couple of months, Benesh
had been loudly riding around the city wearing self-made Hells
Angels colors and making no secret to anyone who would listen that he intended to form a chapter there. Breaching biker
etiquette, Benesh did not ask the Bandidos, who claim Texas
as their own, for permission (and they would not have given
it). In fact, representatives from the Bandidos told him to
stop, through a series of phone calls, or he would have to
face unstated consequences. Benesh didn't stop, though. It

apparently wasn't in his nature. A friend of his told a local reporter, "He was the kind of guy that, if you drew a knife on him, he'd walk toward it."

Although all signs pointed to the Bandidos, their supporters and amateur detectives on social media speculated that the Hells Angels killed Benesh to prevent a war with the Bandidos (or just because he wore their colors without permission), while others opined that the FBI shot him as part of what they saw as a wide-ranging conspiracy to make all 1-percenter clubs look bad.

To what I expect is the utter surprise of those speculating on the case, ten years later, two Bandidos—national sergeant-at-arms Johnny Romo and San Antonio Centro chapter president Robert Romo—pleaded guilty to the killing, and San Antonio Centro sergeant-at-arms Jesse "Kronic" Benavidez pleaded guilty to helping them. The reason, they admitted, was that they wanted to keep the Hells Angels out of Texas. The Bandidos trio has yet to be sentenced as I write this.

It might surprise many readers to learn that the biker wars in the United States have been mere skirmishes compared to what has happened in Australia, Canada and the Scandinavian countries—usually involving clubs based in the U.S. While biker wars in the United States are generally characterized by no more than a handful of deaths, that's not often true in other countries, especially when the big, multinational clubs move in.

A definitive American biker war occurred in the suburban areas around Washington, D.C., in 1991. Before then, several different groups rode in the area, with some level of tolerance for one another, but the amount of money to be made at the time selling cocaine made clubs more territorial and violent.

One of the oldest clubs was the Fates Assembly, which had several chapters in the area. Established in 1974, they were best known for a 1989 Mount Vernon, Virginia, murder conviction that shocked local residents. Sandra Ferguson, a forty-four-year-old mother of three, stopped on her way home from a church meeting when she saw a car stuck in a roadside ditch and offered to help the driver. However, the driver, Gary "Red Neck" Donahue, shot her dead and left her in the ditch. He maintained his innocence but was convicted by a jury and sentenced to life in prison with no chance at parole for thirteen years.

A couple of years later, on the night of May 28, 1991, a few Pagan's walked into a Southeast Baltimore bar that already had a number of Fates Assembly members inside. A brawl broke out, and shots were fired. Three Pagan's were shot. Michael Massaro died that night, Ronald Morris's condition was touch-and-go, but he survived, and Michael Diodato took a bullet to the leg.

On July 26, the Fates Assembly learned that several members of the Pagan's were attending a party in Woodbridge, Virginia, and they set up an ambush. Two of them—Richard "Wolf" Capote and Melvin Payne—recognized Pagan Kirby Gallaghan arriving in his pickup. He must have sensed that something was awry, because he immediately turned around in the parking lot and headed out. Capote asked chapter president John Lea what to do, and he replied, "Go get him."

Capote and Payne got in Payne's van and gave chase. Driving at very high speeds, the Fates Assembly members drew even with Gallaghan's truck and Capote fired two shots. They blew out the driver's side window but failed to injure Gallaghan. He shot back, hit Capote in the forehead, killing him, and drove to safety.

According to testimony at the trial of all the involved members of the Fates Assembly, national president Ronald Fiel declared war on the Pagan's after Capote's funeral and urged every member of his club to kill any Pagan they saw.

The war was kicked off on August 15, 1991, when a pair of Fates Assembly members threw a hand grenade through an open window of Gallaghan's house, according to testimony. It did not explode.

At an emergency meeting called by Ronald Fiel's brother and Fates Assembly full patch Mark Fiel, the Fates Assembly came up with a battle plan. They would find Pagan's hangouts and attack them with pipe bombs and firearms. Member Todd Saulnier would provide surveillance, and a chapter vice-president, Michael O'Bier, would drive the getaway car. Sergeant-at-arms Robert Paris would be in charge of coordinating the war effort.

After several failed attempts, the Fates Assembly decided to attach a remote-controlled bomb to a Pagan's car. Members George Hughes and Lee Clifton managed to make the bomb and duct-taped it to the bottom of a Pagan's car on September 12, 1991. The ensuing blast sent the gas tank and one of the rear wheels flying from the car but failed to injure anyone inside.

At their next meeting, the Fiel brothers called upon the members to make stronger bombs. Lea told them he could supply them with explosives, and Paris said he could build a bomb.

After building the bomb, Paris called Lea for help moving it. Lea, who was flying to Florida later that day, sent Payne and Hughes. As Payne, armed, stood guard, Hughes sneaked into Gallaghan's garage and attached the bomb to the underside of a pickup truck co-owned by two Pagan's who also lived in the house.

On October 4, 1991, the Pagan started up his pickup and drove away as he normally would. The bomb failed to explode. Frustrated, Paris called Hughes and told him to go repair the bomb, which was still under the Pagan's car in the house's driveway.

Hughes, Payne and Paris made another trip to the house under cover of darkness. While the other two stood guard, Hughes got under the car and detached the bomb. They took it to a nearby abandoned warehouse, where Hughes did his best to re-arm it. But he touched the wrong two wires and the bomb exploded. He was killed instantly, while the other two left the industrial park in ambulances.

Fates Assembly member Philip McFarland had had enough and in December 1991 went to the police and agreed to go undercover to help with the investigation of his club. Wearing a wire, he recorded twenty-two separate conversations by Fates Assembly members regarding the war with the Pagan's. In one, Ronald Fiel said that the club was suspicious that Clifton might rat them out to the police, so they were considering killing his wife, Kimberly, to keep him quiet. Saulnier referred to the idea of killing Kimberly—who was serving with the U.S. Army at Fort Bragg—as "doing the obvious."

Clifton did indeed cooperate with the investigation, and he and McFarland faced no charges, but only after he and all the others were arrested. All the rest were convicted of conspiracy to murder (and some of racketeering), with Ronald Fiel getting eight years in prison, Lea and Paris seven, and Payne and O'Bier five years. (Saulnier was acquitted of conspiracy but was convicted of surveillance in aid of racketeering and sentenced to sixty-three months in prison. He later successfully appealed his conviction by arguing that because he was acquitted of conspiracy to murder, his surveillance activities did not constitute any offense.)

With much of their membership dead, behind bars, in hospital beds or in witness protection, the remaining members of Fates Assembly decided to retire the patch. Three chapters patched over to the Hells Angels, while the other—led by a longtime hater of the "featherheads"—became Outlaws.

The Fates Assembly–Pagan's war is typical of biker conflicts in the United States, although not many could claim to share the level of ineptitude that the Fates Assembly demonstrated. It started because one club felt its territory had been infringed upon. It was typified by a low level of targeted violence through which innocent civilians were not likely to be harmed. The body count was low—three, all from the Fates Assembly—and there was a decisive victory.

Biker wars have not historically worked that way in other countries.

Australia has had outlaw biker clubs almost as long as the United States and Canada. They were largely peaceable until the Hells Angels arrived in 1975, and things got even more violent after the Bandidos were established there in 1984.

The Bandidos history in Australia began when a Sydney club called the Comancheros opened a second chapter in the same area. According to published interviews with sergeant-at-arms Colin "Caesar" Campbell, the club's founder and president, William "Jock" Ross, had been found in bed with another member's wife—a clear violation of club rules.

Confronted by his accusers, Ross said that, as founder and president (he called himself "supreme commander"), he was above their rules and that if they didn't like it, they should form their own club.

About half did, sort of. They kicked Ross and his supporters out of their suburban Birchgrove clubhouse and retained their name, colors and constitution. Those loyal to Ross opened a new clubhouse in Harris Park, about a thirty-minute drive away.

The new chapter's president, Anthony "Snodgrass" Spencer, and another member, Charles "Charlie" Scibberas, were invited to a Bandidos party in Texas. While there, they were so impressed that they agreed to become the first Australian Bandidos chapter and, law enforcement in both countries say, import meth from members of the Bandidos to Australia.

Bad blood between the two Australian clubs mounted, leading to several assaults. On September 2, 1984 (Father's Day in Australia, Fiji, New Zealand and Papua New Guinea), the two clubs ran into each other at a motorcycle parts and accessories swap meet held in a restaurant parking lot.

Ross first consulted with the Mobshitters—another club at the event—to make sure they were not intending to get involved. Then he challenged the Bandidos to settle their differences "like men." The two sides, including supporters and even wives and girlfriends, began to brawl. Suddenly a shot rang out, followed by several more. Civilians scattered. After about twenty minutes, two Bandidos—Mario "Chopper" Cianter and Gregory "Shadow" Campbell—four Comancheros—Robert "Foggy" Lane, Phillip "Leroy" Jeschke, Ivan "Sparra" Romcek and Tony "Dog" McCoy—and one innocent bystander, a fourteen-year-old girl named Leanne Walters who was there to buy her dad a Father's Day gift and was shot in the forehead, were dead. Twenty more people were shot but survived. Ross, also shot in the head, suffered brain damage and can no longer read or write.

One woman, not involved with any of the clubs, took refuge under a parked car and snapped dozens of photos of the melee. In no small part because of the evidence she collected, 63 murder convictions and 147 manslaughter convictions were handed down to the participants. Under Australian law, anyone who participates in gang violence in which there are deaths can be charged with murder or manslaughter.

Shock at what media called the Milperra Massacre prompted the state of New South Wales to pass stricter gun control laws, but violence between the two groups continued, as did violence between both and the Hells Angels.

I've written extensively about the biker war in Quebec, so I won't belabor the point here. The short version is that in the 1970s, Montreal—then Canada's largest city—was awash in organized crime. The two branches of the Italian Mafia handled much of the heroin coming into North America, the Irish Mafia controlled the ports, and several dozen biker clubs worked for them all and sold meth, while all of those organizations were involved in large-scale prostitution operations, extortion and bribery of government officials and union leaders. The big biker clubs were well aware of how much money there was to be made in the city and wanted in.

The first to get there were the Outlaws, who patched over several chapters of the English-speaking Satan's Choice, including one in downtown Montreal in July 1977. The East Coast Hells Angels from New York City were auditioning Montreal clubs to sponsor and patched over the French-speaking Popeyes in December 1977.

The Popeyes had earned that honor by violently driving several other clubs out of the East End and consolidating the meth trade there primarily in St. Louis Square Park. Their first task as new Hells Angels was to get rid of the Outlaws. Hells Angels, they were instructed, don't tolerate competition. After a short and bloody war involving several bombings, the Outlaws left Montreal, never to return. The Hells Angels took over their downtown clubhouse and gave it to a support club called the Rockers.

Supplied by all three Mafia groups, the new Hells Angels started to pump cocaine—then a very in-demand drug—all over Montreal and, later, into the rest of Canada and parts of the northeastern United States. The club grew rapidly and split into two groups. One, called Montreal North, on the island of Laval, featured old-school bikers out for a good time; the other, Montreal South, in the suburb of Sorel (which is actually north of Laval), was more business-like. The Sorel president, Yves "Le Boss" Buteau, encouraged his chapter members to cut their hair, wear their cuts only when necessary and avoid any behavior that could end in an arrest—other than trafficking cocaine, of course. They were the first of a new wave of bikers as illegal businessmen, a trend that has flooded through all the big clubs since.

Tension between the two chapters—and mounting debts by members of Laval, who frequently snorted the drugs they were supposed to be selling—led to Buteau and his men inviting the other chapter to a party. With New York's blessing, the Sorel guys killed four members from Laval and disbanded the chapter in what media called the Sherbrooke Massacre.

In the 1-percenter world in Montreal, the killings caused a rift. The two leaders of a local biker club known as the SS—Maurice "Mom" Boucher and Salvatore Cazzetta—disagreed. Boucher thought that Buteau was smart to clean house, while Cazzetta countered that it was wrong for brothers to kill brothers. The two amicably parted and disbanded the SS, Boucher joined the Hells Angels, and Cazzetta formed a new club he called the Rock Machine.

While the Hells Angels were rapidly expanding and attempting to corner the market on cocaine in Canada, a number of disgruntled bar owners and dealers formed a group called the Dark Circle. They wanted cocaine to sell but not at the prices the Hells Angels were demanding. They approached the Rock Machine to do something about it.

That started a war that left 168 or more people dead (Yves "Apache" Trudeau claimed 43 by himself, including some

Outlaws) and lasted until 2002—by which time the few surviving members of the Rock Machine had patched over to the Bandidos.

Most of those killed in the conflict were taken down by firearms, including automatic weapons and other guns not legal in Canada, but many were also killed by remote-controlled bombs, which endangered many members of the public. In 1995, one such bomb, which was hidden under a Jeep with two maverick Hells Angels–associated drug dealers inside, not only killed the intended victims, but also sent a piece of hot metal the size of a roll of dimes into the head of eleven-year-old Daniel Desrochers, who was playing in a schoolyard nearby. Public outcry after his death prompted the Sûreté du Québec (Quebec provincial police) to establish an anti-gang squad, Carcajou (the Wolverines), which quickly made the Hells Angels its primary target.

Since then, biker-related violence has erupted in Vancouver, Edmonton, Calgary, Winnipeg and several other communities after other clubs or street gangs have tried to usurp the Hells Angels' near coast-to-coast hegemony.

While the conflict between biker clubs in Scandinavia did not have nearly as high a body count as the one in Quebec, it was intensely upsetting to many people there because of bikers' cold-blooded disregard for public safety.

In December 1980, the Hells Angels—who had long desired a toehold in Scandinavia—patched over a gang from Copenhagen, the capital of Denmark, called the United MC. That bold move did not sit at all well with the existing gangs in the area. Copenhagen is something of a gateway for illegal drugs to get to the rest of Scandinavia and Finland, and the local clubs had enjoyed a measure of peace and prosperity by essentially sharing the territory and the wealth.

In a move that would later be repeated in Montreal, the other local clubs and drug dealers created a new group, which they called a motorcycle club, and named it the Bullshit MC. It was an appropriate name as very few of them rode bikes, and the club's primary activity was selling drugs.

They set up shop in a place called Freetown Christiania. Almost unknown in North America, Christiania is a strange anomaly within the city limits of Copenhagen. It all began in 1967 when people started breaking into a lightly guarded abandoned military base to walk their dogs, allow their children to play and engage in other activities away from prying eyes. Before long, its reputation for sex and drugs without police intervention began to attract counter-culture squatters from all over northern Europe, and, by 1971, a radical journalist named Jacob Ludvigsen announced that Freetown Christiania had been established outside of government rule.

For the most part, the Danish government has left Christiania to its own devices, even though marijuana and hashish were openly sold on its main thoroughfare—known as Pusher Street—and their sale is prohibited in the rest of the country.

The establishment of the Bullshit MC enraged many Christianites, who had prohibited any other drugs, weapons and private vehicles. But there was little they could do about the heavily armed gang, who came packing heroin and cocaine. Not only did Bullshit take a huge chunk of Christiania's drug market, but they used the lack of a law enforcement presence to store drugs to be sold in much of the rest of the region.

That caused tension with the Copenhagen Hells Angels, and a war of words erupted. In 1984, a group of Bullshit bikers led by president Henning Norbert "Makrellen" (Mackerel) Knudsen walked into Sopromanaden, a bar known to be frequented by Hells Angels, and beat up everyone inside.

It was a bad idea. Bullshit did manage to kill a single Hells Angel and two other people associated with the club but lost eight of their own, including three presidents. When the police finally were able to obtain a search warrant for the Bullshit clubhouse (with rare but utter support from the other Christianites), they found an unidentified corpse under the floorboards. That was it for Bullshit, which folded soon thereafter.

Knudsen was the first to die. He and his wife, Pia Soldthved Larsen, had just pulled up in front of their home when a man jumped out of a parked van. Larsen managed to get out of their reddish-brown VW Microbus and hide behind it, but Knudsen was not quite as quick. The assailant fired a World War II–era Sten submachine gun through the car's windshield until he was out of ammo. He then walked over to Knudsen's bloody body, hanging out of the driver's side door, and blasted him in the head with a sawed-off shotgun. In an extremely European touch, the killer escaped on a bicycle.

The man who killed Knudsen, twenty-two-year-old Copenhagen Hells Angel Jørn "Jønke" Nielsen (his nickname is a play on his first name), fled first to France and then to Canada, where he was harbored by Hells Angels, friends and associates. Four years later, Nielsen returned to Denmark and was arrested in Copenhagen's Kastrup airport after getting off a KLM flight from Amsterdam. He was sentenced to sixteen years in prison and was released after six.

Nielsen rejoined the Hells Angels and has since become a spokesman for them in the Danish media. In fact, he published *The Jackal Manifesto*, an anti-immigrant book that calls itself "a usable tool for understanding those individuals who through threats, terror and violence hold innocent Danes, children, young and older, of all races and both genders, in an iron grip of fear."

One of the Copenhagen biker gangs that did not join with Bullshit in the 1980s was called the Morticians. But after the Hells Angels violently attempted to monopolize the drug market—something they have done in many other places—the Morticians began to grow increasingly disenchanted with their former pals.

Taking heed from what had happened to Bullshit when they took on the Hells Angels, the Morticians changed their name to the Undertakers and reached out to the Bandidos. At the time, the Bandidos were also eager to expand to Europe. Their first chapter outside the U.S. had been established in the tough port town of Marseille, France—one of the highest-volume drug transit spots in the world—and had been very successful.

In 1993, the Morticians-turned-Undertakers became Bandidos. They had a long-standing and close relationship with the Morbids MC, based in Helsingborg, Sweden, just two miles from the Danish coast and an hour's drive from Copenhagen. They too became Bandidos in 1993, establishing the Texas-based gang in yet another country.

Eager to expand into Sweden as well, the Hells Angels approached a group of hot-rodders called the Dirty Dräggels in Malmö, just south of Helsingborg, got them to exchange their cars for Harleys and inaugurated them as the first Swedish chapter of the club in 1993.

The former Morbids had an established beef with another Helsingborg motorcycle club called the Rebels, and—emboldened by their freshly minted status as Bandidos—started pushing them around every time they saw them. Seeking help, the Rebels asked the new Malmö Hells Angels for support. In exchange for becoming a probationary Hells Angels chapter, the Rebels were told they'd be taken care of.

A few weeks later, on January 26, 1994, the Hells Angels started shooting up the Bandidos clubhouse in Helsingborg. But the Bandidos shot back and the Hells Angels took off. One Bandido was seriously injured, but he refused to cooperate with law enforcement. The brazenness of the daylight attack sent shockwaves through the regional media.

Two weeks after that, members of the Rebels led by a Hells Angel shot up the Roof Top Club, a Helsingborg bar well known in the area as a Bandidos hangout. Joakim Boman, a member of the Rednecks, a Malmö club aligned with the Bandidos, was killed, and three others were wounded. A couple of days later, someone shot a rocket from a Carl Gustaf anti-tank rocket launcher through the front door of the Hells Angels clubhouse in Malmö. Although nobody was hurt, the statement was loud and clear: war had been declared. Already-worried Scandinavians were downright frightened of the bikers after they learned about the attack by rocket launcher (which had been smuggled out of a military base by a sympathetic soldier).

After that, gangs across the European north aligned with either the Hells Angels or the Bandidos-Outlaws, and tit-for-tat violence broke out over the region.

The war spread to Finland on June 22, 1994, when Kari Korpi, president of the Klan MC (which was prospecting for the Bandidos at the time), was shot and killed by Juha Nousiainen, president of the Barley MC (which was prospecting for the Hells Angels).

Next was Norway, which first saw inter-biker violence when a group of Hells Angels shot up the Bandidos clubhouse in Oslo on February 19, 1995. Then came Denmark again, where two Hells Angels were beaten up by Bandidos while they were enjoying Christmas dinner at Stardust, a Copenhagen restaurant. They survived by escaping through a window in the women's washroom and swore revenge.

Unlike most gang conflicts throughout history, the participants in what the media started calling the Great Nordic Biker War appeared to show little care about the safety of noncombatants. Shootings in public places, especially international airports, became commonplace. In October 1996, a firebomb at the Malmö Hells Angels clubhouse severely injured twelve people on the street who were not involved with the club. A few days later, a rocket shot from another Carl Gustaf went through the armored door of the Hells Angels' clubhouse in Copenhagen during a party with more than a hundred guests, many of whom had no connection to the club and were there only out of curiosity and the promise of a free meal. Killed immediately were Hells Angels prospect Louis Linde Nielsen and party guest Janne Krohn, a single mother who had responded to a flyer she had been handed describing a free "Viking Feast." Chapter president Christian "Sass" Middelboe was severely injured when a brick wall fell on him. Bandido Niels Poulsen was convicted of the killings and sentenced to life in prison.

That was too much for the Danes, whose government quickly passed what was called the Biker Law. It prohibited bikers from collecting in public places and gave law enforcement significantly more power when it came to surveillance, arrests and charges for people they believed were bikers.

While the violence continued, leadership for both sides realized it was only reducing their numbers and hurting business. So, the top brass from the Danish Hells Angels and Danish Bandidos hammered out a deal. The Hells Angels were granted the right to "operate" (essentially sell drugs) in the major cities of Copenhagen, Aarhus and Odense as well as a few resort towns, and the Bandidos would have the run of the rest of the country. It was a pretty big deal. In fact, the signing of the contract and the handshake between Hells Angels Denmark president Bent "Blondie" Nielsen and Bandidos European president Jim "Big Jim" Tinndahn was broadcast on live national television on September 25, 1997. While the predicted respite from violence was applauded by many, some made it clear that they believed the government had caved in to the demands of the bikers and essentially allowed them to operate as criminal organizations in the territories they had mapped out themselves. "This deal not only gives the two groups a monopoly on crime in their respective territories," said Troels Jørgensen, chief of the National Investigation Center of the Politiet (Danish National Police), but also gives "relative peace and quiet, and freedom from outside competition."

The contract also contained a clause that prohibited the clubs from opening any new chapters in the region, but both sides ignored it after a brief cooling-down period. In fact, the Hells Angels now have thirty-six chapters in the Nordic region (Iceland, Norway, Sweden, Denmark and Finland), up from just fourteen in 1997.

The Danish Biker Law was struck down soon thereafter on constitutional grounds.

Since the signing of the deal, the Hells Angels and Bandidos have largely cooperated in Denmark, frequently meeting to discuss plans or mediate conflicts. There has been little violence between the clubs since then, and the three incidents that have occurred show unprecedented solidarity between the two former enemies.

At the beginning of 2001, Claus "Karate" Bork Hansen was expelled from the Bandidos for stealing money from the club. He had been the European president and Tinndahn's personal bodyguard during the war against the Hells Angels. Eager to get back in the biker game, Hansen and some of his pals started a new club in the Copenhagen suburb of Vanløse. They called it the Red and White MC, a clear signal that they wanted it to become a Hells Angels support club.

That never happened. On the evening of March 21, 2001, Hansen and his girlfriend, celebrated porn actress Dorthe Damsgaard, were getting out of their car after a dinner out when they were ambushed. One of the attackers held Damsgaard down while the others pumped twenty-six shots into Hansen, the last being a shotgun shell to the back of his head as he lay motionless on his front walkway. Witnesses reported a black Audi speeding away from the scene.

After an extensive investigation, Bandidos Kent "Kemo" Sørensen, Karl Martin Thorup, Peter Buch Rosenberg and Jens Christian Thorup were arrested. Jens Christian Thorup was convicted of murder and sentenced to life, while the other three were acquitted.

Although the regional media predicted that the biker war was coming back, they were wrong. It was subtler than that. It came out at the murder trial that the Hells Angels were aware of the planned assassination and had not raised any objection. They had no plans to have any dealings with Hansen or his would-be support club. Hansen was killed not as part of a war, but to reduce tension that could lead to one.

A few months later, a small club called Cerberus MC in the city of Randers was approached by the Hells Angels to become a support club. One of its members, a bodybuilder named Flemming "Philosopher" Jensen, was dead set against it. He had plenty of friends in the Bandidos and wanted to align with them. Refusing to leave the club or to sign on with the Hells Angels, Jensen was stabbed to death in a bar fight in Aalborg, a Hells Angels town.

A Hells Angel named Jesper Østenkær Kristoffersen admitted to the killing and was sentenced to six years in prison. While the Bandidos may well have accepted the stubborn Jensen into their fold, evidence at Kristoffersen's sentencing indicated that they were less interested in him than they were in keeping the peace.

A week after Jensen's murder, there was a major brawl at a Danish beachfront resort when several Bandidos crashed a Hells Angels party. The Hells Angels did not retaliate, because they were in clear violation of the pact by partying in their colors in a town that they knew was not theirs.

All of these wars, but particularly the Great Nordic Biker War, offer object lessons as to why bikers fight one another, often involving civilians. While they invariably say it's about respect (their stock answer to just about any question) and who gets to wear a territory name on their back, that's simply not true.

Look at Denmark, where the war started and ended. Both the Hells Angels and Bandidos (as well as all their support clubs) wear a bottom rocker that reads "Denmark." The two clubs meet frequently and cordially to discuss strategy. And that strategy, at least judging by the outrageous number of convictions, has been drug trafficking and other organized crime activities.

The name on the bottom rocker is meaningless unless it's attached to the exclusive right to sell drugs in the area it represents.

Sometimes those sharing agreements are tacit. Massachusetts, for example, has seen relative peace among its bikers despite both the Hells Angels and the Outlaws wearing the state's name on their bottom rocker. There's no way either would give up that right without a fight. But since both clubs were established there at about the same time and have approximately the same number of chapters and members, any war would be very violent and on a large scale, and neither side would have a decisive advantage.

Instead, they share the state. The Outlaws dominate the south-eastern part of Massachusetts, including Boston and Cape Cod, while the Hells Angels control the north and west regions. Neither side would be proud to admit it, but both tolerate the other as long as they don't cross the invisible but mutually agreed-upon border.

When a workable agreement is endorsed by both clubs, as in Denmark or Massachusetts, or a key victory has allowed a club to monopolize the territory, as in Canada after the war in Quebec and its subsequent spillovers, there is relative peace between clubs. Otherwise, it's open season on anyone wearing the wrong bottom rocker.

In the eastern U.S., the Outlaws and Sons of Silence ended their long-standing kill-on-sight philosophy regarding the other club. The people who started the war were long gone—dead or in prison—and the new guys wanted no part of the inter-biker violence, so they just kind of stopped shooting. According to former Sons of Silence member Nick Nichols, the only ones disappointed were police. "Law enforcement loves it [biker wars], because anyone who doesn't die, they get to arrest."

# CHAPTER 7

# Bikers and Drug Trafficking

Every time I have asked a biker a question about drugs, he's looked at me like I just asked if I could pull out one of his teeth. Of all the bikers I have ever spoken with, the only ones who will talk about drugs are those who have been through witness protection programs, which often work as a sort of de-bikerization rehab. One of them, former Hells Angel sergeant-at-arms Dave, describes how most of the members in his Downtown Toronto chapter made their income from drugs.

The bar they hung out in was something of a flea market for drugs (and stolen goods) that was protected by a Mad Max–style troop of friends, associates and hangers-on who gave early warning if police or a rival gang dared to show up. Their very presence scared off anyone who wasn't involved with the club and thought they might drop by for a draft or a bite to eat. The ongoing cast of regulars included a guy who arrived every morning with cocaine, a ledger and a pen, ordered himself a beer, and distributed individual packets of coke until dinnertime, when he would go back to the suburbs to his wife and kids. Of course, he had to cut the club in on a large percentage of his revenues, but their continued goodwill kept him safe from anyone who might have wanted to take his drugs, his money or his job.

Members traded cocaine and other drugs—including oxycodone, steroids and date-rape drugs—in large amounts, breaking them up into smaller amounts for individual dealers. They even had an elaborate scheme that saw members hide cocaine in packages with T-shirts, hats and hoodies and mail them to a store in New Brunswick almost one thousand miles away. The coke was then handled by Dean Huggan, a member of Bacchus, who got it into the hands of local dealers.

Dave took drugs but was one of the few members who didn't sell them, in no small part because he had a lucrative career in personal security, at least at first. But when his employers found out that he was a Hells Angel, that legitimate career ended. Aware that Dave was down on his luck and unable to get any other work, another member fronted him some cocaine to sell. "To him, it was perfectly natural," Dave told me. "Like, you're one of us now, and now you sell drugs."

I'VE HAD BIKERS who have been convicted of trafficking, even those who have pleaded guilty to it, look me in the eye and tell me with a straight face that they don't sell drugs and never did.

The reason is simple: trafficking is an offense with very stiff penalties that almost always requires the cooperation of several people to pull off successfully. Should those people have the same patch on their back, it opens the possibility for law enforcement to prosecute the chapter or even the club as a criminal organization. Going to prison is one thing, but being known as the guy who made life worse for the whole chapter or being responsible for bringing the club down is another thing entirely.

When they speak about the subject, bikers bitterly complain that the media portrays them all as drug dealers. I wouldn't say that's true, but a remarkable proportion of 1-percenters have been proven to be drug dealers—and I would wager that plenty more are but just have not been caught.

It's not just that drugs are a part of the hedonistic lifestyle—many clubs ban certain drugs, usually injectables, but drug use is rampant among bikers—it's also economics. Being a biker is not cheap. Harleys are expensive to buy, operate and maintain, and many clubs expect their members and prospects to customize their bikes. Insurance rates can be very high for bikers, especially since cops have a habit of ticketing them for even the most minor infractions.

And being in the club is expensive. Besides the dues, there are frequent parties and runs, which members and prospects pay for out of their own pockets, and fines for infractions.

Many find it difficult to be in a club on the salaries of the legitimate jobs they may have.

While it can be tough for members, keeping a legitimate job is virtually impossible for prospects, who are on call 24/7 and frequently find themselves providing their sponsor, his family and friends with gas, food and other expenses. Selling drugs can be the only way for many candidates to survive the prospect period.

How drugs are sold often depends on the source of the drugs, the region and, especially, the type of drug.

Contrary to widespread belief, bikers rarely specialize in or go out of their way to sell marijuana anymore, except in areas where it's in scarce supply and can still draw a big price tag. Weed is just not a high-profit product now. It's bulky and easy for law enforcement to detect. Most weed users, I'm told, consider themselves to be connoisseurs, and bikers often have little patience for their often-picayune complaints about product quality or a lack of choice of strains. Besides, with recreational pot legal in many states, and its legality pending in several more and all of Canada (not to mention the ease of acquiring medical marijuana throughout much of the continent), the bottom has dropped out of the illegal marijuana business. Revenues are so low that in most of North America, most bikers don't consider it worth the risk.

Some do, though. In 2013, Hells Angel Kevin Lubic pleaded guilty to being part of a conspiracy to traffic marijuana in and around New York City. With the evidence piled high against him, he agreed to a plea deal that sentenced him to thirty-seven months in prison and a fine of $50,000. The Hells Angels denied that Lubic was a member of their club, even though many media sources ran several pictures of Lubic wearing a Hells Angels cut and a T-shirt with the death's head on it, including one shot in which Lubic was sitting next to noted Hells Angel Chuck Zito. If Lubic was not a full-patch member, Zito—by his own admission in his memoir—would never have tolerated his wearing the Hells Angels logo and would have reacted violently. Still, his plea deal did not contain wording that made it clear he was a member of the club.

In those jurisdictions where marijuana is not tolerated by law enforcement, street prices can still be very high. According to Forbes, in early 2017, the same quality and strain of weed that would cost $117 per ounce in Portland, Oregon, would fetch $329 in Fargo, North Dakota. Lugging a mere ten pounds of weed from Portland to Fargo could mean a $34,000 profit (although bikers are very rarely street-level dealers, so wholesale prices would apply).

Rather than go to all the trouble of acquiring marijuana and then finding a way to sell it, most of the bikers I've spoken with tell me that the way they, and their chapter mates, make money off marijuana is less direct and very nearly passive.

When someone is making a decent amount of money either growing or selling weed, he can expect a visit from a local biker or bikers before too long. On rare occasions, the grower or dealer can be recruited for the club if he possesses other desirable attributes (many bikers enjoy marijuana, and a reliable source is often considered to be a great asset to the club).

More likely, however, he will be offered a deal in which he pays the biker a portion of his proceeds for the right to grow or sell in his territory. It's like the old protection racket, although they rarely go through the song-and-dance pretense of providing any protection unless there is a significant external threat—like a rival biker club—to the supplier.

Those few growers and dealers who do not go along with the deal, or who fall behind in payments, can expect a second, much less pleasant visit. When that occurs, the grower or dealer will have his product and cash taken by force and will perhaps be roughed up a little until he agrees to return to the conditions stipulated by the previously offered deal.

"I laugh whenever I see them talk about 'home invasions' on the TV news," said Sean, who had been with an independent club but quit when it patched over to the Hells Angels. "They always play it off like some innocent family is being robbed, but it's always some dealer getting his stash taken." Maybe I looked skeptical when he told me that, because he added, "You'll notice that it's never the guy whose home got invaded that calls the cops; it's a neighbor, always a neighbor."

More than any other drug, in both popular media and their own culture, methamphetamine is associated with bikers. And for good reason: bikers helped spread meth for decades and are still considered by most users as a good way to find the drug.

It came about naturally, almost innocently at first. Throughout much of the twentieth century, amphetamine was a legal drug, available over the counter and recommended for energy boosts, staving off sleep and even weight loss. Side effects included an increased libido and a feeling of confidence. That potent combination led to it quickly becoming popular with bikers, who found amphetamine invaluable for cross-country rides and all-night parties.

Once it became illegal to sell, bikers became its primary source. Of course, the best way to afford drugs is to sell them to someone else, so many bikers, particularly Hells Angels, began to sell amphetamine.

But it also became harder for bikers to acquire. The solution was a revelation that the drug could be manufactured using easily and legally obtained ingredients—the most important being ephedrine or pseudoephedrine, the active ingredient in many popular over-the-counter nasal decongestants. The resulting drug was an even more powerful and more addictive variation on amphetamine called methamphetamine.

For decades, meth was a mainstay of biker culture. It was, for them, an almost perfect product. It could be made anywhere out of cheap, easy-to-acquire ingredients, it was small, and it was easy to hide. It was intensely addictive, and there seemed to be no limit to the number of people who wanted to try it. "We sell a lot of cocaine," said Big Larry, "but our drug that we sell the most is crystal meth because that is our money."

But three factors conspired to put a serious dent in the meth business for bikers.

The most important was competition. While the kind of small-scale meth-manufacturing operations—members of law enforcement call them "mom and pop labs" or "Beavis and Butt-Head labs"—bikers have traditionally depended upon can make a steady supply of product, they can't compete with the massive meth factories operated by the Mexican cartels. After they essentially cornered the cocaine trafficking market from the Colombians, the big Mexican cartels had the manpower, infrastructure, firepower and will to exert themselves in the United States and Canada. One smaller group, known as the Colima Cartel, led by José de Jesús Amezcua Contreras and his brothers Adán and Luis, started to make meth in the early 1990s. With the aid of very relaxed Mexican drug and importation regulations and many corrupt officials, the Colima Cartel was able to import tons of pure ephedrine from India and Thailand and employed thousands of people, mostly women, to cook meth in factories in southwestern Mexico. The industrialization of meth manufacturing led to the Mexicans having a huge supply of high-quality meth that the unsophisticated, small-scale cooks in Canada and the United States couldn't hope to compete with. As they became more successful, the Colima Cartel was absorbed by the much-bigger Sinaloa Cartel, which has intensive connections throughout North America.

Since 2006, the Mexican cartels have been fighting each other and the government in what could be labeled an undeclared civil war. Frequently referred to in media as the Mexican Drug War, the conflict has resulted in more than 100,000 deaths since 2006. The terrifying conflict has seen hundreds of beheadings, bodies hung from traffic overpasses, grenades thrown into crowds of innocent people, bars and restaurants raked with machine gun fire and even rehab centers destroyed by bombs and rocket launchers. Many of the cartels are emboldened by the fact that some of the best-trained and -armed units of the Mexican military defected en masse to their side. Specialists in urban warfare, well armed and battle hardened, the cartels' forces have little to fear from North American biker clubs. As one DEA supervisor said, "When these guys show up, the bikers leave."

But the cartels need manpower to move product, and they prefer to use people with an intimate knowledge of their area, a tough-guy reputation, an ability to keep their mouth shut and, often, an ability to speak English. That, of course, describes all kinds of groups but especially biker clubs. Suddenly, North American gangs with close ties to the Sinaloa Cartel, like the Mexican Mafia, had quick and easy access to massive quantities of better-quality meth at a far lower price than the bikers. Clubs like the Vagos and Mongols, with good relationships to Mexican and Mexican-American gangs, could buy from them, while other clubs had to rely on contacts like the traditional Italian Mafia, who bought from the same guys. That extra layer of revenue-taking meant that clubs like the Hells Angels and Outlaws were paying a higher price for the same meth that other groups bought.

Even in places beyond the reach of the Mexican cartels, things were tough for meth makers. In many places where meth is popular, items that contained pseudoephedrine, the primary active ingredient of meth, were removed from store counters. Anyone buying those products in many areas afterward has had to produce identification, and there are often limits to how much they can buy.

At the same time, law enforcement developed more sophisticated methods to find and dismantle meth labs.

That led to a situation in which the bikers were scrambling to find home-grown meth to compete with the flood of product coming from Mexico.

As that was happening, a third factor struck: meth quickly became far less in demand. The popular image of users—widely

The Hells Angels' patch features the death's-head logo. The club is very protective of its name and logo and allows only full-patch members to wear either. (COURTESY GREEN HOUSE)

The first Hells Angels chapter in Canada was established in Laval, Quebec, in 1977. Yves "Apache" Trudeau (*bottom row, second from the right*) would later admit to killing forty-three people on the club's behalf. He lost his protected witness status after being caught having sex with an underage boy. (COURTESY RCMP)

Although he stood just 5-foot-4, Walter "Nurget" Stadnick was national president of the Canadian Hells Angels and extended the club's reach from the Atlantic to the Pacific. (COURTESY ONTARIO PROVINCIAL POLICE)

The Para-Dice Riders were a successful Toronto club that patched over to the Hells Angels in 2000. (COURTESY ONTARIO PROVINCIAL POLICE)

The original Rock Machine began in Montreal and fought a bloody war with the Hells Angels before patching over to the Bandidos in 2000, and ceased to exist in 2006. Clubs using the name and logo have emerged since in Canada, the United States, Australia and Europe with varying levels of success.
(Courtesy Green House)

The Texas-based Cossacks do not wear a 1-percenter patch, but, after a series of violent run-ins with the Bandidos, they are considered to be 1-percenters by law enforcement. The club says it has banned Confederate flag and SS patches, but several members still wear them.
(Courtesy Green House)

The recently restyled Bandidos patch reflects a split between U.S. chapters and those in the rest of the world. Note that the mascot's sleeve patch features the Texas flag, which Bandidos patches in other countries don't.
(Courtesy Green House)

It was briefly against the law to distribute the Mongols patch in the United States, but that ban has been rescinded. Note the "Laughlin 2002" patch, which commemorates the River Run Riot, a brawl in a Nevada casino that led to the deaths of two Hells Angels and one Mongol.
(COURTESY GREEN HOUSE)

The Outlaws patch features Charlie, the club's skull mascot. The AOA patch—which represents the American Outlaws Association, the club's corporate entity—is worn on the front.
(COURTESY GREEN HOUSE)

The Vagos wear green patches and refer to themselves as the Green Nation.
(COURTESY GREEN HOUSE)

When the Hells Angels and Bandidos fought a war in the Nordic countries, both sides used Carl Gustaf rocket launchers, like this one, against each other. (Courtesy Wikimedia Commons/Försvarsmakten Sverige)

Vladimir Putin (*left*), president of Russia, greets Alexander "The Surgeon" Zaldostanov at a gala reception at the Kremlin. Zaldostanov is president of the Night Wolves, an activist motorcycle club funded by the Russian government. (Courtesy Wikimedia Commons/Government of the Russian Federation, Office of the President)

While passing through Utica, New York, I came across this pro–Hells Angels message carved into the sidewalk on Genesee Street, the town's main drag. The Hells Angels have a chapter in nearby Troy, New York. (Jerry Langton)

Members of various support clubs gather on a street corner before being allowed into the Hells Angels clubhouse in the Alphabet City neighborhood of Manhattan. The man holding the coffee in the center of the photo is the doorman for the nightclub on the corner and is not a member of any of the clubs. (Flickr-SliceofNYC)

When police raided the Hells Angels Downtown Toronto chapter's clubhouse in 2006, they considered the armored metal door so tough to open that they instead used a tow truck to drag down an exterior wall. Someone trying to remove the death's-head sticker after the raid did a bad job. (Flickr-Chris Huggins)

This member of the Kingsmen MC demonstrates many traits of the traditional biker look. The Kingsmen claim not to be a 1-percenter club, but in 2016, sixteen of its members were indicted on forty-six counts, including murder in the aid of racketeering and several drug trafficking charges. (FLICKR-DBKING)

Members of the Bronx-based Satan's Soldiers, a Hells Angels support club, park their bikes on a busy Manhattan street. All of them are Harley-Davidsons with varying levels of customization. (FLICKR-SLICEOFNYC)

Members of several Hell Angels support clubs, including Trashed from Staten Island, arrive in New York City to join the Hells Angels on a run. The man on the far right, in front of the minivan, is wearing a hoodie that reads SUPPORT 81 NEW JERSEY. The "81" is a nickname for the Hells Angels. (FLICKR-SLICEOFNYC)

Members of some Hells Angels–associated clubs get ready for an annual run. Note that they are all wearing leather vests, Levi's-brand jeans and no helmets, and all their bikes are Harley-Davidsons. (Flickr-SliceofNYC)

This is an excellent representation of a Hells Angels full-patch member's colors. Note the top and bottom rockers, which name the club and its territory, the iconic death's-head logo and the MC (motorcycle club) patch. This member does not wear a 1-percenter patch. (Flickr-SliceofNYC)

known as meth-heads—emerged as unhealthily thin, half-mad toothless hillbillies. According to the U.S. Department of Health and Human Services' Substance Abuse and Mental Health Services Administration Center for Behavioral Health Statistics and Quality, the number of people trying meth for the first time dropped from a record high of 318,000 in 2004 to just 97,000 in 2008. That was the same year that *Breaking Bad*—a compelling TV show that presented meth use and its results in a frank and accurate way—debuted.

Meth is, of course, still around, but the meth industry is nowhere near the big-money bonanza for bikers that it was even just a few years ago.

All the major clubs have had plenty of convictions related to trafficking meth, but in recent years, the Bandidos—the FBI alleges that they have a solid working relationship with the notorious Los Zetas Cartel—have been the most frequently arrested and convicted club when it comes to that particular drug.

In the wake of the 2015 Bandidos-Cossacks shootout at the Twin Peaks restaurant in Waco, Texas, combined law enforcement agencies conducted a massive investigation of the Bandidos. As a result, the club's top brass—international president Jeffrey Pike, vice-president John Portillo and sergeant-at-arms Justin Forster—were arrested on a variety of charges. While many of the counts involved Portillo's alleged declaration of war against the Cossacks, many more were related to the large-scale distribution of meth and massive money-laundering operation required to keep it going. The indictment alleged that the Bandidos were the primary source of methamphetamine in Texas and several surrounding states. Forster pleaded guilty to several charges, including trafficking meth, and has yet to be sentenced. Pike and Portillo have yet to be tried. Both have pleaded not guilty to charges but have acknowledged their positions with the club.

One of the primary reasons meth was so popular with bikers was that they did not have to deal with foreigners to get it, at least at first. That was never true of cocaine, which is grown primarily in Bolivia and Peru, processed in Colombia and is now imported north almost exclusively by Mexicans.

But the lure of cocaine was too great for many to resist. It shared several of the same qualities as meth but offered even higher, actually far higher, profits—at least in the early days. Cocaine started to trickle into the United States, primarily through Miami by Colombian smugglers, in the 1970s. It caught on because the disco generation considered it a classy way to get high, associating it with jet-setting celebrities, many of whom admitted to using the drug. By the middle 1980s, cocaine was in such high demand that it was making millionaires overnight.

The early importers were looking for English-speaking dealers to move product, especially in large cities. Many of them were bikers or their associates. In several larger cities, the Colombians sold to the Italian Mafia, who in turn sold to bikers.

Law enforcement acted quickly on cocaine, making it their top priority. Large-scale investigations and mass arrests for trafficking cocaine became regular occurrences, as did long prison sentences for major traffickers. If you're dismayed by how well armed and militaristic police forces have become, you can blame the cocaine trade—particularly one single event called the Dadeland Massacre. The call for more firepower and specialized tactics for police forces was kicked off in 1979 when a group of Colombian traffickers shot up a liquor store and parking lot at Miami's Dadeland Mall with automatic weapons while assassinating a rival and his bodyguard. Their armored truck was found to be full of automatic weapons and explosives, prompting the Miami-Dade force to claim they were outgunned by the traffickers. Soon, the desire to equip police forces with military weapons and tactics spread throughout the U.S., Canada and other nations.

Many noteworthy bikers, along with other smart traffickers, protected themselves from law enforcement by distancing themselves from the final buyer. By selling to subordinates who sell to others, who in turn may sell to others, the biker might lose some revenue (as every person who handles the product takes a cut) but is much better insulated from prosecution. If a street-level dealer gets arrested, he can give up only his contact, and so on up the line. Since every person in the chain is sworn to secrecy and afraid of retribution if they talk, the likelihood of the top guys getting caught is greatly reduced.

The effects of meth and cocaine also overlap a great deal, and bikers who traffic them usually sell one or the other, as their community prefers. Take Massachusetts, for example. In the more rural, less prosperous western part of the state, meth is more popular, while in the eastern, wealthier region, cocaine is preferred.

When informants told police in the area in 2004 that the Outlaws were running the cocaine market in eastern Massachusetts, several agencies joined forces for Operation Roadkill. The centerpiece of the operation was an undercover FBI agent who posed as a wealthy businessman from Texas who liked to dabble in various illegal activities as a hobby.

He quickly befriended several Outlaws, including Timothy Silvia of the Brockton chapter, treating them to drinks and dinner at local bars and restaurants.

After two years of gaining their trust with minor deals, the agent was surprised when two Outlaws drove up to his house in an unfamiliar pickup truck. The two men from the Taunton chapter— former president Joseph "Joe Doggs" Noe and sergeant-at-arms

Brian "Clothesline" Delavega—told him that they had just car-jacked a guy at gunpoint outside the Sportsman's Café, a modest bar and restaurant located in an old barn in nearby Norton. They told him he could have the Chevy Silverado for $6,000 cash, per-haps a quarter of its actual worth. Eager to gather incriminating evidence and to gain their trust, the agent paid them.

After that, many members of the Outlaws were happy to work with him. He targeted two in particular—Silvia and Todd Donofrio, also of the Brockton chapter—because they seemed to have more money than the others. When he told Silvia that he could let him have ten kilos of high-quality cocaine for the bargain-basement price of $180,000, the Outlaw was interested. But he had a problem: he didn't have that kind of cash on hand. So he made a deal. He told the agent he could get $50,000 in cash right away and would let him hold on to his customized Hummer H2 SUV and his brand-new Harley-Davidson FLHR Road King motorcycle as collateral until he raised the rest of the money. The agent agreed.

On the warm evening of July 30, 2007, the agent waited with another undercover agent in a Cadillac parked next to a tractor-trailer in the massive parking lot of the Brockton Holiday Inn. At 7, as agreed upon, he saw a car he recognized as Donofrio's green Ford Crown Victoria, followed by Silvia's Hummer, which was pulling the Harley on a trailer.

Silvia parked and walked over to the two agents. After a few pleasantries, he handed the original agent $25,000 in cash. Donofrio arrived and handed the agent $30,000.

The agent then went into the truck and brought out a box. He handed it to Silvia, saying that it contained cocaine, and told him to test it. The Outlaw slit the packing tape on the cardboard box, pulled back the flaps, and stuck his finger into the white powder for a little taste.

That's when the agent gave the signal for the dozens of heavily armed and armored cops in the parking lot to converge and arrest Silvia and Donofrio. In all, eighteen Outlaws and their associates were arrested and charged for a variety of offenses, mainly trafficking. Silvia was sentenced to twenty-one years, Donofrio to ten and the others to shorter terms.

While certainly not as closely associated with coke as they are with meth, bikers do sell plenty of it regionally. They essentially cornered the market in Canada, being supplied by both branches of the Italian Mafia (La Cosa Nostra and 'Ndrangheta) as well as their own contacts in South America. The Montreal Hells Angels had befriended Guy Lepage—a former Montreal cop who had been kicked off the force when it was discovered he was part-owner of a nightclub that was a notorious venue for cocaine trafficking—and convinced him to go to Colombia in 1997 to negotiate directly with the Mejia Cartel in Barranquilla. By sailing the cocaine from Colombia directly to the remotely populated Gaspé Peninsula in eastern Quebec, they bypassed strict and technologically sophisticated U.S. authorities. The plan worked for years until a series of informants provided law enforcement with small bits of information that had to be painstakingly put together to unravel it.

But, as with meth, competition with Mexicans and decreasing demand (cocaine is more closely associated with homeless crackheads than movie stars these days) have combined to greatly reduce the revenue that can be gained by trafficking cocaine.

While the arrow might be pointed down at the moment for stimulant drugs like meth and cocaine, the opposite is true of opioids, whether prescription drugs or heroin.

The most common way for bikers to get their hands on prescription drugs is through scrip scammers. These are people who visit doctors, complain about chronic pain—real or imagined—and are given a prescription for opioid painkillers. Instead of using them, the scammer sells the pills to a dealer, often a biker. If they're left alone for a moment in the examination room, scrip scammers will usually try to steal as many prescription pads as they can, to be forged for more pills.

Of course, it's not that uncommon for doctors to be intimidated into providing bikers or their associates with prescriptions, and there have been several instances of doctors who have been caught supplying bikers with medically unnecessary opioids for their own financial gain.

One of them was William J. O'Brien III, who liked to call himself "Doctor Bear" and advertised his practices with a teddy bear mascot with a cast on its leg and crutches. He was an osteopath, which meant that although he did not study traditional medicine and did not have an M.D. degree, he was entitled to write prescriptions. O'Brien's services were popular in the Philadelphia area, and he opened seven locations under the Doctor Bear name, employing ninety people. But by 2010, he was in financial trouble. He had purchased a huge ten-person hyperbaric chamber at great personal expense and advertised that he intended to use it to treat autism, attracting many desperate parents who were not satisfied with traditional treatments for the condition. The problem was that since the FDA had not approved such a treatment for autism, he was in breach of several federal regulations. The FBI raided his Middletown, New Jersey, office and seized the chamber.

With his legal costs and the loss of his investment in the hyperbaric chamber, O'Brien filed for bankruptcy.

But he did not lose his osteopath license or his right to prescribe drugs. Desperate for money, he spoke to an old friend, Joseph Mehl, in early 2012. Mehl was a tow truck driver who, in exchange for opioid prescriptions for his own use, would direct anyone he met who had been in an auto accident to visit Doctor Bear in case they needed something to handle any pain. O'Brien told Mehl about his financial problems, and Mehl quickly came up with a solution. He introduced O'Brien to his boss, Sam "Bullet" Nocille.

Nocille was a full-patch member of the Pagan's, and he already had a large network of drug dealers under his sway. He and O'Brien hit it off right away, and together they came up with a plan. Nocille would recruit his dealers and other associates to make appointments with O'Brien, for which they would pay him $200 cash, which he would not report to the IRS, his creditors or the bankruptcy court. In exchange, the fake patients would be given prescriptions for opioids. They would then turn the pills over to Nocille, who would distribute them to his dealers in eastern Pennsylvania and western New Jersey. It seemed like a win-win situation for all parties, especially since single oxycodone pills sold illicitly for as much as $25 at the time.

It was immediately successful, and demand very quickly outstripped Nocille's crew of trusted dealers. He designated two of his oldest friends, Michael "Tomato Pie" Thompson and Charles Johnson, as recruiters, responsible for bringing more fake patients to O'Brien. They then added Pagan's supporters Frank "Stalker" Corazo and Peter "Petey Nose" Marradino to their group. But even that couldn't fill the seemingly limitless demand. Nocille cut two other Pagan's full patches—Patrick "Redneck" Treacy and Joseph "Body Parts" Mitchell Sr.—into the scam.

The large group started recruiting anyone they could, with a preference for people with Medicaid insurance, which would pay for the prescribed pills, increasing their profits at taxpayers' expense.

They even started to have fun with it. O'Brien designated Pagan's members as his VIP patients and met with them in a separate office in Levittown, Pennsylvania, near their clubhouse. Treacy, a forty-eight-year-old man, wrote on his official medical history form that he had been pregnant "lots of times" and had requested a PAP test for cervical cancer.

The Pagan's hung out at a strip joint called the Oasis Gentlemen's Club in Southwest Philadelphia near the airport and started to recruit dancers to visit O'Brien. On several occasions, Doctor Bear waived the $200 co-pay in exchange for oral sex.

At the end of every day, O'Brien and his receptionist, Angela Rangione, would shred any evidence that cash had changed hands. Every week, O'Brien would take about $20,000 in cash to a luxurious house that officially belonged to his ex-wife, Elizabeth Hibbs. Just before he declared bankruptcy, O'Brien and Hibbs went through a quick, uncontested divorce in which he claimed no property. That kept her assets safe from seizure. They continued to live together in the house, and the FBI maintained that they, "by outward appearances, continued to act as husband and wife" (there was testimony that O'Brien had asked several Pagan's if Hibbs could be "beaten or killed" for the right price, but no charges were laid).

O'Brien became quite chummy with the Pagan's—although Nocille frequently complained he wasn't getting paid enough, since it was all his idea—and started hanging out with them. When one of his patients, a South Philadelphia recruit named Anthony Rongione, fell $2,000 behind in his payments, O'Brien asked the Pagan's to do something about it. Days later, Treacy and Mehl knocked on Rongione's door, but when he, his brother and two friends emerged armed with baseball bats, the Pagan and his supporter friend quickly left, shouting threats. The next day, Rongione and friend Michael Sperling were found inside the house dead, each with a bullet hole in the back of his head. No charges were ever laid in connection with their deaths.

Nocille's whining and a few unpaid bills notwithstanding, the operation was humming along successfully until one of the Pagan's directed the wrong person to O'Brien—a real patient. A Bucks County, Pennsylvania, man named Joseph Ennis had been hit by a van in a snowstorm and suffered from chronic pain but did not have enough medical insurance to see a doctor. Through friends, he was recruited by a biker who directed him to O'Brien, who prescribed a ridiculously large amount of opioids in exchange for $200 cash. Instead of selling the pills to the bikers, Ennis took the prescription as advised and promptly died of an overdose.

An investigation into how and where he acquired the pills led to the arrest of O'Brien, Rangione, the bikers and the other recruiters. Despite a paucity of records, investigators determined that O'Brien had prescribed at least 378,914 oxycodone pills and 160,492 methadone pills over less than three years, many of them well over standard-strength doses.

At his trial, O'Brien admitted that he had made some mistakes and defended himself with witticisms like "That's why they call it a medical practice and not a perfect." Eschewing a lawyer to represent himself, he had a juror read *The Cat in the Hat* aloud to test his English skills, frequently made sexual comments about prosecutors and other people in the court and blamed the whole thing on his "greedy" patients. He called investigators "bullies" and accused them of calling him the "fat doctor" behind his back. Despite his efforts, O'Brien was convicted by a jury of 123 counts, including drug trafficking, money laundering and lying in a bankruptcy proceeding and was sentenced to thirty years in prison. He was not charged in relation to the death of Ennis.

Nocille died of a heart attack before he could be tried. After the jury was played secret recordings of Treacy clearly claiming, "I'm part of an organized crime family" and Mitchell saying, "Working is for the birds . . . it ain't for Pagan's" in court, they both pleaded guilty but still got twenty years each. The others, including Mefl, Thompson, Johnson, Carrago, Marradino and Rangione, were also convicted of trafficking and received lighter sentences. Hibbs was convicted of money laundering.

While O'Brien was certainly the prime mover in the Philly case, his efforts would have been in vain had he not been supplied with patients by the Pagan's, and had the club's members not had the drug distribution network to make the scheme profitable. And, although his case had its own special flair, it's hardly unique. In 2010 alone, 650 million oxycodone pills were imported into Florida. The FBI claimed that there were 856 illegal pill mills like O'Brien's in the state that year. Without bikers, they'd find that kind of volume almost impossible to move.

For bikers, the benefits of trafficking opioids are numerous. They are fairly easy to acquire in great numbers and usually require no contact with other crime organizations (which could lead to violence). There are an almost unlimited number of customers, and the drugs themselves are quickly and profoundly habit forming. And there's an added bonus: unlike with users of cocaine, meth and heroin, there is no lasting negative public image of a prescription opioid user. While the image of what cocaine, methamphetamine and heroin can do to a person are common enough to have become cliché in mainstream media, and a walk through many neighborhoods can confirm its truth, opioid users tend to appear to be living normal lives, and most overdoses happen quietly in the user's home.

Heroin is still around as well. An illegal opiate made from poppy seeds, it was very popular in the late 1960s and early 1970s, but—as with meth-heads and crackheads—the image of what the drug did to frequent users (called "junkies") severely cut into the drug's popularity. It is, however, making a comeback. According to the Centers for Disease Control, the rate of heroin overdoses per 100,000 people reported in 2016 was double that of 2012.

Traditionally imported from Thailand or Afghanistan, more and more heroin is now being manufactured in Mexico as the cartels that had specialized in cocaine or meth work to find additional revenue streams.

But it's rare to the point of exceptional that you'll see bikers selling it these days. In the 1960s and early 1970s, when heroin first became popular in North America, many bikers took it, and plenty—including Sonny Barger—sold it. But the devastating toll heroin takes on people hit the bikers just as hard as it did their customers, with frequent overdoses and numerous destroyed lives. By the end of the 1970s, all the big clubs had banned the use and sale of injectable drugs by their members. While several clubs have rules against selling other drugs, they often turn a blind eye or even give a knowing wink to dealers in their midst. That tolerance, however, does not extend to heroin, and any biker dealing in it would have to keep it secret from the rest of the club, knowing that his punishment if caught could be dire.

Many chapters, however—tacitly or at least unofficially—will waive their no-needles policy for steroids. Because fighting, bodybuilding and other displays of machismo are so ingrained in biker culture, steroids have become a distinct, even necessary, part of life for many of them.

Steroid users are generally a tight-knit community who are loath to expose their suppliers, and only rarely do law enforcement officers hear about trafficking. Often, arrests for steroid trafficking occur when police are targeting bikers for other drugs, like cocaine or meth, and happen upon a stash of 'roids. It's usually just a matter of getting lucky, as police did with Hells Angel William Bettencourt in 2010. After he was positively identified in an alleged assault and battery case the night before, police raided Bettencourt's home in Live Oak, California. Ten heavily armed officers stormed the house because Bettencourt had already had two violent felony convictions and was believed to be armed. They did indeed find a semiautomatic handgun—itself enough to put Bettencourt in prison for a very long time—but were surprised to also find ten vials of anabolic steroids and twenty-five more containing what Bettencourt himself identified as human growth hormone, a similarly illegal bodybuilding drug, and which he admitted to trafficking.

Another illegal substance frequently associated with bikers, after a steady stream of convictions, is the family of three common compounds known as "date-rape drugs" or "roofies."

In January 2006, a man named Mark Figueiredo aroused suspicion when police watched him walk into the home of a full-patch Toronto Hells Angel—who was under investigation as a drug trafficker—with a set of plastic shopping bags and leave with a different set of very cumbersome bags.

A month later, in the same house, an undercover agent asked Figueiredo if he wanted any drugs. The members of the Downtown Toronto chapter normally sold cocaine, so the agent was surprised when Figueiredo asked for GHB, a date-rape drug.

In May, police raided Figueiredo's home and found 375 liters (99 gallons) of GHB. Since 5 milliliters is generally considered more than enough to knock a person out, the amount found at Figueiredo's home was good enough for 75,000 doses.

When Figueiredo was sentenced to six years, he wept uncontrollably and then hugged and kissed his wife, sister and niece. The five Hells Angels members and prospects he was arrested with were convicted of conspiracy to traffic.

While talking about drugs might be a prominent taboo in the biker world, dealing them seems to be acceptable, even encouraged.

## CHAPTER 8

# More to the Life than Just Drugs

**A**ll day, every day, boosters would come into the bar we hung out in and try to get someone interested in what they had," Frankie, a former Outlaws prospect, told me. Boosters, if you don't know, are professional thieves, and Frankie says they approached bikers in an effort to sell them items they had stolen. "It was mostly the full patches, because everyone knew they had money."

I asked him what kind of items they would bring in.

"You name it . . . everything," he told me. "Lots of electronics, jewelry, anything they could get their hands on that had any value."

"And what would the bikers do with it?" I asked.

"Sell it or give it to family and friends."

"Why wouldn't the boosters just sell it themselves?"

"That's a good way to get the shit kicked out of you."

IN THE SUMMER of 1997, Bob Henderson of the National Insurance Crime Bureau went to the Hennepin County Sheriff's Office in Minnesota desperately in need of help. He told them that over the past three years, more than five hundred Harleys had been stolen in Minnesota alone and that virtually none of them had been recovered. It was costing insurers millions, pushing them literally close to bankruptcy. Henderson pointed out that most of the thefts had been pinned down to the Minneapolis–St. Paul area and wanted to know if the sheriff's office could get to the bottom of it.

A few days later, three Harleys were stolen from a garage in the southern part of Minneapolis, but one of the thieves who was riding away spun out on an on-ramp. The thief fled on foot, but a pager was found at the scene of the accident. It belonged to Kami Gorham, whom investigators knew to be the girlfriend of Antonio "Tony" Morales, who had a long record of theft arrests and convictions for a variety of non-violent crimes.

About a week later, a Harley owner heard noises in his garage and called police. They arrived to find Morales, his leg in a cast after he'd broken it crashing the stolen Harley, pushing the man's motorcycle down a street about a block away.

Caught red-handed, he explained that he had been stealing bikes for two members of El Forastero (a 1-percenter club associated with the Hells Angels) named Patrick Smith and Jay Puig.

The cops got permission to search Smith's mail and telephone records. Much of both were to and from Paul "Rooster" Seydel, vice-president of the Hells Angels' Minneapolis chapter.

Not long after that, a local meth-head named Ronnie Bowles, trying to get off a trafficking charge, offered information on local motorcycle thefts in exchange for cash. He told police that he had been approached by Morales—before he broke his leg—and a man named Burronie Brosh to help them steal a motorcycle. Bowles agreed to take on the job, and when he broke into the garage they led him to, they were delighted to discover that there were four complete Harleys, two more in stages of disassembly and two kilos of cocaine. They took everything, even the tools in the garage.

It was an extraordinarily bad idea. They should have known something was up when they saw the "fuck with it and find out" sticker on the most customized of the bikes.

The next day, handwritten posters offering $3,000 in cash for information leading to the thieves' identities appeared all over the neighborhood. It did not take long for word of who had stolen the stuff to make its way to the bikes' owner—Pat Matter, founder and president of the Minneapolis chapter of the Hells Angels. He had hired the same private investigator he used to give polygraph tests to prospects.

Without making any specific threat, Matter sat down with the three, demanded back his bikes, coke and tools, plus $10,000 for each of the thieves for his aggravation over the incident and to make up for any missing cocaine. Once they complied, Matter told them to get out of town.

Brosh and Bowles laid low, but Morales kept stealing bikes in and around Minneapolis, although he was more careful about whose bike it was. When he was arrested again, he gave more evidence on Smith, allowing police to surveil his home and the storage lockers he rented.

When they finally arrested Smith and Puig, they seized more than $750,000 worth of Harleys and parts.

The revelations about Matter bore more investigation, and police, led by sheriff's detective Chris Omodt, found that he was buying custom frames from a Hells Angels–associated company in Alberta and transmission cases from a business operated by another Hells Angels chapter president in California. With those key parts, Matter was able to make custom bikes using components from stolen Harleys (supplied by the guys in El Forastero) and make them appear to be legal. In fact, in his first year of selling bikes made from stolen parts, he said, the business brought in more than $250,000. His second was in excess of $750,000 and his third cleared "well over" $1 million. That was more than he was earning from selling cocaine and methamphetamine.

Motorcycle theft is incredibly lucrative for bikers and their allies for a number of reasons. One is that it's surprisingly easy— you don't even have to know how to ride a motorcycle to steal one.

The heaviest stock Harley maxes out at about 870 pounds, while most are much lighter, and choppers—by their very definition—are even lighter still. While all motorcycles are heavy for one person, it's not a huge problem for four or five guys to lift even the biggest ones for a moment or two, and it's easy for most thieves to roll one into a van. All locks can be defeated with wire cutters, bolt cutters or canned Freon, and alarms can be disconnected and silenced. Insurance companies and law enforcement advise that the best way to keep your bike from being stolen is to keep it concealed, but if you've got a Harley, the whole neighborhood knows—they've all heard it.

Once the Harley is in the hands of the builder, it's a pretty simple job to conceal its origin. The vehicle identification number (VIN) is located on the front of the frame, and the transmission case also has a serial number that indicates year and model (if not the individual bike). The VIN is the only way to accurately determine the bike's origin. All the other parts are essentially interchangeable from bike to bike and have no individual identifying characteristics. The builder can simply swap out the frame—cheap frames can be had for as little as $300 and are frequently sold by biker-associated or biker-owned companies—and the even less expensive transmission case. Or, he can manually change the VIN to one taken from a bike that has been crashed or is otherwise unsalvageable. It doesn't even matter if the VIN matches the type of frame, because it's not like the man or woman at the licensing office is going to force the builder to prove his 1999 Wide Glide is actually a 1993 Fat Bob, especially if the final product is heavily customized.

And there's no shortage of people lining up to buy custom Harleys. Matter invested almost none of his own money into the business, other than buying frames and transmission cases and paying thieves, and sold most of his bikes from $10,000 to $12,000, a few in excess of $30,000 and one for more than $50,000.

He kept meticulous, if not entirely accurate, records and paid taxes on the revenues. Unless he was informed on, it would be virtually impossible for police to determine the true nature of his business.

Pat Matter was very good at his business but far from unique. Many bikers who have jobs work in motorcycle customization and repair or do similar work on cars and other vehicles, and some do it just for fun. Stolen cars are reduced to component parts at chop shops, and the parts can be sold individually in a store or, increasingly, online. Several bikers on the Pacific coast of Canada and the U.S. have been convicted of sending cars, motorcycles and their parts to China, where certain brands of cars and bikes are rare and the replacement-parts market is expensive.

An August 2012 raid of a motorcycle repair shop in Nanaimo, British Columbia, called Cycle Logic found dozens of stolen vehicles, ranging from pickup trucks to speedboats, and several

Harleys. The shop's owner, John Newcombe, pleaded guilty to altering the VINs on vehicles and dealing with stolen property. Police said that the vehicles had been supplied to Newcombe through members of the Hells Angels and two associated clubs, the Throttle Lockers and Kingpin Crew.

Documents recovered at the Nanaimo site connected it to the Edmonton Hells Angels. And in 2016, police served warrants on several properties and came up with seventeen camper trailers, three pickup trucks, six all-terrain vehicles, a snowmobile, two off-road bikes, eighteen rifles, two shotguns and a handgun, all stolen. Ten men were arrested: police allege two were Hells Angels full-patch members, seven were members and prospects of support clubs and one was an associate of no fixed address. They have yet to be tried and have pleaded not guilty.

Another way bikers have been known to make a little extra money is to misrepresent vehicles for sale. Cars and trucks damaged in natural disasters can be bought at auction for very little, get a new VIN and sell for a heck of a lot more.

In several cases involving the big clubs, insurance fraud goes hand in hand with Harley ownership. A good example of that occurred in 2010 when the Massachusetts State Police infiltrated the Taunton chapter of the Outlaws. An undercover agent managed to befriend Scott Towne, who was not an Outlaw but hung around with them, worked with them, and earned their respect—and clubhouse privileges—by beating up two Hells Angels full-patch members, stealing their cuts and giving them to the Outlaws.

Towne introduced the undercover agent to Joseph "Joe Doggs" Noe, president of the Outlaws' Taunton chapter, and was present while Noe sold him a Kawasaki Vulcan for $7,000 under the condition that he change the VIN. The undercover agent asked why, and Noe told him that the bike's owner—a friend of his from nearby Avon—had bought the bike, sold it to him, reported it stolen and collected the insurance money. The undercover agent checked with police, and the Vulcan had indeed been reported stolen and the insurance company had paid its owner.

Pretending to want in on the action, the undercover agent approached Noe about buying more vehicles. When the investigation ended, the undercover agent had purchased thirteen vehicles from club members, some of them acquired through violent carjackings.

While not all bikers have great mechanical aptitude, all of them know how to fight, and that can be used to make money. Of course, there are legitimate jobs in which fighting ability is a requirement—like bodyguard, bouncer, mixed-martial-arts instructor and professional wrestler—and I have met bikers who have held each of them.

However, the legitimate job openings available for people who know how to fight (and have few other marketable skills) are far outnumbered by the sea of suitable applicants. That puts many into the muscle-for-hire business. Many people engaged in illegal activities need tough guys to collect debts, intimidate witnesses or protect prostitutes from their clients. That's often where bikers come in.

A definitive example of how it works occurred in Connecticut in 2016. A man, his identity now protected by court, approached James Broderick III for a loan. Broderick lent the man $1,500 on the condition he pay him back $2,000 four days later (that's a more than 30,000-percent rate of interest per year). When the debtor did not return with the money on the agreed-upon day, Broderick called Howard Hammer.

Hammer was a full-patch member of the Charter Oak MC in Stamford, a Hells Angels support club that law enforcement says answers to the chapter in Bridgeport. He texted the debtor, telling him to pay or face severe consequences. When the man did not reply, Hammer and a few other bikers paid him a visit.

According to Yale New Haven Hospital, the victim was stabbed eight times (one of which perforated his spleen), he had multiple skull fractures, his cheekbone was "completely shattered," his jaw bone was "reduced to minute fragments and pulverized particles," his lip was "completely destroyed," he was missing eleven teeth and his left eye was hanging out of its socket.

An informant let police know that Hammer was a prime suspect, so they were awarded a warrant to tap his phone. What they heard—including "I'm gonna be the fall guy, take the hit" and "I don't wanna see no one else get in trouble; I don't want to see nothing, you know what I mean"—meant to them that, if caught, he would not identify the other participants in the beating.

They also determined that by taking the fall for the group, Hammer was positioning himself to become a candidate for Hells Angels membership, citing to a friend over his tapped phone a meeting with Bridgeport chapter president Sean Oldroyd: "Sean took me to the side and he goes, 'I don't talk to many people like this,' he goes, 'but your guys' club, you guys are top notch in our book, you know.' He goes, 'you know,' he just praised us like crazy, and he goes, 'and you for helping us out, you hold our card in your pocket.'"

Both Hammer and Broderick pleaded guilty. Hammer received a thirty-month sentence in prison, and Broderick was fined. No charges were laid against Oldroyd.

Of course, using violence or the threat of it isn't something bikers do exclusively for other people. Being a biker, especially a full patch in a big club, brings many privileges. In many bars, bikers expect not to pay for drinks, food, lap dances and other goods and services.

Often, these agreements are tacit and in place simply because the owner or manager of the establishment wants to avoid trouble.

When the deal becomes spoken, however, what might be a friendly gesture becomes extortion. There are plenty of ways I've known bikers to extort. The simplest is by demanding free drinks. I've seen that grow into bikers demanding money from an establishment not to show up there. It works like this: The biker shows up a few times and acts as obnoxiously as possible, stealing drinks, breaking bottles, assaulting staff and doing whatever he thinks will annoy management the most. If they manage to eject him or call the police, he'll come back with friends and do the same thing. He, possibly accompanied by his friends, keeps up the destructive behavior until the establishment's management pleads with him not to come back. At that point, they hammer out a deal in which the management pays the biker a certain amount every week in exchange for him not showing up anymore. Even with just a few establishments paying, I've known bikers to make a better-than-decent living off nothing else.

Of course, the old protection racket, in which the biker offers protection from disasters like arson in exchange for cash while intimating that he's the one the business needs to be protected against, is alive and well and popular among bikers.

A great example of how extortion works for bikers occurred on Long Island. It was uncovered in 1998, but how long it had been going on is still a mystery. Long Island is home to about eight million people, is primarily suburban and is dominated by the Pagan's. Before the explosion of porn available on the internet, it was also home to many strip joints, topless bars, peep shows and porn stores. And, according to police, a series of informants told them that every single one of the businesses had been the victim of extortion attempts by members of the Pagan's.

Here's how it worked. The owner or manager of each business would be told that they had to pay $400 a week to the club or face assault or arson. Further, any salaries due the dancers would be forwarded to the Pagan's, forcing the performers to rely solely on tips for their income.

And every one of them agreed to it, except one. Sean McCarthy—who was both manager and primary bouncer for the Carousel Club, a topless establishment in Huntington Station—refused. On no less than seven occasions, the Pagan's arrived at the Carousel Club and attempted to beat McCarthy into submission. There was a problem with that plan, though. McCarthy, aided by friends, never lost any of the fights—although he was stabbed on two occasions.

Frustrated, Bay Shore chapter president and national sergeant-at-arms Keith "Conan" Richter put out an order to the Long Island Pagan's that McCarthy had to be killed. Luckily for McCarthy, two of the people who received the order told police, and Richter and thirty-three other Pagan's were arrested. Richter pleaded guilty to conspiracy to murder in aid of racketeering and was sentenced to sixteen years in prison.

Often, though, biker extortion is less organized and ambitious than that. Sometimes the very signs of "disrespect" that often elicit a beating from a biker can instead result in intimidation. More common in Australia than North America, a biker will "fine" someone who breaks his rules, like talking to the wrong woman or wearing the support gear of another club. The person could be an associate but could also be a neighbor or a stranger the biker happens to run into. Should the person fined not pay, they can expect a beating or damage to their property.

Similarly, witness intimidation is commonplace, according to the bikers I have spoken with, either to keep themselves out of jail or just to make a few bucks.

The matter of whether biker clubs operate as crime organizations continues. After the 2011 killing of San Jose Hells Angel Jeffery "Jethro" Pettigrew at the Sparks casino in Reno, Nevada, by a member of the Vagos, the FBI put together a multi-department task force to look into the club's activities.

By 2016, they came up with an indictment, naming twenty-three individual Vagos, alleging that among other offenses, Vagos traffic several different types of drugs, including cocaine, methamphetamine and steroids; assault debtors; order subordinates to carry out assaults on the club's behalf; illegally seize property (often motorcycles and other vehicles) of debtors; assault women who refuse their sexual advances and anyone who tries to come to their aid; steal and resell consumer items stolen from ports; habitually lie under oath; punish members and associates who cooperate with law enforcement, sometimes with death; conduct kidnappings for the purpose of intimidation; sell stolen motorcycles; and engage in murder, conspiracy to murder and arranging to murder members and associates of rival gangs, specifically the Hells Angels and Sons of Silence.

The case, which could change the way biker clubs are treated under the law, has yet to be tried. While the U.S. Department of Justice frequently refers to several clubs as criminal organizations, as does the RCMP in Canada, attempts to convict any club under RICO laws, which would legally label them gangs, have failed. However, in 2005, a Canadian judge ruled that the Hells Angels were indeed a criminal organization after two members, Steve "Tiger" Lindsay and Raymond Bonner, were convicted of extorting a debtor by using nothing other than the intimidating reputation of the club. While the judgment did not outlaw the club, it did give law enforcement more powers of surveillance and judges more leeway to impose heavier sentences. Although subsequent trials of

Hells Angels in Ontario have not specifically mentioned the club as a criminal organization, several people close to the club have told me that members, prospects and their friends and associates have appeared, in their opinion at least, to suffer harsher sentences than others convicted of the same or similar offenses.

Similarly, a long-term investigation of the Rock Hill, South Carolina, chapter of the Hells Angels alleged that they were a multi-faceted crime organization, dealing not just in methamphetamine but also in firearms. And while some of the participants pleaded guilty to racketeering, making them individually gangsters, some did not, and the crime organization label could not stick. Again, the prosecution could not prove that the members of the club banded together to commit crimes and not to ride motorcycles.

Gun-running is not uncommon for biker clubs, particularly when they are located in places with relaxed laws and restrictions on firearm acquisition and ownership and are not far from places with stricter statutes. It should be remembered that Jay Dobyns's infiltration of the Arizona Hells Angels was not prompted by their war with the Mongols, nor their drug trafficking, but by their business of importing firearms—many of them illegally converted to automatic-fire capability—into Mexico. And business was booming: Mexico has just one legal gun store and is in the throes of a war between the government and drug cartels, which has left more than 100,000 people dead.

No matter which criminal enterprise bikers—or anyone else—take on, money laundering is an essential tool for staying out of prison. Ever since it became known that it was an IRS tax evasion investigation and not the police that put away Al Capone in 1931, people involved in organized crime have made scrupulous efforts to keep from being found with money that they can't explain how they acquired.

Although there are many, often sophisticated, ways to launder money, bikers—according to the ones I have interviewed and from what law enforcement tells me—generally use two surprisingly simple methods.

One process that bikers have told me about simply involves visiting a casino. Upon entry, the money launderer exchanges cash for chips. Casinos will not accept credit cards or debit cards for chips, so large cash transactions are not uncommon and do not raise undue suspicion. Although the casino will keep a record of the transaction and issue a receipt, no identification is required, and the amount exchanged is not associated with the person buying the chips, so it leaves no paper trail. The person laundering the money then hangs around the casino and maybe plays a game or two in front of security cameras. Again, no identification is required to gamble, and winners and losers are not required to provide their names. After a while, the money launderer cashes in all the chips. The casino then issues a check with the launderer's name on it.

Should the launderer have to explain the amount of cash, he or she simply attributes it to good luck at the casino and presents the canceled check to prove that the money did indeed come from the casino, and prosecutors are almost powerless to prove that the launderer brought the money into the casino in the first place.

It's not foolproof, of course. Casinos are under extreme scrutiny from federal authorities and are in no hurry to be associated with that kind of crime. And the lucky-at-gambling method can only be used sparingly, as frequent wins at casinos can stretch the money launderer's credibility, which often proves detrimental in jury trials.

More consistently reliable, my sources tell me, is to operate or invest in a cash-intensive business and inflate its revenues on its ledgers. For example, let's say a biker owns a tattoo business (it doesn't have to be tattoos; it can be any product or service that people generally pay cash for). And let's say the biker charges an average of $100 per tattoo and regularly sees forty customers a week for an average weekly revenue of $4,000. But if he writes receipts for a hundred tattoos per week, he can claim the shop brought in $10,000 or even more (he can also claim higher prices were paid for each tattoo). Should an inspector visit the shop and see that there are far fewer customers than the biker claims, he simply declares that the inspector visited on a particularly unlucky week.

Unless an informant is involved, money laundering is difficult for law enforcement to track down, and bikers are generally only charged with the offense alongside other offenses, such as trafficking.

Sometimes, bikers get caught when they slip up. In a 1969 interview, Sonny Barger bragged that he paid a guy $12,000 to customize his car. Angrily, he wrote in his memoir that an "IRS creep" happened to hear the comment, determined that Barger claimed just $6,000 income on his taxes and started the process for an audit.

Of course, he should have followed his own rule and not snitched on himself.

# CHAPTER 9

# Your Friendly Neighborhood Biker

"Do you want to know how dumb civilians are?"

I hadn't asked, but now I was eager to hear the rest of the story anyway.

"I'll tell you how fuckin' dumb civilians are," Pete told me, and then dropped this on me: "They actually asked the Hells Angels to get drugs out of their neighborhood."

He tells me that he was prospecting with the Hells Angels in a southern Ontario city when he was approached by a full-patch member (not his sponsor) with a task. Pete knew that a prospect couldn't say no to a request from a full patch, especially if it's for the good of the club, so he simply answered, "Great, what do you need?"

The full patch told him that there was a problem in the neighborhood and that the two of them were going to get rid of it.

"That kind of scared me a bit," Pete told me. "See, this guy had a lot of friends in Quebec, especially Sherbrooke."

Pete was referring to how violent things had gotten in Quebec from 1994 to 2002 when the Hells Angels were fighting the Rock

Machine, the Dark Circle and some other groups. The Sherbrooke Chapter was particularly notorious for violence and had a reputation for killing not just the enemy, but civilians and even other Hells Angels who didn't abide by their rules.

"Relax," the full patch told Pete, clearly aware that he was concerned. "Nobody has to get hurt; we just want to teach this guy a lesson."

Pete said that he knew why he was picked. Not only was he a solid 6-foot-4, he had served as a doorman for a boisterous nightclub, and he was also a part-time mixed-martial-arts instructor.

The problem, the full patch told him, was that there was a guy selling crack in a residential neighborhood not far from where the full patch lived. Pete laughed. He knew that several members of the chapter sold cocaine at least, if not crack. He assumed that the chapter was upset because some interloper had encroached on the club's turf.

He was wrong. The full patch told him that a couple of neighborhood moms had knocked on his door a few days earlier and asked to speak with him. He invited them inside and they told him about the kid who was selling crack. They didn't want that kind of thing in their neighborhood, they said. It was right near their kids' school. He knew about the guy already but thought he was too small of a fish to bother with. If the guy made a couple of hundred bucks a week, it would have surprised him.

The full patch was skeptical at first, Pete said, not sure if he was being set up or not. He had seen both moms around before— he also had a kid at the same school—but couldn't be too careful. He asked them why they didn't just go to the cops. They had, they told him, but it didn't do any good. From his own experience, the full patch knew that it was difficult for the police to build a case against any drug dealer unless they could get an informant or some other way to get a judge to grant a search warrant.

So he asked them what they wanted him to do about it. Without hesitation, they asked if he would pay the dealer a visit and, you know, maybe, convince him he was in the wrong neighborhood.

It was at that point, he told Pete, when he really started to relax. He had heard of the police setting up stings for drug trafficking and weapons sales but never for intimidating a drug dealer. Even if the police recorded everything, what would they have him on—being a concerned citizen?

He told Pete that he had agreed in principle to have a talk with the boy. But what, he asked, was in it for him? The moms, he said, were flabbergasted. They clearly had not thought about that part of the deal before knocking.

Finally, he said, one of them told him they didn't really have any money. The full patch laughed, he told Pete. First, he said, the fact that they didn't come up with a solid cash price proved they weren't working for the cops. The cops would have provided money. And second, he hoped they weren't going to offer him sex in exchange.

He let them hang for a moment, he said, and then told them he'd do it free of charge.

And then he recruited Pete. The instructions were simple: meet the full patch at a Tim Hortons near the dealer's house. It was crucial that he be unarmed, the full patch told him, and that he not wear anything that identified the club. If Pete showed up wearing a club T-shirt, boots or belt buckle, the full patch said he'd tear it off him, throw it in the trash and send him home to change. That order extended not just to anything with the name Hells Angels or its logo, but to words like "Support 81" or "Big Red Machine" or even the name or logo of Harley-Davidson.

Pete understood why; every Canadian biker did. In 2005, a couple of Hells Angels were convicted of extortion after they leaned on a Barrie gambler. Since they were wearing club gear, the judge decided that they were using the club's reputation as a weapon, added years to their sentences and managed to get the Hells Angels declared a criminal organization. It didn't stop the club from operating; it just gave police extra powers to investigate members and associates, and it gave judges the ability to issue them all stiffer penalties upon conviction.

Like every successful prospect, Pete did exactly as he was told. He arrived at the Tim Hortons in jeans, work boots and a T-shirt, without any jewelry. He left his ID at home and his phone in his car. The full patch looked even less like a biker than he did. He was wearing a navy golf shirt and khakis. He stood up, took a long swig out of his large double-double and said, "Let's go."

They wordlessly walked up to the low-rise apartment building and waited until they saw a woman leaving to let themselves in through the security door. They ran upstairs to the dealer's apartment on the third floor. The prospect pounded on the door. No answer. He did it again, saying firmly, "Police, open up." Pete said he heard a voice from inside say, "Just a minute."

The full patch laughed and covered the door's peephole with his index finger. After a moment or so, the door opened a crack. Pete told me he shoved it wide open, and the guy behind it tumbled to the floor.

"You're not cops," the kid said. "I know who you guys are." The bikers let the dealer get up, and the full patch told him that he was wrong, he did not know who they were. The dealer then offered them money to leave. "That's when we told him he was wrong again," Pete said with a laugh. "He was the one who was going to leave."

Did you beat him up? I asked.

"Nah, nah, nah, nothing like that," he told me. "Didn't have to." He explained that the "kid" was maybe twenty-one, weighed no more than 140 pounds and "had never been in a fight in his life."

He knew it was a bad idea to start playing the tough guy. There was an aluminum baseball bat beside the door, but the full patch had grabbed it on the way in. "He was shittin' his pants," Pete told me with a laugh.

Instead of hitting the kid, the two bikers explained that there were no hard feelings, that he just had to get out of the business or move out of their territory. The dealer promised he would leave.

Just for fun, Pete said, he asked him where he got his product. "At first he said, 'Just a guy in Toronto,'" he told me. "But it didn't take him long to give his guy up . . . neither of us had heard of him."

Less than a week later, Pete went to check on the situation. The apartment was empty. The kid had fled. "Later, I heard he got arrested near Peterborough," he told me. "Not our problem."

I asked Pete why they did it. I mean, they weren't getting paid and the dealer was no threat to the club or to its members.

"For the PR, man," he said. Then he explained what happened next. The moms had noticed that the dealer was gone. One of them saw the full patch downtown and thanked him. The full patch said that he had no idea what she was talking about, but smiled and winked.

"They believed that they had gotten the Hells Angels to chase a dangerous drug dealer out of their neighborhood," he told me. "I guess we did, but that didn't mean that crack didn't get sold in the neighborhood."

It did, he said, just more discreetly, and by dealers sanctioned by the chapter who kicked a significant share upstairs. "You can't buy that kind of goodwill for any amount of money," he told me.

There's an old biker saying, generally associated with the Hells Angels but used by most clubs and chapters, that goes like this: "When we do right, nobody remembers; when we do wrong, nobody forgets."

Indeed, the Hells Angels and other outlaw motorcycle gangs do their best to maintain an image of benevolence within their communities. As organizations, they might take part in toy drives, food drives and other charitable undertakings, and they frequently invite the public to motorcycle shows, barbecues and similar events that show them in a positive, or at least non-aggressive, light.

As individuals or small groups, bikers might help someone in their community financially, provide security for a person or group, or take on other tasks that appear to be for the common good.

Randy, the former Outlaw full patch, says that bikers' community involvement is not by accident—and it's not because they are great guys. "If the civilians in your area like you, they are much less likely to call the cops or talk to them when they show up," he told me. "Besides, you have to live and work near them . . . you want them to be on your side."

The art of public relations is actually a big part of being a biker. And it goes much farther than simply publicly denying that the club is a gang and claiming that every member who goes to prison was working on his own, not on behalf of the club.

If you live in a community with any 1-percenter clubs nearby, you've probably seen or heard of their annual toy drives. Every year, close to Christmas, bikers give free toys to children and try to ensure the event is well attended and covered by local or regional media.

While it's not always an all-out scam, three of the bikers I spoke with for this book—Randy, Mitch and Frankie—told me that it's often not as altruistic as it appears from the outside. Here's how, according to them, it happens: Late in the year, usually around Halloween or Thanksgiving, the chapter will hold a party open to anyone they find acceptable. Along with the usual admission fee, guests are strongly encouraged to bring a toy. Toy drops are also usually established at the clubhouse and at bars and restaurants frequented by the chapter and its associates.

The toys are gathered up, wrapped and then brought to the Christmas event by the bikers, to be given to children. Rarely, and only in front of cameras, do the bikers themselves buy any of the toys. According to Mitch, the children sometimes belong to the bikers themselves, or their friends and associates.

For years, biker toy drives were a mainstay feel-good holiday story for local news, but more and more editors and broadcasters now see these drives as a ham-fisted publicity ploy, and they rarely make the papers or TV news any more.

The last time a biker-related toy drive made a big-time newspaper, it was because it did not go exactly as the club planned. In conjunction with local firefighters, the Hessians MC (a medium-sized 1-percenter club associated with the Hells Angels) were taking part in the 2005 version of the Sparks of Hope toy drive in Norco, California, not far from Riverside. While the bikers, firefighters and others were preparing for the event, they were set upon by some passing Mongols. Angry words became punches, which evolved into gunshots. Three people—including a firefighter—were shot, although none was critically injured.

Many cops have told me that bikers like to conduct illegal activities at fundraisers because the police would look bad if they arrested a biker when he was appearing to do some good for the community, and it would be especially bad optics if there was a scuffle.

But that doesn't mean bikers always get a free ride from cops when they are involved with charity events. In 2013, Thomas Napoli, an eleven-year-old boy from Seaford, New York, was diagnosed with brain cancer. His plight stirred many, and support came from the John Theissen Children's Foundation, Seaford Little League, Adelphi University and the Long Island Hitmen lacrosse team.

Two years later, police in the area noticed posters advertising an event called Bikers for Thomas Strong that was also celebrating the fiftieth anniversary of the founding of the Pagan's and the reopening of their Long Island chapter. The Pagan's had shut down the chapter after mass arrests stripped them of members— the result of a murder conspiracy against the Hells Angels.

Police showed up en masse at Duffy's Ale House in Lindenhurst but did not enter the building. Outside, they arrested eleven bikers—Michael Parsnip, Jason Craft, Boudewijn Rob, Kenneth Reynolds, Adam Sockriter and Todd Hathaway of the Pagan's; Julio Rosa and Manuel Tull of the Dirty Ones; Edward Otto of Steel Wheels; Mark Harmon of the Black Sheep; and Eneldo Rivera of the Armored Saints—and seized five handguns, a rifle, a shotgun and a club, as well as marijuana, cocaine and methamphetamine.

The party had three hundred attendees and reportedly raised $3,000 for Napoli, who was not in attendance. The eleven arrested bikers have yet to be tried and all have pleaded not guilty.

Even if there are not arrests, cops tell me that they take the opportunity to watch the participants at such events very closely, in hopes of uncovering previously unknown alliances and membership changes.

When bikers hold charitable events or make other displays of community spirit, it frequently involves the concept of helping children. It makes perfect sense, since few people would regard helping children as anything but good. And those who abuse or harm children are often held in the lowest regard by the public.

Not only are there toy drives and fundraisers for sick children, but there are several nonprofit, tax-exempt organizations. They range from the absolutely ridiculous Bikers Against Bullying (the dripping irony of a group that uses violence or the threat of it against anyone who behaves in a way they consider in contravention of their rules portraying themselves as anti-bullying seems to have eluded them) to the very popular Bikers Against Child Abuse (BACA).

BACA was started in Utah in 1995 by Brigham Young University professor and therapist John Paul "Chief" Lilly, who was disappointed that courts frequently returned children to parents who he believed abused them. In an unusual move, he took one shy eight-year-old named Alec who he believed was sexually abused to a barbecue party with some local bikers. Since Alec reacted positively at the barbecue, Lilly surmised that exposure to bikers was somehow therapeutic for young victims of abuse. Lilly formed the organization, which aims to fight child abuse by having bikers, in their colors, stand guard outside the homes of alleged victims and accused and to escort both to and from courtroom visits. They say it's "showing support"; others counter that it's intimidating potentially innocent suspects against whom nothing has been proven. Perhaps appropriately, their symbol is a fist. "We are not concerned with what is legal or ethical," Lilly wrote in a media release. "We are only concerned with what is right."

And their efforts have been known to backfire. In 2014, a Florida man named Brian Scott Long—who had been convicted in 2012 of two counts of lewd and lascivious molestation and one count of sexual battery of a person in familial or custodial authority under the age of twelve and sentenced to thirty years in prison—appealed his convictions on the basis that two members of BACA were present during the trial, wearing their colors in full view of the jury. He claimed that both his defense team and the prosecution had instructed the bikers not to wear their colors in court as it could prejudice the jury.

In a 2–1 decision, the judges ruled that the bikers showed "reckless advocacy" and retracted Long's convictions, stating that "there is no room at any stage of judicial proceedings for such intervention; mob law is the very antithesis of due process." Long was remanded for a new trial, and his name was taken off Florida's public sexual offenders database. His second trial ended in an acquittal.

Despite BACA's stated disinterest in ethical or legal niceties, it has won widespread public support. As one noted podcaster, Dr. Linda Tucker, said, "When you think of bikers, you might think of gangs, thugs and tattoos. John Paul Lilly has changed all of that." I hate to disagree with the good doctor, but no, he hasn't.

Indeed, there have been many, many, many convictions of bikers abusing and even killing children, their own and others. One case in particular continues to draw great ire among bikers.

Back in 2013, a Kansas City, Missouri, man was cruising through the escorts listings on the local edition of Backpage.com—a site for buying and selling goods and services that had acquired something of a notorious reputation for its "adult" section—when he saw the almost-nude photos of a girl he thought he recognized. If it was who he thought she was, that meant trouble, because she was not close to being eighteen years old yet.

An investigation into the ad determined that it was placed by eighteen-year-old Kayla "Foxy" Pinkerton, and the escort in question was indeed her younger friend. Pinkerton had even taken the pictures. The testimony of both of them, and others, led to an indictment for Milton Charles "Barbwire" Wilson, who was president of the Kansas City chapter of the Sons of Silence.

He later pleaded guilty to transporting the underage escort to a Kansas City hotel room and an Overland Park, Kansas, hotel with the knowledge that she was performing sex acts in exchange for money. Pinkerton, who was also indicted and convicted for her role in luring the child into prostitution and for taking the pictures and buying the ad, testified that Wilson had threatened her life if his participation in the operation was ever revealed to police, but he was not charged with that offense. Wilson, who was determined to be the prime motivator in the scheme, was given a sentence of ten years in prison, and Pinkerton was sentenced to sixteen months. Both were compelled to register as sex offenders. In March 2017, Pinkerton moved without informing the state, and is—as I write this—still a wanted fugitive.

The Wilson-Pinkerton case brings up a great deal of emotional response when discussed with bikers. While the old adage that boys will be boys can be used to excuse overtly illegal acts like trafficking and violence, there seems to be little that can be said in support of someone convicted of pimping a child, especially when the clubs work so hard to portray themselves as pro-family and concerned about the proper treatment of children.

Most of the bikers and supporters I brought the case up with denied it had ever happened, claiming that the government persuaded Pinkerton to make up a story about Wilson, just to weaken the Sons of Silence. Others took a more stoic and realistic approach, labeling Wilson a rare bad apple among their bushel. One Sons of Silence associate, clearly frustrated, told me (I'll spare the reader the all-caps), "So? I bet there are plenty of pedos in what you do too."

With so much media and law-enforcement focus on how closely biker gangs are associated with drugs, it makes sense for them to project an official anti-drug message. Many famous bikers claim they don't do drugs—most of them appear to be sincere to me—and they sometimes say that the other members of their club don't either. Chuck Zito, who has been a member of three different New York City–area Hells Angels chapters, maintained in his memoir that he never did drugs and that members of one of his chapters would be expelled for dealing drugs, but he also recounts a harrowing tale of how a four-hundred-pound Hells Angel who had an unfortunate "fondness for drugs" attacked him with a knife. Zito, of course, also served a six-year sentence in prison after pleading guilty to conspiracy to traffic methamphetamine. He pleaded guilty, he wrote in his memoir, because he was "tired" of fighting against a federal government that was determined to put him behind bars even if they had to break the law to do so.

In 1974, almost a decade after the Hells Angels decided to start selling methamphetamine, some of the club's brass felt it would be smart to distance their club's image from drugs. The innocence of the '60s was over, overdose deaths were making the newspaper with surprising regularity, and a surge in crime was attributed mainly to "drug addicts." President Richard Nixon was winning many converts to the War on Drugs he had declared in 1973. If the Hells Angels wanted support from the public, a good way to get it would be to make it appear as if they were against the scourge that many North Americans believed drugs had become.

Fillmore Cross, president of the San Jose chapter, took the reins of an operation that saw the Hells Angels buy billboard space—at charity rates—all over southern California and put up the phrase "No Hope in Dope." They also went on a blood drive, donating 160 pints of blood to southern California hospitals.

It worked. Soon, politicians and clergy all over California were praising the Hells Angels for their anti-drug stance. At the head of them was Canadian-born TV personality Art Linkletter. He had become one of North America's leading anti-drug advocates after he blamed the tragic death of his twenty-year-old daughter, Diane, on drugs. He widely promoted the story that she walked out of a sixth-floor kitchen window because, high on LSD, she "believed she could fly." He claimed that her death "was not a suicide, but a murder" and labeled everyone who manufactured or sold drugs "murderers." Although toxicology tests determined there were no drugs in Diane's system at the time of her death, Linkletter managed to sell two popular spoken-word records about the incident, and one even won a Grammy.

With his help, Cross became a minor celebrity, frequently speaking at anti-drug rallies and appearing on radio and TV programs. But San Jose police acquired enough evidence that he was actually a drug dealer that a judge allowed them to bug his phone. On a day in which he was scheduled to appear on a TV talk show to deliver his No Hope in Dope message, they recorded him talking to a Hells Angels associate. When his friend started taking too much time with small talk, Cross cut him off and told him, "Hey, I've gotta split to be at the TV studio to do my number." Aware that time was short, the two then struck a deal that would have Cross supply his friend with several pounds of meth. Cross was quickly arrested and convicted, and the Hells Angels' No Hope in Dope operation fizzled.

A ridiculous number of convictions since then have squashed any chance that 1-percenter clubs could convincingly portray themselves as anti-drug crusaders. But they have cultivated another image that has won them favor with many people, especially those in remote or criminally active areas—the widespread belief that biker clubhouses or members' personal residences brings down the amount of street crime in a neighborhood.

The belief comes from the idea that small-time crooks are so afraid of bikers that they vacate any place near them. The logic is set in the truth that bikers react with violence or the threat of violence to people and groups who offend them, and then people extrapolate the idea that since crime in their neighborhood would probably offend them, bikers will "take care of it" without the need for any of that messy and time-consuming due process that maintains our current level of freedom from government harassment.

It's an absurd, but pervasive, belief. When the Hells Angels rolled into Alberta, they were greeted by a large group of well-wishers who sought them out for pictures and autographs. I've spoken to dozens of neighbors of bikers and their clubs who confidently maintain that their region is safer because of them. I've interviewed those same people when they are utterly shocked and surprised that a violent event—like a shootout or firebombing—happened in their neighborhood, often related to the very same bikers.

It's not hard to understand the frustration of people who see criminals operating in their neighborhood. Time and time again, I have been told that the "police don't do anything" about small-time drug dealers or other criminals. Police, of course, can act only with credible evidence, which is hard to come by when people in their community adhere to the "stop snitchin'" ethos bikers like to encourage.

Bikers, of course, often take advantage of that disconnect between law enforcement and the communities they serve. Bikers frequently post articles featuring cops who have broken the law on social media, claiming, ironically, that those examples are representative of the profession as a whole, and they sell support items with sayings like "All cops are bastards" and "I don't call 911," which encourage people not to rely on law enforcement, or other items with threats for "snitches."

While I'll admit I've met my share of racist, sexist, otherwise intolerant and even downright dumb cops, their careers rely on properly interpreting the law and serving the people it protects. Limitations on who they can arrest and charge and how long it takes and how difficult it is to make a conviction serve to protect members of the community from being wrongly or inhumanely punished. When bikers attempt to deflect from their own activities by promoting the idea that cops, in general, are law breakers, they are claiming that if a police officer breaks his or her oath to maintain the law then the whole profession is invalid. They are engaging in what might be called a *tu quoque* fallacy in philosophy class, or—as it's more commonly known—the "I'm rubber, you're glue" defense.

Those who would prefer that bikers protect their neighborhoods risk essentially handing their community's security over to a group that has no vested interest in eliminating crime (unless it competes with their own operations), uses the threat of violence to enforce their will and is accountable to nobody but themselves. The idea that bikers make a community safer by their presence just because they are willing to beat up people who cross them is the same kind of thinking that gives rise to regional warlords in places like Somalia.

But it persists.

Even in communities where people have great faith in law enforcement, the belief that bikers make the neighborhood safer is endemic. It certainly was in Chino Valley, Arizona, in 2006. The large but sparsely populated town had a very low crime rate, in a state with a higher-than-average one, and many people told media that they believed it was in no small part due to the Hells Angels' clubhouse on North Yuma Drive.

The clubhouse had once belonged to the Dirty Dozen, a homegrown Arizona club that fought viciously to keep other clubs from wearing an Arizona bottom rocker in their state. Usually, a warning or a beating was all that was required, but at the same time as the drug trade heated up in the area, things changed.

In 1985, a club from New Mexico called Bad Company set up a chapter in the historic town of Globe, not far from Chino Valley, and started wearing an Arizona bottom rocker. As is biker custom, the Dirty Dozen's Robert "Chico" Mora summoned them to a meeting to discuss the bottom rocker situation. Two members of Bad Company arrived, and Mora shot and killed them both. He was unrepentant about the killings and claimed self-defense. He also pointed out that he considered his opinions to be laws the Bad Company members were breaking, as though he and he alone established community standards. "I told them to behave themselves and respect my authority," he explained to a reporter. "Then one of them pulled a gun on me, so I defended myself." He was convicted of manslaughter and served three years in prison.

In 1990, with Mora freshly out of prison, the ambitiously expanding Vagos set up a chapter in Phoenix, led by Donald "Arizona Don" Halterman, who was returning to his home state after becoming a Vago in California. There would be no meeting to discuss the bottom rocker this time. According to Steve Trethewey, who was an officer in the Chino Valley Police Department's anti-gang unit, "there was some shooting and pipe bombs" directed at the new chapter's clubhouse and its members' residences. When Halterman found a pipe bomb on his front porch one morning, he decided to pack it up. The Vagos left Phoenix, never to return.

Not long after, the Hells Angels made it clear that they were auditioning clubs in Arizona for a potential patch-over. At the same time, the Dirty Dozen were hoping to make an alliance with a bigger club because they did not feel safe wearing their patches outside of Arizona. Openly admiring how well they had kept opponents out of their state, the Hells Angels looked to the Dirty Dozen to patch over, and they—under Mora's leadership—became the Arizona Hells Angels in 1997.

When ATF agent Jay Dobyns set up a fake Solo Angeles chapter in Arizona, several Hells Angels advised him not to cross Mora, who had emerged from prison a trim three hundred pounds after spending most of his time behind bars working out and training in boxing. "Mesa Mike (Kramer) warned me never to tangle with Chico," Dobyns wrote, "that he'd kill anyone—cop, woman, child, dog, bunny rabbit, even a Hells Angels brother if he deserved it, without losing a wink of sleep."

For several years, the Hells Angels expanded in Arizona. Even Sonny Barger—who had been in prison there from 1988 to 1992—took a shine to the state and moved from the Oakland chapter to Cave Creek. The chapter in Chino Valley was named Skull Valley. It shut down in 2006, due to an aging membership and several arrests. Those members who still wanted to be Hells Angels left for other chapters in the state.

The area saw little biker-related violence until several Vagos started moving in from California. A number of Vagos established themselves in towns with little Hells Angels presence, like Bullhead City and Havasu. At first, the Hells Angels tolerated them, in no small part because they continued to wear California bottom rockers.

But by 2009, meetings between Vagos and Hells Angels (and their supporters) were routinely resulting in brawls. The Vagos, as is their habit, started to taunt the Hells Angels, and many started wearing Arizona bottom rockers.

They upped the ante even further in 2010 when Vagos full patch Michael "Mad Dog Mike" Diecks moved into a house at

2920 North Yuma Drive in Chino Valley, just three doors down from the old Hells Angels clubhouse at 2640. Although the club no longer met at the house, it was still occupied by a veteran Dirty Dozen and Hells Angels member, although age and ill health had sentenced him to wearing a respirator and riding in a mobility scooter, making him little threat to Diecks or the friends who visited him in Chino Valley.

Before long, neighbors and law enforcement reported seeing Hells Angels prospects and members of support clubs riding down North Yuma Drive and making threatening gestures at Diecks and his house.

On the morning of August 21, 2010, guests began to arrive at Diecks's house for a barbecue. It just so happened that on the same day, the Hells Angels and their friends arrived just up the street for their own barbecue.

At 11:30, witnesses told investigators, the Vagos started riding up to the Hells Angels barbecue. Once they were close, the Hells Angels opened fire. The Vagos side got off their bikes and fired back. In the ten-minute firefight, those same eyewitnesses said, they counted more than a hundred shots fired, although investigators could find evidence of only fifty. When the smoke cleared, five bikers had been injured, all of whom survived. Seven men—Michael Koepke, John Bernard, Kevin Christiansen, Kiley Hill, Larry Scott Jr., Robert Kittredge and Bruce Schweigert—were charged after neighbors positively identified them as the shooters.

Suddenly, however, every single one of the eyewitnesses—all of whom lived on North Yuma Drive between or alongside the two properties—refused to testify or speak to law enforcement or the media. The seven accused men subsequently saw the charges against them withdrawn.

Nobody other than the alleged combatants were hurt in that melee, but fifty to a hundred stray bullets sprayed around a residential area isn't anyone's idea of safe.

Of course, that was but a minor skirmish compared to some of the wars biker gangs have fought in the United States, Canada and overseas, many of which featured bombs, automatic weapons and even rocket launchers, and—of course—civilian casualties.

But biker clubs don't have to be at war for non-bikers to get hurt or killed around them. Many people have been assaulted by bikers for the slightest of affronts, and the methods used by bikers—gang assaults, kicking and stomping on people once they are down—can easily lead to deaths.

The fact that bikers consider violence an appropriate answer to "disrespect," combined with their reluctance or inability to recognize the rights of non-bikers, can make for dangerous situations even for passersby.

There are plenty of examples, but the most definitive, I believe, is one that occurred in Melbourne, Australia, in 2007.

In late 2004, a member of the Finks MC, Christopher "Huddo" Hudson, patched over to the Hells Angels. The Finks are an Australia-only club with a reputation for territoriality—their motto is "Attitude & Violence"—that has a long history of run-ins with other clubs. They are particularly hostile to the Hells Angels, and some Finks chapters have recently patched over to their archrivals, the Mongols. Hudson had gained even more ire from the Finks by openly recruiting their members and prospects for the Hells Angels, intimating that the Finks were bush league in comparison.

Having found out that Hudson and some other Hells Angels would be attending a mixed-martial-arts event at the Royal Pines Resort, outside Brisbane, about a thousand miles up the Pacific coast from Melbourne, in May 2006, the Finks decided to teach him a lesson. After the fights had begun, at least forty Finks barged their way into the arena, ticketless, and began to stare down the Hells Angels. "When a group of Finks trooped in—and the way they were standing, their demeanor, the way they were staring at the Hells Angels—I knew something was going to happen," said off-duty cop Robert Wilkinson, who was in the crowd.

He and the two on-duty cops who'd been hired for security were unable to prevent the brawl that broke out moments after the Finks arrived. Chairs were thrown, knives were quickly unsheathed and several bikers were stabbed. Then the shooting began. "When the gunshots started, it was a bit surreal," said Wilkinson. "It was hard to believe they were gunshots because we didn't expect it."

The event—which the Australian media called the "Ballroom Blitz"—was caught on video, and a high-ranking Fink, Shane Scott Bowden, was arrested and charged with attempting to murder Hudson, who was shot in the chin, and for assaulting the fight promoter. Nobody was killed, but several bikers (or as Australians say, "bikies") were rushed to nearby hospitals for treatment of their bullet and stab wounds.

After he recovered, Hudson became even more vocal about his affiliation. He wore his colors frequently and threw his weight around at several downtown Melbourne bars. His favorite hangout was the Spearmint Rhino, an outlet of an international group of strip club franchises. The management there made sure that Hudson's drinks and lap dances were free, not because he was a great guy, but because they feared retribution from him and the club if they weren't. He, and they, had already established that kind of reputation in town.

"Huddo had informed me that he was part of the Hells Angels motorcycle group," a stripper who gave her name as Jazz later told reporters. "I don't know why he told me he was with them; however, he was very proud of belonging to them."

On June 28, 2006, Hudson spotted Australian-rules football star Alan Didak in the Spearmint Rhino with a friend. Didak was drowning his sorrows after his Collingwood Magpies lost to the Melbourne Demons. Eager to get to know him, Hudson kept a series of free drinks coming for Didak, until the friend left. Then, Hudson approached the footballer, who told the Hells Angel that he was drunk and wanted to go home. Hudson offered him a ride back to Collingwood, just three miles away.

Although Didak was a highly paid professional athlete, he said he was impressed by Hudson's expensive twelve-cylinder Mercedes-Benz. The biker made lots of money with an identity-theft operation he had been at for years.

With Didak in the passenger seat, Hudson took off, driving at frightening speeds, making dangerous lane changes, and cutting off several other drivers while playing music at deafening volumes. "I was shitting myself," Didak later said in an interview. Things got worse for Didak as Hudson pulled out a handgun. Laughing, he stopped the car, rolled down his window and fired eight shots at nothing in particular. Didak said he could barely hear the shots over the music.

Then Hudson roared off, and stopped again, not at Didak's home in Collingwood, but at the Hells Angels clubhouse in nearby Campbellford. Didak, fearing for his life by that point, followed him inside and stayed for "another drink or three."

They then stumbled back into the Mercedes, with Hudson again roaring off and driving to Collingwood. Officers in a police car saw them and gave chase, so Hudson fired three shots at them, then floored the accelerator in the mighty car, losing them.

Unable to find Didak's house, Hudson let him off in the neighborhood to make his own way home.

Less than a week later, Hudson was partying at the Spearmint Rhino again when, at about 5 a.m., he invited club manager Steve Kyriacou, a waitress and five dancers to go drinking with him at Bar Code, a nightclub next door.

One of the dancers, Brianna, noticed Hudson coming out of a restroom for disabled people agitated, sweating and shaky, and she later said that she assumed he had just taken a hit of cocaine or meth.

At about 6, he texted his on-again, off-again girlfriend, stripper and aspiring model Kaera Douglas, to join them. At first she declined, but when she realized her car keys and all her money were missing, she decided to go to the bar to confront Hudson, the likely culprit, about it. Douglas had been planning to break things off with Hudson anyway, because his drinking and drug use had gotten out of hand.

Hudson got into an argument with a stripper named Autumn Daly-Holt (who performed as Savannah), then she began to perform a lap dance for Kyriacou. Drunk, Daly-Holt took her clothes off and got on top of Kyriacou in the crowded bar. Angered, Hudson grabbed her by the hair and started to pull. Daly-Holt screamed, and Hudson let her go.

He then approached the bar, where plenty of men were watching, and pulled up his sleeves to show them his tattoos. "Do you know who I am?" he screamed at them. "I'm a Hells Angel!" Then he lifted his shirt to show them a handgun tucked into his jeans and stormed out of the bar.

Douglas arrived in a taxi at about 8 a.m. to see a still very drunk Daly-Holt attempting to get her clothes back on and leave the bar. Still topless, she stumbled out of the bar and sat down on the front steps. The streets of downtown Melbourne were rapidly filling up with people starting their Monday morning and getting to work. Regardless, Hudson approached her threateningly and started yelling at her to stand up and get into his car. Daly-Holt, later saying she felt her space invaded, feebly tried to brush Hudson away with an open hand.

That sign of "disrespect" was too much for Hudson. He kicked Daly-Holt in the face, then grabbed her hair with his left hand and lifted her into a standing position, punched her square in the face and threw her to the pavement. Daly-Holt woozily made it up to a seated position and Hudson kicked her in the face again, knocking her unconscious and sending several of her teeth flying. She collapsed in a pool of her own blood.

Douglas rushed to Daly-Holt's aid (they had been friends since childhood) as Hudson stormed off. She then confronted Hudson about her car keys. He showed her his gun and then grabbed her by the arm and forced her to walk into a parking garage with him. He grabbed her by the hair and forced her up against a cement wall.

At that moment, they were approached by Brendan Keilar, a forty-three-year-old lawyer and father of three who had just got out of his car, who tried to help Douglas out of what appeared to be a rough situation. "Hey, what's going on here?" he asked.

Douglas started screaming for help. A twenty-six-year-old Dutch tourist named Paul de Waard then joined Keilar in an effort to separate Douglas from Hudson. He had seen TV commercials about helping prevent violence against women in Australia, and he felt it was his duty to intervene, despite Hudson's size and obvious ferocity.

As Keilar and de Waard approached, Hudson released his grip on Douglas's hair, pulled out his gun and shot all three of them. The victims fell to the ground, and Hudson shot Keilar and de Waard again. Keilar died where he fell, at one of Melbourne's busiest intersections; the other two survived after hours of surgery. Douglas lost one of her kidneys after spending three days in a coma. Daly-Holt survived, but her facial injuries were too severe to be totally erased by reconstructive surgery, and her scars ended her fledgling modeling career.

Hudson fled—after dropping his gun, a .40-caliber MiniMax, in a nearby dumpster—to a Hells Angels clubhouse. While he thought they would hide him from authorities, his "brothers" had another idea. They tore off his shirt and chained him to a chair. Then they burned off his shoulder-to-elbow death's-head tattoo and threw him out the front door. They kept his bike. The bikers I spoke with told me he was almost certainly being punished for bringing bad publicity to the club.

Hudson made his way to a hospital where he was promptly arrested.

He pleaded guilty to all charges (the entire attack had been caught on security video with Hudson's face and tattoos clearly visible, and there were hundreds of eyewitnesses). At his sentencing hearing, Hudson's psychologist testified: "Although anabolic steroid abuse and the lifestyle led by Mr. Hudson suggest narcissistic and anti-social features, it is more likely that he was seduced by the lifestyle offered by joining motorcycle gangs—and that his peer group and lifestyle encouraged self-centered and aggressive attitudes."

Hudson was sentenced to life with no chance at parole for thirty-five years.

Of course, the daily newspapers aren't filled with stories of bikers like Hudson kicking strippers in the head and shooting innocent people, but where bikers go, violence often follows.

Every biker I have ever spoken with admits, often with pride, that if they detect any sign of "disrespect" by anyone, the affront will be met with violence. In the Hudson case, those signs could have been Daly-Holt not standing up when ordered, Douglas not getting into Hudson's car immediately or Keilar and de Waard verbally confronting him while he was clearly assaulting Douglas as she cried for help.

"If people don't know they'll get their ass kicked," Randy, a former Outlaw said to me, "how are they going to know to respect bikers?"

If he wanted to get away with it, Hudson's mistakes were that he executed his rampage on a busy downtown corner during rush hour (in front of high-resolution security cameras) and that he brought a gun into play. Had he only crushed Daly-Holt's face with his punch and two kicks and maybe been able to drag Douglas into his car, the event certainly would not have made the newspapers and probably not even the police blotter. It should be noted that nobody called 000 (the Australian equivalent to 911) until after Hudson pulled his gun out.

Countless biker assaults go unreported each year, mostly because of fear of retribution. And many of those that are reported are withdrawn due to victim and eyewitness intimidation.

For neighbors of bikers and clubhouses, the obvious problem stems from the fact that they can't always know exactly what any biker might define as "disrespect." I know of people who have been assaulted by bikers because of the color of their car, their haircut, wearing a non-local sports team hoodie and several other tiny and often unwitting infractions of the bikers' seemingly arbitrary code of other people's conduct.

When I co-wrote a book about the life of Dave, a biker who turned informant, he told me that he sincerely regretted something about the witness protection process: it was that he had to put up with disrespect all the time and couldn't just beat up the person who offended him. He was, as he put it sadly, "just like everyone else."

Between the shootouts and fire-bombings that occur when rival clubs get too tense, and the almost random beatings of whomever the biker chooses, I'd have to say that the widespread belief that a biker's residence or clubhouse in your neighborhood makes it safer is false. In fact, if you do find that a biker has moved in next door or that there's a clubhouse on the next block, I'd advise that you be extra careful about what you say and do.

# CHAPTER 10

# Dealing with Disrespect

In the summer of 2009, a Hells Angel named Adam Lee Hall was unloading his pickup truck in Peru, Massachusetts, in the Berkshire Mountains near Pittsfield. When he came back out for a second load, he noticed that a carburetor was missing.

As is club policy, Hall did not go to police, instead taking the matter into his own hands. He had seen David "Drummer Dave" Glasser, a neighbor with a mild learning disability who occasionally did odd jobs for Hall, in the area that day and surmised that he must have been the thief, despite having no actual evidence.

Hall grabbed a baseball bat and went over to Glasser's apartment. He questioned Glasser, who denied that he had stolen anything. When he would not relent from his story and produce the missing carburetor, Hall beat him with the baseball bat. Still unable to get Glasser to confess, Hall threatened to kill him unless he signed over the ownership of his own pickup truck as restitution. Glasser did, even though he still maintained that he had not taken the carburetor, and Hall had him drive himself to Berkshire Medical Center in his Hummer H2, while he rode in the passenger seat. As he left him, bloody and bruised, he told Glasser that he'd "put two bullets" in his head if he dared to report the beating to the police.

Glasser didn't have to, because the police came to him. Alerted to the obvious signs of a brutal assault by hospital staff, Massachusetts state trooper Dale Gero questioned Glasser about who beat him up. Glasser said he didn't want to say, that he feared for his life, and then inquired about the state's witness protection policies. Gero convinced him to talk, and Glasser admitted it was Hall who had assaulted and threatened to kill him. Gero visited Glasser at home two days later and interviewed him again. Glasser again told him that the culprit was Hall but said he was scared Hall would kill him when he found out he'd talked.

Hall was quickly arrested, and the club put up money for his bail. Because Hall was already on bail for several other charges—including allegedly sending sexually explicit texts to an underage girl—he needed $50,000 to walk free. Gero also managed to get Glasser his truck back.

Hall had a long record of accusations of violence. Four years before the Glasser beating, local police responded to 911 calls about a "dead man" in Peru. Several officers approached Hall's property and discovered an unconscious man lying in a pool of blood in the bed of Hall's pickup.

The man later told police his story. He had been drinking in a dumpy little Pittsfield bar called the Crossroads Café when he got into an argument with the bartender over how much he owed. Nothing major, just a little heated discussion. Hall then grabbed the man and dragged him out of the bar. Once outside, he told him, "This is a Hells Angels bar, and you are a punk." Before the man could respond, Hall began punching and kicking him, finally pulling a knife and stabbing him in his right arm. Bleeding profusely, the man passed out, and the next thing he remembered was being woken up by cops and being told an ambulance was on its way. Hall was not convicted of the assault after the witness changed his mind and refused to testify.

A year later, another man parked his green Jaguar in front of the Crossroads. He alleged that Hall emerged, wearing his colors, and asked the man if the car was his. The driver said it was and stuck out his hand to shake Hall's. Instead, he claimed, Hall punched him in the face five times. With the man down, he started kicking him with steel-toed boots. Again, the alleged victim refused to testify and the case did not go to trial.

Earlier, Hall had been driving with another Hells Angel in Pittsfield when some guys blew an airhorn at them from inside an apartment. Hall stopped the car, and he and the other Hells Angel started pounding on the apartment door with hammers until they were stopped by police.

Not long after, a man told police that Hall nearly ran him over in Pittsfield. Unhappy with the man's reaction, the pedestrian claimed, Hall got out of the car, carrying a pair of bolt cutters. The man said that, wisely, he ran away. Once it was clear Hall wasn't going to catch him, the pedestrian alleged that Hall threw the bolt cutters at him, narrowly missing his head.

In fact, Hall had faced charges related to ten incidents of kidnapping, assault and aggravated assault over the years with a positive identification every time, but it resulted in just a one-year sentence behind bars in 1997 after a conviction stemming from the time he used a hammer to try to knock a door down, which the police witnessed. He was also charged with inciting violence, and witnesses said that he forced three local women to have sex with his friends for money, which he reportedly kept. When one of the women refused, the witness said that he responded, "You work for me now; there's no way out." One of the clients later told a court that, "the girls never looked happy about having to have the sex but did it out of fear of physical harm from Hall if they refused." In all of the charges except the one that sent him to jail, the cases fell apart after witnesses who were initially willing to cooperate with the district attorney later changed their minds.

The police and district attorney, understandably, were more than a little eager to get Hall behind bars. So they leaned heavily on Glasser to testify. The district attorney, David Capeless, said that Glasser had been relocated twice but chose to go back to his apartment both times, saying he felt safer in his own home. Several of his friends, who acted like something of a surrogate family for Glasser, later told reporters that, as far as they knew, he was never offered anything like that and would have jumped at the chance to relocate. Either way, he continued to cooperate with the prosecution.

Hall, enraged that Glasser was going to talk, started to panic. He enlisted the help of a man, Scott Langdon, who lived in a tent in Hall's unfinished basement and was something of a friend of Glasser's. Like Glasser, he performed menial odd jobs for Hall, who paid Langdon in lodging and food. Hall gave Langdon $3,000 in cash and instructed him to offer it to Glasser in exchange for not testifying. Langdon ran over to Glasser's, showed him the money and told him he could have it if he changed his mind about testifying against Hall, but Glasser turned him down.

In August, Hall borrowed a car from his girlfriend, Nichole Brooks, to attend his cousin's wedding in Indiana. When he returned it, Brooks found a greeting card wishing congratulations to the happy couple signed by Hall and Alexandra Ely.

Brooks confronted Hall about the card, and he admitted that he had lied about breaking things off with Ely, the mother of one of his children, and that he was still seeing her. He told Brooks that he wasn't going to stop seeing Ely but that he also wished to stay in a relationship with her. She agreed.

Hall invited Brooks to his house the next day. When she arrived, Ely—whom she had never met before—and Langdon were already there. Hall showed Brooks a .22-caliber revolver and told her he had a plan to fix Glasser. He told her that she was going to fake an armed robbery and he would use it to frame Glasser. Brooks agreed to play her part. Then they drove to Wells, New York—a quiet little town surrounded by wooded mountains about 120 miles away from Peru—and Hall shot a bullet into a tree near a rest stop.

The following morning, Langdon went to Glasser's house and asked him for a ride to Wells. At first, Glasser was reluctant, but knowing Langdon's relationship with Hall, he agreed because he "didn't want to get beat with a baseball bat again." Langdon was carrying the gun and $800 in cash in a bag and made a point of hiding it in Glasser's truck.

Brooks arrived after she was sure Glasser and Langdon had come and gone. After a short wait, she called 911. When a state trooper named Samuel Thompson arrived, she told him that Glasser had pulled a gun on her and demanded cash. She said she gave him the $800, and he demanded she get in the truck with him. She refused, turned and ran, and said that Glasser shot at her, instead hitting the tree.

Thompson, a veteran cop, had a feeling that Brooks was lying. Her story was too precise, too practiced. How many people, he thought, while running from an attacker with a gun, take the time to see where an individual bullet landed?

He did a little digging. He found a receipt in her wallet that indicated she had been in Pittsfield just before the time of the alleged incident. Thompson also looked into Glasser's case against Hall and found that Brooks and Hall were Facebook friends.

When he presented her with his doubts and the inconsistencies in her story, Brooks agreed to cooperate and told Thompson all about Hall's plot to frame Glasser. Hall was rearrested, and, this time, his bail was set at $250,000.

Realizing how much evidence the district attorney had stacked against him, Hall called for a meeting with the FBI. He promised to tell them all they wanted to know about what the Hells Angels were up to in western Massachusetts in exchange for leniency in his own case.

While bikers always tell me that law enforcement is out to get them at any cost, this time they preferred to see Hall go down rather than any number of his "brothers."

Unaware of his attempt to sell them down the river to save his own skin, the Berkshire chapter bailed him out. They put up the clubhouse in Lee as surety.

A few days later, on August 19, Katelyn Carmin, an ex-girlfriend of Hall's, agreed to go out with Hall and two friends that night. Hall arrived with David Chalue and Caius Veiovis.

Chalue was a member of the Aryan Brotherhood and later said that he had befriended Hall in part because he wanted access to what he heard was the Berkshire chapter's extensive collection of guns. As sergeant-at-arms, Hall would have a big say if not outright command as to who was allowed to use the chapter's weapons.

Veiovis was something of a character in the Pittsfield area. Born Roy Gutfinski in Maine, he was arrested at age thirteen for bringing a large, double-bladed, military-style knife to school. A psychiatrist who examined him said that he had an obsession with the occult, particularly devil worship, and a defiance of authority. He told her that he was adopted, even though he wasn't.

While on probation for the knife charge, Gutfinski was treated for substance abuse and mental instability, but he was thrown out of one hospital after assaulting a worker there. In and out of hospitals and group homes, he applied for Social Security disability payments due to his consistent mental illness, which he received.

A year later, at nineteen, he assaulted his girlfriend and her employer with an ax handle. His next girlfriend sliced a sixteen-year-old rival's back open with a straight razor, and she and Gutfinski drank some of the resulting blood. He was convinced he was a vampire but—when pressed by friends—could not adequately explain why he had no fangs and could walk around in sunlight with no ill effects.

After he was given probation for his part in the slashing, Gutfinski began to change. He altered his appearance first with tattoos (including a stylized 666 on his forehead), then piercings. Later he would get implants on his forehead to make it look as though he had horns. He ran a blog under the name "Trash" and wrote that he was fond of body piercing, torture and necrophilia and was looking for work in the music business.

In 2008, he legally changed his name to Caius Domitius Veiovis. He said that the Caius Domitius part came from a lesser Roman emperor, Domitian, who was known as something of a tyrant before his assassination. Veiovis, he said, was derived from a Roman deity, normally spelled "Vejovis," who was officially god of medicine, although later scholars attributed many other responsibilities to him.

By 2011, Veiovis had wound up in Pittsfield, where he worked as a gardener, hedge-trimmer and contractor's assistant. He befriended Hall and was known to party at the Hells Angels' clubhouse in nearby Lee frequently. Despite what several media sources said about him later, Veiovis never had any confirmed status as a

Hells Angel, but Hall told several people that he planned to sponsor Veiovis as a prospect once he bought a motorcycle.

The night they picked up Carmin (who started dating Hall when she was thirteen and he was twenty-three), she could tell Hall was agitated. In the car, he said that Glasser (whom she knew only as "Drummer Dave") had ruined his life by agreeing to testify and that he was "going to kill that motherfucker." Chalue and Veiovis (whom she knew just as "Trash") tried to calm him down, saying that they would "get him." Later, Carmin would testify that she didn't pay much attention to Hall's threats because he was "talking about killing people all the time."

Carmin later said that Hall also mentioned that he was angry with a friend named David Casey because he would not lend him the keys to his backhoe.

The little group went to several bars in Pittsfield and ended up at the Hells Angels clubhouse the chapter had put up as surety to get Hall out of jail. Drunk and smoking marijuana, they started messing around with some ATVs. Carmen said that Hall took her aside and told her not to ride so aggressively with Chalue and Veiovis because he needed them "for a job" later.

Carmin said that Hall started acting a bit weird after that, and—fearing for her own safety—she called a friend for a ride home.

A few days later, on August 24, the Pittsfield Home Depot was swamped with anxious customers. Hurricane Irene had been downgraded to a tropical storm, but it still threatened to bring plenty of havoc to the Berkshires.

Despite the deluge of customers eager to buy items to protect their houses and vehicles, clerk William Gregory said that he noticed Chalue and Veiovis right away—facial tattoos are one thing, but a guy with horns is altogether different. "It was nothing I'd seen before," Gregory later said. It also struck him as odd that the two men were interested in saws and hatchets when everyone else was clamoring for tarps and sandbags to deal with the oncoming storm. Gregory showed them what the store had and left to help other customers. Security footage shows the two men trying out different saws and axes, but they didn't buy any, leaving instead with a Star-Fold, which is kind of like a Swiss Army knife that has hex keys and screwdriver tips instead of blades and a corkscrew.

On Saturday, August 27, the Berkshire Hells Angels threw a party. Police photographed Hall, Chalue and Veiovis arriving in an old Buick that Hall had recently purchased for $800 and licensed in New Hampshire, which has much more relaxed vehicle insurance laws than Massachusetts does. They were also photographed leaving the party at 4:30, headed to the McKinney & Burbach Tavern. Leaving there at 6:30, they went to some friends' houses, showing them several firearms they had with them.

His own friends later reported that Glasser was tense that day. He asked a friend named Andrew Johnson to drive him to work the next day because he told him that he was scared Hall would kill him.

At about 10:30 on the evening of August 27, Glasser's downstairs neighbor, Lisa Archembault, knocked on his door. Glasser had parked his truck in such a way that she couldn't get into her parking spot, so she had to ask him to move it. When Glasser opened the door, Archembault noticed there were three other men in the apartment. Glasser moved his truck, and one of the guests left, leaving him with his close pals Edward Frampton and Robert T. Chadwell.

Shortly after midnight, Archembault reported that she heard some banging and other loud noises from Glasser's apartment, along with voices that she did not recognize.

At about 1:30, Hall and Veiovis showed up at the house of Rose Sutton, where Ely was staying overnight. Hall borrowed Sutton's cell phone and left.

At 5 in the morning, Hall showed up at the A-Town convenience store in Pittsfield, wet, muddy and disheveled. Not long after Hall, in the old Buick, and Veiovis, in his Jeep, parked on Sutton's front lawn, and Ocean Sutton—Rose's sister and Chalue's girlfriend, who was just returning from the Hells Angels party herself—let them in the house.

At 9:30, when Ely woke up, Hall asked her to take Rose to Price Chopper to buy breakfast and bleach. He was wet, dirty and shoeless. The money he handed her, she said, was "nasty" with "some kind of liquid" soaked into it.

They left in Hall's Buick and were not quite to the store when he called her. She answered, and he told her to forget about getting the bleach and not to look in the McDonald's bag in the car. She agreed, but curiosity got the better of her. All she found inside was a pair of dirty gloves.

Meanwhile, Hall was burning his clothes. Ocean Sutton didn't think much of that because, as she said, Hells Angels frequently burn their old clothes to save them the indignity of being put in the garbage.

After Frampton missed an early morning appointment with his social worker and Chadwell didn't show up at the apartment of his boyfriend, Willie Haywood, as he had promised, police investigated their homes and then Glasser's. Finding them all empty and all three men's cell phones at Glasser's, they opened a missing persons investigation.

When Ely and Rose Sutton returned from Price Chopper, Hall gave Rose back her phone and told her to delete the call log and to deny she had ever lent it to him if anyone asked.

A few hours later, Casey was napping at his home in Canaan, New York, when he heard an urgent-sounding knock on his door. It was Hall. He had previously hired Casey to install a fish pond in his own backyard and to do some landscaping work on the Hells Angels clubhouse.

Hall asked him if he knew a place where he could park his car safely overnight, and Casey made arrangements. Hall then casually admitted that he had "offed" Glasser and had also killed "a fat guy and a nigger" (Frampton was obese and Chadwell was African-American).

Stunned, Casey asked for details.

Hall told him that he, Chalue and Veiovis had taken the three men into the woods and he held Glasser down, aimed a gun at his head and pulled the trigger. Nothing happened. As he was putting another bullet in the chamber, Glasser struggled out of his grip and ran. Hall ordered Chalue to bring him down, so he shot him in the leg. He walked over to the bleeding and crying victim and dragged him back to Hall. Hall angrily told him that he wanted to kill Glasser. While Glasser begged for his life and promised not to testify, Hall said to him, "I told you what would happen if you witnessed against me" and shot him in the head.

Hall then stabbed Chadwell and Chalue shot him in the face. Veiovis shot Frampton five times. Hall then slashed at the fallen Frampton, managing to cut into his spinal cord. Assuming the victims were all dead, they left.

Realizing they had to dispose of the evidence, they returned not long after. Hall was surprised to find Chadwell sitting up, moaning and holding his hands against his belly wound. They all took turns stabbing the poor man, at first just to inflict pain, then to kill. "I didn't mind killing the nigger," Hall told Casey with a chuckle.

He explained to Casey how they dismembered the bodies. He laughed when he recalled that he had held Glasser's severed head up by the hair and berated him for being ugly and missing teeth, and he said that cutting Frampton into small pieces was a huge chore because of his size.

Casey asked how he felt about it. Hall told him that the guys really enjoyed the torture and mutilation and that he felt no guilt because he had "done the right thing."

He then asked Casey if he had any shovels. Casey lied and said he didn't. He didn't want bodies buried on his property with his tools. Hall asked him if he was still working at the home of a man named Dan Cole. Casey said he was, and Hall told him that he wanted Casey to dispose of the body parts on Cole's property. Casey refused but reluctantly agreed when Hall said that if he helped, there would "be no harm done" to him, his girlfriend, his sister Teresa Cunigan (who was dating Langdon and also frequented the Hells Angels clubhouse) or Langdon.

Although buried in a trench and covered with boulders, the remains were found on September 10, just nine days before Glasser was due to testify against Hall.

Hall, Chalue and Veiovis maintained their innocence, but they each were found guilty of all three murders. (All other charges against the three were dropped to simplify the case.) It didn't help their case that Veiovis had a diagram of the proper way to dismember corpses in his house (and it matched the state of the victims' bodies when they were found) along with machetes and meat cleavers. Nor did the fact that Chalue admitted to his part in the killings to roommate Christopher Letalien.

When his verdict was read, Hall shouted that he had been "twenty miles away!" and claimed he had been in the clubhouse when the murders happened. Veiovis was more stoic and told the jury he'd meet them in hell.

All three were given three life sentences. Langdon, Brooks and Ely saw their charges, including conspiracy for all three and lying to police for Brooks, dropped in exchange for cooperating with the prosecution.

I include the Hall-Glasser story not because I believe his behavior is typical of bikers—there haven't been that many beheadings, after all—but because I think that Hall acted under the biker code.

All the major clubs forbid their members from seeking help from police in the event of a conflict, urging them to take care of such matters by themselves. They don't expressly say it in their constitutions, but it's widely understood that the primary, if not only, way to resolve such problems is by violence or the threat of it.

To Hall, who believed Glasser stole his carburetor, beating him with a baseball bat and extorting him for his truck seemed perfectly in accordance with the biker ethos. He was taking care of business, as they so frequently say.

Similarly, when Glasser spoke with police, that made him a rat or snitch, the lowest creature in existence, according to the big clubs. In Hall's world, Glasser deserved nothing but punishment, if not extermination, simply for seeking help from law enforcement after he was beaten and lost his truck through extortion. After all, if Glasser testified, unlike Hall's other alleged victims, Hall could have gone away for a very long time.

The bikers I spoke with all agreed that Hall was right to confront Glasser. "If he stole his carburetor," Frankie told me, "he has to man up and get it back . . . the cops won't do anything." They were careful not to condone the beating, the stealing of the truck, the threats, the murder and the beheading, but they did say that turning "snitch" deserved some form of punishment.

And that encapsulates the biker's view of the world: I can do anything I want to you, but if you dare fight back or get law enforcement involved, you will only suffer more. If that ethos reminds you of the behavior of a junior high school bully, you're not alone.

Bikers I know—and I have spoken with dozens if not hundreds since my first motorcycle-gang-related book came out in 2006, many of whom have reached out to me—consider violence against those who offend them, although they always say "disrespect," to be mandatory, routine and fully justified.

While bikers generally claim that allegations of drug trafficking and other criminal enterprises and acts are the invention of law enforcement and other enemies, they freely speak of illegally and frighteningly using violence for even the most minor of conflicts.

In his memoir, Barger practically gushes over how many times he and his friends have beaten people up, sometimes leaving permanent or even fatal wounds. He talks with pride about sticking a .25-caliber pistol into the mouth of a motorcycle customizer who said something he didn't like. When the man apologized, he put away the gun and started to leave. But when the man yelled at Barger's friend's girlfriend, he bashed him in the head with the gun. It went off on impact, sending a bullet into his head. "The first shot had been an accident," Barger wrote, "but since the motherfucker was already shot in the head, I bent him over a pool table and shot him again."

A few days later, Barger heard that a friend, Terry the Tramp, had gotten into an argument with someone at a bar and the man had fled into his house nearby. When Barger arrived, he wrote, Terry was on the house's front lawn threatening the occupants.

Barger convinced him to kick the door in. Once they illegally entered the home, they "fucked up everybody in the house." He did not specify the number of victims, their genders or their ages.

The victims called the cops, and Barger was arrested and quickly bailed out. He was grabbed by police again and told them he had already been bailed out for the house invasion and beatings. He was surprised to learn that he was actually being arrested for other charges, those relating to the beating and shooting of the motorcycle customizer he called "chrome boy." Barger said he was surprised the man had survived.

Due to a dearth of people willing to give eyewitness testimony, Barger walked in both cases.

Similarly, in his own unambiguously titled memoir, *Street Justice*, Hells Angel Chuck Zito also shows pride and no shortage of delight in violently punishing those who crossed his personal demand of obsequious behavior. He once cut off a car, forcing it to the side of the road, intent on "kicking the shit" out of the two guys inside simply because he thought they were making fun of his outrageous look-at-me custom car. Only when they, terrified, told him how much they actually liked his car did he soften his stance.

On another occasion, when a car came too close to his bike while changing lanes, Zito said he used nunchakus—a traditional Okinawan weapon with a chain linking two sticks that is illegal in many states and countries—to shatter the windshield of the still-moving car, sending it careening over the roadside barrier and into a nearby field.

It's a hallmark of biker gangs to make sure that the punishment far outweighs the crime and frequently to commit the same crimes that had put their victims in their sights in the first place.

Back in the '70s, Barger's customized bike, which he called Sweet Cocaine, had been stolen. Instead of going to police, he conducted his own investigation, and a witness told him that he had seen a biker with just a bottom rocker ride off on Sweet Cocaine. From the description of the thief and the rocker, Barger and his friends determined that the bike had been stolen by a prospect from a nearby club called the Unknowns.

Barger and a number of Hells Angels collected all the members and prospects of the Unknowns and took them to Barger's house. With Barger's wife, Sharon, holding a gun on them, the captives were beaten with bullwhips and spiked dog collars, then had their fingers broken with ball-peen hammers. The carnage was so bad that one of them, Barger recounts in his memoir, screamed, "Why don't you just kill us and get it over with?"

Unable to recover Sweet Cocaine (it had been dumped in the Oakland Estuary), the Hells Angels took all the Unknowns' motorcycles and sold them—making themselves motorcycle thieves.

In general, bikers have three methods of fighting—and the difference reflects their attitude toward themselves, rivals and others.

When a biker fights another biker from the same or allied club, it's a one-on-one match that more or less follows schoolyard rules. There will be no weapons (even rings are removed), no outside help and no kicking when an opponent is down.

These rules apply not just to members of the same chapter, but also to members of chapters from the same club. Prospects and members of support clubs are included on the list of people who get this type of preferential treatment but—depending on the club, chapter or member involved—know better than to win a fight against a full-patch member of the big club.

Duane, a former California Hells Angels full patch, told me that when he was on a run with the club while still a prospect, a full patch from another chapter was giving him an unnecessarily hard time. Before long, they were fighting. Just as Duane realized he might be jeopardizing his status by beating up a full patch, he heard someone shouting encouragement at him from the side-lines. He told me that he was stunned to see that it was Barger himself, yelling, "Come on, prospect, kick his ass!"

It's not unknown for full patches to order two prospects to fight each other, just for entertainment, and bets to be made on the outcome.

Most clubs have a fine—from $5 to $25—for fighting among members and prospects, and it's about as effective a deterrent as you probably think it is.

Fighting against rival clubs, as we have seen, can range from fists and boots to rocket launchers and firebombs. No matter which weapons are used, the end goal is to cause as much pain and suffering to the individuals on the other side as possible. Forget the rules of fighting that apply to members of the same club. Bikers generally do not seek fights with rivals unless they outnumber their opponents, usually by a wide margin. In those cases, all the club members, prospects, hangarounds and even supporters available are supposed to participate in the beating. Some clubs, particularly the Hells Angels, refer to the concept of many guys on their side against one or a few on the other side as "rat packing."

The primary focus in such fights is to get the opponent off his feet and on the ground. That way, he can be kicked and stomped by the collected bikers and can offer little in the way of defense.

Once an opponent has been rendered harmless—either by injury or by threat, like having a gun held to his head—bikers do their best to cause lasting pain and permanent disability. Breaking fingers and hand bones is commonplace, especially if the victim in question works with his hands, as are blows to the knees.

Special care is taken to humiliate members of rival clubs. Taking his cut is considered a primary goal, and erasing club tattoos with cheese graters or blowtorches is far from unknown. If possible, they will also take his bike by forcing him to sign it over or changing its VIN.

Finally, there are fights with civilians. These can arise from a variety of reasons, but two are most common. The first is that the victim has shown some form of "disrespect" to the biker. That can be anything from touching his cut, talking to his old lady or just looking at him the wrong way. Many beefs come from not giving a biker enough room in traffic, but I know of bikers who have beaten people up for wearing a tie, for driving a car they didn't like (or liked too much) or even for ordering the wrong brand of beer in "their" bar.

Similarly, civilians can incur the wrath of bikers by not cooperating with their demands. I know of at least two tattoo artists who have had their hands broken because they did not allow bikers to take a cut of their revenue. Bikers regularly punish drug dealers who sell for opponents, as they do prostitutes or strippers they employ for various infractions. Civilians can also fall victim to a beating if they choose to defend an item that a biker wants. That frequently includes women, who many clubs admittedly regard as property. Of course, witness intimidation also supplies a steady stream of victims.

The methods used to fight civilians are basically the same as those for fights with other clubs, with large numbers and weapons encouraged. The differences are subtle but significant. The first is that, while a full-patch member might throw the first punch, he generally delegates the beating, kicking and stomping to prospects, hangarounds and even supporters. The second is that greater care is taken to make sure the victim survives the ordeal. It's far easier to fight an assault or aggravated assault charge (especially if any witnesses or victims are intimidated into not testifying) than it is any form of homicide, and the potential sentences are much lighter.

But heads hit pavement and kicks damage vital organs, and sometimes beating victims die. One interesting example, which Barger mentions with little if any hint of regret in his memoir, was the case of Bradley Parkhurst. In 1972, he visited a friend, Connie Perry, at her house while some Hells Angels were also there. He went down to the basement, where Marvin "Mouldy Marvin" Gilbert was working on his bike. The two began to argue, and Gilbert threatened the other man's life. Parkhurst offered to shake hands as a gesture of putting their differences behind them, but Gilbert did not like the way Parkhurst wanted to shake. "That's a nigger's handshake," eyewitness testimony entered into court records said he yelled. "Shake hands like a white man!"

A scuffle ensued and Perry, who was also in the basement, ran upstairs to get the other bikers to help break it up. Though giving up more than forty pounds on his opponent, Parkhurst seemed to be winning the fight. The three other Hells Angels put a stop to that. Russell Beyea, a hundred pounds heavier than Parkhurst, landed two punches to his head from behind while he was busy with Gilbert. Reeling from those, Parkhurst took a punch to the middle of the chest from Gilbert that sent him to the ground. The collected Hells Angels then kicked and stomped on his prone body for approximately fifteen minutes. Parkhurst died of a ruptured spleen.

Beyea and Gilbert were both arrested and charged with second-degree murder. Even though Gilbert had been a member of the club since 1964, considered Barger his "best friend" and even had "Sonny" tattooed on his right arm, the club decided that he should take the fall and do his best to claim full responsibility for Parkhurst's death because Beyea was more valuable to the club. When Gilbert demurred, he later testified, the lives of his wife and child were threatened.

Gilbert did his best to take all the blame but was not very convincing. Both he and Beyea were convicted of second-degree murder.

Having his family threatened to force him to perjure himself in court did not seem to deter Gilbert's fondness for the club, and after his prison term, he rejoined the Hells Angels, although he moved from Oakland to the fledgling Spokane, Washington, chapter.

Prison time did not gain him any contrition over the death of Parkhurst, either. When he was arrested for trafficking in 1996, a reporter asked him about the incident. "He was disrespecting some girl I was with, and he had it coming," Gilbert told him.

While the Parkhurst case is an old one—there have been plenty of accidental beating deaths by bikers since—it's a definitive study of how bikers see the world, and their place in it.

While the argument, according to Gilbert, began over Parkhurst's comments about "some girl," punches were not thrown until Parkhurst refused to follow an order by the biker.

When Parkhurst was getting the better of the biker, his friends stepped in and made it a decidedly unfair fight. Once Parkhurst was on the ground and defenseless, they kicked and stomped on him as long as they felt like, and he ultimately died.

Neither Gilbert nor Barger showed any remorse for Parkhurst's death, and Gilbert even told a reporter that Parkhurst deserved to die because of his "disrespect."

Every biker I have ever spoken with, or have read the writings of, has steadfastly maintained that their club is not a gang, nor is it a criminal organization, because it does not engage in drug trafficking as a group—although they readily admit that individual members of their club do that.

However, not one has ever shied away from the fact that any sign of "disrespect" would be met with violence. While even those who believe the line that biker clubs are not gangs because not every single one of their members traffics drugs—though, admittedly, many do—and, keep in mind that only one jurisdiction has declared only one 1-percenter club a criminal organization, it's hard to believe that a uniformed group of men who reserves the right to determine what is acceptable behavior by those around them, and to mete out violent punishments to those who disobey them, is anything but a gang.

# CHAPTER 11

# Bikers and Cops

'll tell you why we hate cops," said Randy, a former Outlaws full patch. I hadn't asked him, but I was interested in what he had to say. "They judge us. As soon as they see a patch, they've already decided you're a bad guy, and they'll do anything to bring you down."

I told him that bikers weren't the only group with that problem, but he didn't seem to pay any attention to that. He was in full tirade mode and would not be stopped until he was finished. I'll save you the long, loud details, but the gist of what he said was that cops aren't interested in justice, just arrests and convictions and seizing people's property. They target the bikers, he said, because the public and media have already decided that all bikers are criminals. By arresting bikers, he maintains, it makes it look like they're doing their jobs.

I pointed out that cops only make arrests that they believe will lead to convictions.

"Well, *they've* got it in for us too."

"Who?"

"Judges, lawyers, the legal system."

As YOU MIGHT expect, cops and bikers usually do not get along very well. One group is sworn to be dedicated to upholding the laws of the community, and the other is just as dedicated to ignoring them, and instituting their own.

The odd part of that relationship is that the memberships of both groups are largely cut from the same cloth. Police forces often prize many of the same qualities biker clubs do—a strong belief in hierarchy, a dedication to obedience, an ability to make quick decisions based on training and an ability to handle one's self in a scrap—and recruit many of the same type of people (men, at least).

In fact, every biker I have ever spoken with has pointed out that he knew some of the local cops while they were growing up together. Cops and bikers were often friends, teammates or rivals in high school, and sometimes even worked together in security or other jobs before their paths diverged.

That similarity has led to a phenomenon that many on both sides find bizarre—police biker clubs. One cop, who is not a member of such a club but does ride a Harley, told me that "cops like to ride, drink and chase women as much as anybody."

Clubs like the Blue Knights, the Enforcers, the Roughnecks and the Expendables are made of entirely or primarily active or retired law enforcement, although some will also allow corrections officers, firefighters and military as members.

They wear cuts and colors, use the same number-corresponds-to-letter codes and have three-piece patches with similar logos to outlaw clubs. They have chapters and constitutions with many of the same rules as outlaw clubs. They look and sound like outlaw biker clubs, but they maintain they don't break any laws.

Most bikers I have spoken with find the concept confusing at the very least, as though the members of law enforcement clubs (LEMCs) are playing an adult version of dress-up. A couple have openly mused that it would be no stranger if the cops put on fedoras and dark suits and pretended to be mafiosi.

The concept is more concerning to cops, many of whom have told me that they believe the interest in behaving like bikers reveals that the officers involved support, or at least have sympathy for, the outlaw clubs.

Steve Cook, a veteran biker investigator, told CBS News that some LEMCs actually ask permission from the local 1-percenter clubs to start their clubs. "You've got to pick a side," he said. "You're either a cop or a biker."

Of course, the very existence of LEMCs often enrages the actual 1-percenter clubs, and violence can result. On January 30, 2016, clubs like the Bandidos and Mongols attended the Colorado Motorcycle Expo at the Denver Coliseum. So did the Iron Order, an LEMC. Both sides tell very divergent stories as to how it happened, but a brawl broke out between some members of the Mongols and Iron Order. The Iron Order says that it all started when a Mongol assaulted an African-American Iron Order member, ordering him out of the event because of his skin color, while the Mongols say that the same officer assaulted one of their members. According to the Mongols, one member of the Iron Order, a corrections officer named Derrick "King" Duran, pulled out a gun and started waving it around. Mongol Victor "Nubz" Mendoza, they say, rushed him in an attempt to disarm him and was shot and killed. The Iron Order countered that Duran shot in self-defense as Mendoza stormed at him in the middle of a brawl. The incident prompted a deluge of finger-pointing and name-calling on both sides in the form of press conferences and social media posts. The Denver district attorney's office decided not to file charges against Duran because they said they could not fight his claim of self-defense.

The owners of the Colorado Motorcycle Expo have since banned attendance of both the Mongols and Iron Order.

Despite their often-shared backgrounds and interests, however, few cops that bikers actually run into are members of LEMCs. For the most part, the feelings between them are an uneasy détente. "He's got his job to do," Randy said. "And I've got mine."

The question of LEMCs aside, cops can look the other way from time to time or even occasionally break the law to help them.

One instance occurred in 2010 in southern California. Santa Clara police arrested William "Billy" Bettencourt for a laundry list of violations, including trafficking steroids and illegal possession of a semiautomatic firearm.

As part of the investigation, police seized his BlackBerry. Of the more than 50,000 text messages they found on it, one frequently used number stood out. Two cops recognized it as the personal number of one of their own, Clay Rojas.

Two officers went to Rojas's home to question him and were surprised to see a "Support 81" banner hanging in his living room. Confronted with his hundreds of incriminating texts, Rojas admitted that he had given Bettencourt sensitive information, including the home addresses of the owners of license plate numbers the biker provided. He also told them that he borrowed "a thousand here, a hundred there" from Bettencourt and that feeding him information was his way of paying him back. And, finally, he told them that he honestly believed he had done nothing wrong.

Later, Rojas, still maintaining that his offenses were "a slip" of his "ethical code," was sentenced to forty-one months in prison. Bettencourt, his other two strikes long used up, went down for life.

The bikers I've spoken with categorize local cops in order of how dangerous they are.

The first category—often called "Barneys," in reference to Barney Fife, the bumbling and nervous deputy played by Don Knotts on *The Andy Griffith Show*—are cops who are easily intimidated by bikers. While they do their best to put on a brave face, their stress can be obvious, and bikers like to play with them a bit, making them more nervous.

After them are the macho men. These are cops who try to intimidate the bikers. The rule of thumb with them, I'm told, is just not to give them a reason to get violent—comply with their requests and say and do as little as possible.

Far worse, from the bikers' standpoint, are the old pros. These are cops that are neither intimidated nor intimidating but can be successful in getting a biker talking. While the biker will try to keep conversation to motorcycles or the weather, any slip could help an investigation into the club. These are the cops that stop the bikers frequently for minor infractions—Dave, a former Hells Angel, told me he had been stopped on his bike maybe once or twice a year before he put on the patch and about three times a day afterward—hoping to gain some information, or at least remind the bikers they're out there.

But, for the most part, bikers and local cops live in an uneasy equilibrium that rarely threatens the chapter but might lead to the arrest of individual members.

Besides the threat of retaliation for calling police, bikers also do their best to undermine public confidence in law enforcement by posting links to police wrongdoing on their own sites, internet forums and social media.

Things are different when the club or chapter is targeted by federal agencies like the FBI, DEA, ATF or RCMP. While local law enforcement is generally looking only to maintain peace and order in their communities, bigger agencies are actively looking to undermine and take down clubs.

To do that, they need eyes and ears within the club.

Traditionally, the only way to find out what's going on inside is through turning a member, prospect or someone else close to the club. That's not easy. Clubs constantly remind the people they come in contact with that they consider "snitching" the most repulsive act, and any instances of it will be met with violence, probably fatal, when uncovered.

Consequently, most of the people turned by law enforcement are desperate enough to take that risk. They might be facing a long prison term, owe immense sums of money, have a debilitating drug habit or have committed some other offense the club is ready to punish them for. Law enforcement can also sweeten the deal by offering entry into a witness protection program and sometimes even large sums of cash.

While informants can be invaluable for law enforcement, their testimony in court can be and often is challenged by smart lawyers who point out that desperate people will do just about anything to save their skins. If the case comes down to an informant's word against that of the accused, the fact that the informant stands to gain significantly from his or her testimony often weakens its credibility.

To avoid having to rely on the informant's word in court, members of law enforcement go to great lengths to have their agents record conversations, copy documented evidence (such as business ledgers) and photograph or even take physical evidence. All of those actions, of course, make life much more dangerous for the informant.

Still, clubs work very hard not to allow the people close to them to get into such situations. Debts are collected before they get too large, the use of injectable drugs (aside from steroids) is not tolerated, and members and friends facing time behind bars are often buoyed up by parties and fundraisers in their honor and a promise of protection from gangs once inside. Every major club also campaigns heavily to encourage its supporters to send letters and gifts to members and friends behind bars to remind them they have not been forgotten. The belief is that incarcerated people are less likely to turn informant if they feel goodwill from the club and have the hope that they will be welcomed back after release.

Even more important are prison runs. Clubs, support clubs, allied clubs and others will take part in a mass ride—sometimes as many as two thousand strong—past prisons that have bikers inside. It's an obvious show of strength as well as a demonstration that the club has not forgotten the guys inside, and it can be a very effective way of keeping morale high—not to mention its value in impressing potential recruits.

Alternatively, the police can get one of their own into a club. That's a tremendously difficult task, as clubs have become paranoid about admitting new members and have instituted intense and far-reaching background checks to weed out any potential informant, let alone actual cops.

The best way around that is for undercover officers to form their own club or chapter of an existing club (usually without the club's blessing or even knowledge). Nearby 1-percenter clubs will take notice of them and—if the cops play their cards right—will befriend them or even patch them over. When it works, it's because the bigger club believes that the members of the fake club have already been vetted and need no further background checks.

These sorts of infiltrations can lead to mass arrests, but many are concerned about the effectiveness of them. I've had two different cops tell me that they've been thanked by rival bikers after they took down a chapter, with one even being told by a member of another club, "Thanks for giving us the city."

And while mass arrests might cause headlines and allow police to seize assets—often clubhouses—they can be big and cumbersome and end badly. For example, in 2009, Operation SharQc led to the arrest of 156 people in Quebec, including 111 full-patch Hells Angels. Much of the evidence was supplied by members-turned-informants Sylvain Boulanger and Dayle Fredette. Boulanger, it was later revealed, was paid $2.9 million for his efforts. The case was made that the Hells Angels and their support clubs waged war against the Rock Machine and their supporters, with at least 168 casualties, in an effort to corner the province's cocaine market.

The government of Quebec, however, found the mass trials to be too time consuming and expensive. Most of the suspects who were convicted took sweetheart plea bargains to lesser charges with light sentences, and thirty-one—including some accused of murder—walked when the court decided it no longer had the time or funds to continue the trials.

While unthinkable today, the police and 1-percenter clubs used to work together on occasion. In the late 1960s, the Oakland police and the local chapter of the Hells Angels had a common enemy—anti-war protesters. With the war in Vietnam becoming increasingly unpopular and Cold War hysteria at its height, Sonny Barger made Oakland police sergeant Edward Hilliard an offer: the Hells Angels would uncover any stashes of weapons made by "radical leftists" in the area and turn them over to Hilliard in exchange for the release of any club members who were arrested. Hilliard enthusiastically agreed.

Of course, the weapons caches by leftist radicals were nothing more than a paranoid fantasy of Hilliard's that Barger was eager to exploit. The Hells Angels were stealing and even buying weapons to use as get-out-of-jail-free cards for their chapter.

When Barger revealed the reality of his deal in court, Hilliard defended himself by saying that at least he didn't take the Hells Angels' offer of trading favors for the corpses of dead leftist fugitives.

Years later, Barger became something of a spokesman for the "We don't dial 911" movement, encouraging not only Hells Angels, but everyone to take care of emergencies by themselves either by fighting back against any aggressors or shutting up and taking what's coming to you.

But, if you believe former Hells Angel George Christie—and it's nearly impossible not to—Barger broke his own rule, which calls for immediate expulsion from the club, at least once.

According to an article in *Phoenix* magazine, Barger's wife, Noel, was driving in Arizona on July 13, 2003, when she saw Sonny with another woman on the back of his motorcycle. Enraged, she tried to run them off the road with her Camaro.

On his return to their home Barger, the story continued, kicked Noel, knocking her senseless. An alarmed Barger, it said, then called 911 at 2:26 the following morning.

After police and an ambulance showed up to sort things out, the article said, a neighbor found Barger in a state of nervous delusion so severe that he had to be hospitalized.

For years before the incident, Barger and Christie had been very public rivals. Christie, president of the Ventura, California, chapter, had taken on increasing responsibility for the club while Barger was behind bars and later when he was treated for throat cancer. As Barger sought to reclaim his number-one Hells Angel status, two sides formed with a great deal of tension. Several violent incidents, including the death of Barger's right-hand man, Cave Creek president Daniel "Hoover" Seybert—shot by a sniper as he mounted his Harley in 2002—and that of Ventura's Josh Harber, a close friend of Christie's, two weeks later were attributed to the rivalry.

At a West Coast officers' meeting, Christie brought up the alleged 911 call. Barger, he said, claimed it never happened, but Christie dropped what he said were both a transcript and tape recording of the call on the table in front of him.

Christie then said that Barger had obliquely threatened to fight him, so Christie handed his glasses to a Ventura member who had come with him. No punches were thrown, though, as the pair sat down and argued for two hours. Christie said he encouraged Barger to admit he had broken a club rule and try to move on, accepting the club's punishment. Barger, Christie maintains, told him, "I don't answer to anyone" and explained to the other members at the meeting that the voice on the call was not his and that Christie had faked the whole thing. Christie, sensing support for Barger's chain of events, later quit the club.

When Christie published his memoir in 2016 and mentioned the alleged incident, media picked up on it. The New York *Daily News* (a publication I once worked for) ran an article with the headline "Former Hells Angels boss Sonny Barger was a fraud who beat his wife and fourteen-year-old stepdaughter, ex-gangster George Christie writes in 'Exile on Front Street' tell-all."

According to police, when they arrived Barger told them that Noel had pulled a gun on him, so he kicked her. Noel, police said, claimed that she had not pulled a gun and that Barger had kicked her, grabbed her by the hair and punched her before kicking her. Sarrah, her thirteen-year-old daughter from a previous relationship, claimed she had been punched twice in the head by Barger and said, "He hits my mom all the time. He's going to kill her. I hope he goes to prison forever. I hate him."

When it was announced that Christie would discuss the matter, and other topics, on the History Channel TV show *Outlaw Chronicles*, a lawyer representing Barger (who has copyrighted his name and likeness) sent a letter to its producers. It made clear that the show was under no circumstances to make it appear as though Barger was pursuing charges against or protection from his wife—as Christie maintains is in the edited portion of the 911 call. Although the letter did not admit that Barger called 911, it did note that Noel "insisted in prosecuting Mr. Barger for aggravated assault."

The show did indeed play the recording, with a warning that several minutes had been cut out. It began with a voice that, in my opinion, sounded like Barger's introducing himself as Ralph Barger, complaining that his wife is "paralyzed" and admitting that her injuries were the result of an "altercation." The voice then admits there is a pistol in his wife's car. Then the show said that several minutes were edited out. It then returned to the original caller telling the operator that the police had arrived, thanking her and hanging up. Police charged Barger with aggravated assault, but that was later reduced to misdemeanor assault. And that charge was dismissed after Noel changed her version of the events several times.

If the voice on the call is Ralph Barger—it does sound like him to me and the caller identifies himself by that name—and the recording is authentic, then it indicates that Barger not only called 911 but that he also told them about the pistol (which many bikers would interpret as cooperating with police), regardless of what's in the edited portion.

Judging by Barger's response, even if it's acceptable under the Hells Angels' ethos to kick your wife into paralysis, it's not okay to let the police know she had a gun in her car.

CHAPTER 12

# Bikers and the Rest
# of the World

I asked Randy, the former Outlaw, to tell me his opinion of how
bikers see the world differently than civilians.

"In our places, our bars, our clubhouses, whatever, we make
the rules, not the cops or [the] government. We do, and if you don't
like it, fuck you," he told me. "Break a rule, we'll fuck you up; call
the cops, we'll fuck you up. Like it or not, we're in charge."

THE HELLS ANGELS certainly are the best-known motorcycle
gang, but they are far from the most powerful in a strategic sense.

Look at it this way: Suppose the United States intended to
invade and occupy Baja California. They set up some flimsy reason regarding the safety of tourists and expats on the Mexican
peninsula and unilaterally mount a military operation to seize
it. The Mexicans officially opt to cede the territory rather than
risk all-out war, but some holdouts do their best to defend their
sovereign territory.

Now imagine the Hells Angels fighting on the front lines, capturing sites of key military importance, recruiting rebels from the local population and patrolling the city streets at night to keep terrified people in their homes and any hint of resistance down. Now imagine them doing this while the U.S. president calls them his "friends," rides a Harley with them in parades and sends millions of dollars in federal government money to keep them going. Under this hypothetical scenario, a Hells Angel would even become a governor of a small but vitally important state.

Sounds ridiculous, right? But it actually happened, if you change a few names. The club wasn't the Hells Angel but the Night Wolves. And it wasn't really the Americans invading Baja, but the Russians annexing the Crimean Peninsula from Ukraine. The president, of course, was Vladimir Putin. And the state governor was actually Ramzan Kadyrov, president of Chechnya, a full-patch member of the Night Wolves.

The club's origins go back to the early 1980s, when the Communists were still in power in the Soviet Union, which included both Russia and Ukraine. Back then, entertainment was strictly regulated by the state, which jammed foreign radio broadcasts and operated all legal live music venues. Many people were dissatisfied with the bland, out-of-date and often condescending acts that the government would allow to perform.

Naturally, people started putting on their own shows, surreptitiously, in defiance of the government. One group of guys who specialized in illegal heavy metal shows started referring to themselves as the Night Wolves because they operated under the cover of darkness and these kinds of guys often seem to have a particular fondness for wolves.

In the late 1980s, under the leadership of Mikhail Gorbachev, the Soviet Union began to relax many restrictions on its citizens, including those surrounding entertainment. Freed from having to put on their shows in secret, the Night Wolves quickly became very wealthy. Already clad in denim and leather and with many of them already riding motorcycles, in 1989 the Night Wolves organized themselves as an outlaw motorcycle gang along the lines of what they had seen in the West.

At the time, the Communist Party in the Soviet Union was weakening. Not only were Soviet Republics like Lithuania and Ukraine demanding independence; people in the streets were openly flouting Communist rules. Hard-line Communists in the government attempted a coup in August 1991, seeking to bring back the old ways. It was quickly put down, but Gorbachev and the party were clearly finished. The day after Christmas 1991, the Soviet Union ceased to exist, and the new Russia emerged with Boris Yeltsin in charge.

It was a wild period of history and a good time to be a Night Wolf. Yeltsin severely mishandled the transformation from a communist to capitalist state, and Russia was soon swamped with incredibly wealthy oligarchs who openly operated crime organizations to earn more and keep their riches safe.

An inveterate alcoholic who had become a national embarrassment, Yeltsin resigned from office in 1999, with a 2-percent approval rating. He was replaced by Putin, who has been the ultimate power in Russia ever since, alternating his title between premier and president to retain a legal status under the constitution. Although much of the obvious Wild West–style crime that haunted Yeltsin's Russia has since been greatly reduced, crime organizations have become far more powerful and politically influential.

One such organization that has benefited from Putin's rule is the Night Wolves. Their president since 1989 has been his friend, Alexander "The Surgeon" Zaldostanov. He was born in 1963 in

Ukraine to a Georgian father and a Russian mother (his last name at birth was Zaldastanishvili, but he changed it to sound more Russian); the family moved to Moscow when he was young.

Zaldostanov began riding Czech-made Jawa motorcycles to rock shows in Moscow, getting to know the players and making an image for himself. When the Night Wolves were formed in 1989 as Russia's first official motorcycle club, he joined. He was still studying to become a surgeon specializing in facial reconstruction—an operation in high demand with the shocking amount of violent crime in Moscow at the time. But then the money started flowing in. The Night Wolves traded in their Jawas and Russian-made Urals for Harley-Davidsons. Zaldostanov quit medicine to become a full-time biker.

Like many bikers, Zaldostanov is fiercely jingoistic and xenophobic, in favor of separating people by ethnicity. While far from a communist, he believes in a union of Slavic states. He believes that ethnic Slavs should be regarded as one people, who should be in one nation and strictly follow the teachings and rules of the Russian Orthodox Church whether they want to or not. He has referred to people who do not share his beliefs as "possessed" by the devil.

When Ukraine—one of several breakaway republics that separated and declared independence just before the final shutdown of the Soviet Union—made steps to leave the Russian sphere of influence, he, like Putin, was enraged. The movement in Ukraine to become more pro-Western is called Maidan, so Zaldostanov and several other Russian right-wingers formed their own movement called Anti-Maidan.

Since about 2000, Zaldostanov and the Night Wolves have been traveling activists, even evangelists, for the Anti-Maidan call. They put on elaborate shows with rock music, lasers and

other special effects. The highlights are always mock gun bat-
tles between valiant Russians and bumbling Westerners that the
Russians always win. Westerners and their allies are continually
denounced as fascists, criminals and degenerates. Zaldostanov
once told a reporter that "Death to faggots" would be an appropriate motto for the Anti-Maidan movement.

A former bouncer who admits to "constant fighting" as a
younger man, Zaldostanov frequently talks of violence but says
he won't ever start anything. "I'm not a provocateur, and neither
is Anti-Maidan, but we will not be pushovers," he told Vice. "We
won't allow ourselves to be humiliated. If they don't use violence
against me, I won't use it either. But if they try to rape us, they
will get an even worse response." He appears to be obsessed with
that last concept, bringing up rape imagery repeatedly.

While many clubs have been accused of bankrolling their
activities by trafficking drugs and other crimes, the Night Wolves
don't have to. They are paid handsome sums by the Putin government to put on their shows and run their club.

In fact, Putin and Zaldostanov have become close friends, and
Putin even appeared—riding a customized Harley three-wheeler—
in a 2009 Night Wolves parade. Putin awarded Zaldostanov the
Russian Medal of Honor for "activity in the patriotic education
of youth" and arranged for him to be a torch-bearer for the Sochi
Winter Olympics in 2014. In a televised speech, Putin said of the
Night Wolves, "You do not just ride your motorcycles; you also
perform military patriotic work. Historical memory is the best
cement that binds people of different nationalities and religions
into one nation, in one powerful country—Russia."

While all that was happening, pro-Western and pro-Russian
demonstrations became violent in Ukraine. Pro-Russian groups
received military aid from the Kremlin, and in 2014, Russian

troops invaded and annexed the valuable Crimean Peninsula, which had been sovereign Ukrainian soil. The excuse was that Crimea had a large Russian-speaking population and that the Ukrainian government was not treating them fairly. Since then, a long and bloody war has been fought in eastern Ukraine, the region bordering Russia, between the Ukrainian government and fighters who, judging from the weight of evidence, are Russian soldiers, which the Kremlin denies.

According to many media reports, the Night Wolves were active participants in the invasion, not as a formal military unit, but wearing their cuts. They are widely reported by media on both sides as having stormed a lightly guarded natural gas facility, holding it secure until the military arrived.

After the Russian military had secured Crimea, the Night Wolves were brought in to patrol the streets at night, to ensure there was no rebellious activity.

Once the area was stable, Zaldostanov put on an elaborate pro-Russian concert and show, complete with military re-enactments and Ukrainian officials operated by American puppet masters, that had 100,000 in its live audience and was broadcast live on Russian state television. Zaldostanov himself acted as emcee. He kicked it off by announcing, according to *Rolling Stone*, "We are celebrating our sacred victory at a time when fascism, like putrid, poisonous dough, has overfilled its Kyiv trough and begun to spread across Ukraine. The new battle against fascism is inevitable. Stalin's eleventh strike is inevitable." Josef Stalin, if you don't recall, was the Soviet Union's Georgian-born leader from 1924 until his death in 1953. Through purges, the "liquidation" of certain economic classes and intentional famines (mainly against Ukrainians), the ruthless dictator is estimated to have been responsible for the deaths of twenty million to forty million people, not including those lost in World War II. Zaldostanov frequently praises Stalin and says that his "work" should be continued.

Since the invasion of Crimea, the Night Wolves and Zaldostanov have been the subjects of sanctions by many countries, including the United States and Canada, both of which have banned known Night Wolves from entering their countries. He later tongue in cheek thanked U.S. President Barack Obama for recognizing the work he was doing for the motherland. And Night Wolves have been denied access to Poland and Germany, where they planned an elaborate celebration of Germany's defeat in World War II.

There's a lot of debate about what Putin has and has not done as leader of Russia. But we do know that under him, the state has invaded a sovereign country (a Western ally) and bankrolled a motorcycle club modeled on the 1-percenters of the West that was also involved militarily in the invasion. As well, the club does its best to spread its violently anti-Western message throughout Eastern Europe and incite violence.

Only in Russia, right? Not so fast. The Night Wolves are a group with secret rituals and meetings. They espouse inequality of sexes, ethnicities and sexual minorities. They put their country first and put on shows that indicate they believe they can solve all conflicts with violence. They attract attention and recruits by showing off a fun, hedonistic lifestyle and justify their existence by saying they do a lot of good for their community.

That is, of course, much like how the biker gangs in North America act.

And don't think they have not been militaristically minded as well. I'm not talking about bikers going to war with other bikers; I mean bikers actually going to war.

Back in the 1960s, the Hells Angels hung out frequently with hippies and other counter-culture groups. They bonded over drugs, a shared mistrust of government and outsider status. But they differed over one important issue—U.S. military involvement in the conflict in Vietnam. The bikers believed that protesting the war was un-American and tantamount to aiding and abetting the enemy. Calling the protesters "a mob of traitors" and threatening violence by adding, "our patriotic concern for what these people are doing to our great nation may provoke violent acts by us," Sonny Barger sent a telegram to President Lyndon Johnson that read, "I volunteer a group of loyal Americans for behind the line duty in Vietnam. We feel that a crack group of trained guerrillas could demoralize the Viet Cong and advance the cause of freedom."

The answer from the White House was that if the Hells Angels wanted to fight in Southeast Asia, they could join the army. That disappointed Barger, who pointed out in his memoir that nobody in his chapter could join the army because they were all convicted felons.

Not long after, the Hells Angels planned a military-style assault on Rolling Stones singer Mick Jagger. There had been bad blood between the club and the rock superstar over the events at the ill-fated Altamont rock festival in 1969.

On the advice of the Grateful Dead, the Rolling Stones hired the Hells Angels as security. Not surprisingly, it didn't go well. Before long, beer-fueled Hells Angels were beating concert goers with sawed-off pool cues.

In his memoir, Barger blames the Rolling Stones, particularly Jagger, for the violence, citing poor event organization—the band was just three feet off the ground—and the band's egging on the crowd. He did, however, admit to kicking one woman in the head because she was trying to get onto the stage.

One fan—an African-American man named Meredith Hunter—was stabbed and killed by a Hells Angel, Alan Passaro, who was later acquitted on grounds of self-defense. That ended the show. Some say it ended the '60s.

It also ended any relationship between the Hells Angels and the Rolling Stones, with both sides talking smack about the other in the media.

Later that year, though, the Hells Angels engaged in an ambitious operation. According to the FBI, the plan was to infiltrate Jagger's walled and heavily guarded beach-house compound in the Hamptons on Long Island. To evade the guards, they decided to make an amphibious landing from the beach under cover of darkness.

They loaded up a boat with guns and took off from a nearby launch, intent, the FBI alleges, on making a quiet landing on the beach by moonlight, storming the house, killing Jagger and escaping before his security team could mobilize.

But they hadn't accounted for the weather. Strong winds and driving rain churned the ocean off the Hamptons, and their boat was swamped. All the Hells Angels aboard were thrown into the sea.

The would-be invaders all survived, and the boat was salvaged the next day. The plot to assassinate Jagger, which he did not know about until many years later, was called off. The Hells Angels alleged to be involved were never charged.

More recently, many bikers announced that they were prepared to go to war against Islamist fundamentalists in the Middle East. A few, mostly from the Netherlands and Germany, actually went. A group of them, under the name FCKISIS, set up a crowd-funding project, hoping to collect one million euros. They fell a bit short, raising just 364 (about $425 U.S.). Video of one of them—who gave his name as "Ron" and said he belonged to the

No Surrender MC in Eindhoven—armed with an assault rifle and saying he was fighting Islamic State, with some armed men carrying a Kurdish flag, became very popular in international media, especially in Russia.

While Ron was in Syria fighting ISIS, his mates back in Eindhoven were also busy. Weeks after the video surfaced, another video of No Surrender emerged that put a different light on how they operate. On October 4, 2014, several of them—in their colors—approached a house in Eindhoven, had words with two men over the fence, then burst through the gate with guns out. Several of the No Surrender guys shot at the two men, who shot back. Somehow, nobody was injured, although one of the bikers was bitten by a dog that had initially been quite friendly when they arrived.

About a year later, the club announced that Ron had been killed in Amsterdam when a train collided with his motorcycle.

While North American bikers have not gone to war for the government like the Night Wolves have, or to fight in actual wars as independent contractors (and at least one Dutch biker seems to have), they have gone to war against the government.

An attempt was made by the Montreal Hells Angels, under the command of "Mom" Boucher, to intimidate the government of Quebec by killing any judges, prosecutors, police and prison guards who made life difficult for the club. Their theory was that if everyone in the province who could make a dent in the club's cocaine business feared for his or her life, the Hells Angels would have no problems. The club did manage to kill two prison guards—Diane Lavigne and Pierre Rondeau—in 1997 but lost its desire to take on the government after Boucher went to prison.

A year earlier, members of Satan's Choice detonated a bomb at police headquarters in Sudbury, Ontario, in retaliation for being thrown out of a strip joint for violating a "no colors" rule. Nobody was hurt, but the message was clear. The chapter later patched over to the Hells Angels.

Bikers are much less likely to take on law enforcement directly in the United States, where police are more heavily armed and more likely to use military-style tactics.

But that doesn't mean that the threat is not there, at least in the minds of law enforcement officers.

On December 31, 2009, two officers of the Hemet, California, gang task force walked into their unmarked headquarters and smelled gas. Instead of turning on the lights, which they believed might have ignited the gas, they called the local hazmat team.

Quickly, the Hemet police force surmised that it must be the work of the Vagos, the biggest club in the area. The local police had been leaning on the Vagos heavily in the previous few months, sifting through active warrants and arresting several of them. The day before, police and Vagos faced off against each other angrily but not violently at a nearby church. The Vagos were there attending a funeral of one of their members.

An investigation determined that someone had indeed rigged a gas pipe to flood the task force's headquarters. But there was no physical evidence linking it to any specific person, let alone the Vagos.

Less than two months later, February 23, 2010, a task force officer opened the front security gate at the group's headquarters and was shocked to hear a loud bang. Someone had rigged a homemade gun to fire when the gate was opened. The officer was unharmed. Again, there was not enough evidence to link the crime to anyone or any group.

The cops were tense after that. On March 5, 2010, another officer gave his car a quick check and found a pipe bomb underneath it.

That was enough for the cops. On March 17, they rounded up thirty Vagos, seizing several illegal weapons and coming upon a meth lab in the process.

But the attacks continued. Two men were seen on the roof of the Los Altos Meat Market attempting to fire a rocket launcher at a car driven by task force detective Chuck Johnson, but the World War II–vintage bazooka failed to ignite. An investigation later determined that the rocket was a training round with no explosive material.

Later, Johnson found boards with rusty nails pointed up on his front porch. Johnson, a former Marine, and his family were taken into government protection.

That was followed by an arson in the task force's evidence room.

The police had offered a $200,000 reward for information leading to the arrest of the attackers, and a local woman decided to collect. She had overheard her friend's boyfriend and another man discussing the attacks. The boyfriend was being berated for supplying a faulty bazooka for $3,000. The angry man wanted another bazooka, she told police.

Five days later, the task force arrested Nicholas Smit and Steven Hansen. Smit was found guilty of being behind the gun, bazooka and pipe bomb attacks. He had been arrested by Johnson in June 2009 on five felony drug trafficking charges and was attempting to eliminate Johnson or at least intimidate him enough to prevent him from testifying against him. He was out on bail during the attacks and later pleaded guilty to the drug charges. He received four consecutive life sentences for his violence against Johnson. Hansen, Smit's roommate, took a plea deal and pleaded guilty to helping Smit acquire and try to fire the bazooka. That allowed him to escape a life sentence, instead getting him twenty years.

While the attacks had all the hallmarks of organized crime trying to intimidate police and destroy evidence, the Hemet cops and prosecutors could never link them or Smit or Hansen to the Vagos. In fact, the Vagos sued for defamation. The two sides settled, and the Hemet police had to remove any mention of the Vagos in their reports on the crimes and issue a public apology.

"This was never about money; it was about clearing their good name," said Vagos attorney Joseph Yanni. "They've been trashed and mistreated. I'm just glad the county saw fit to restore the reputations of these good men."

While wars between biker gangs and law enforcement and government are thankfully very rare, many in law enforcement tell me that subtler one-on-one intimidation takes place regularly. A biker might tell a cop that they know the names of the cop's spouse or children or their home address, especially in remote communities where the cops might be outnumbered and outgunned.

"While they are rare, assaults on law enforcement officers by outlaw motorcycle gang members do occur. Still, threat and intimidation of officers are routine and commonplace, although the bikers rarely follow up. When assaults on officers do occur, they are rarely planned. Instead, they occur when tempers flare at routine road stops or other contacts," wrote Steve Cook, a law enforcement officer who has gone undercover as a biker. "And there have been killings of law enforcement officers by outlaw motorcycle gangs, but again they are more often spontaneous incidents, rather than premeditated murders, and they are exceptionally rare."

The difference between most bikers and those that have made their presence known in a military way has been their charismatic leadership. Without the tough-talking Zaldostanov—and his close relationship with Putin—the Night Wolves would be just another Moscow gang, not a government-financed paramilitary power. If Barger had not been in charge of the Hells Angels, it's unlikely they would have had the chutzpah to offer to fight for the U.S. in Southeast Asia. And if it wasn't for Boucher's charm and drive, his vision of a government terrified into submission would probably have been laughed off.

# CHAPTER 13

# The Biker Mentality

If you're still unclear what the biker mindset is like, consider the case of Daniel "Diamond Dan" Bifield. He was a Hells Angel in upstate New York, and he was successful enough to be able to start a chapter in Bridgeport, Connecticut, and serve as its president.

But in 1980, he was convicted of extortion and firearms offenses and went to prison. After a few weeks behind bars, he noticed that a guard had left a window open in a room he had access to, and Bifield escaped.

After a report that his body had been found in a nearby river made its way into several newspapers, Bifield sent a picture of himself with two guns to the local district attorney's office. He was eventually captured in Denver—after hiding out in the Bahamas—the culmination of what the FBI called an "international manhunt." He told a judge that he escaped only because he was seeking better treatment for his kidney stones.

Bifield was released in 1982 and was promptly put back behind bars after another extortion conviction.

He was paroled in 1997 and was sent back to prison in 2000 for his role in a money-laundering scheme. While he was doing that stretch, he was convicted of fraud after an operation was uncovered in which he and other inmates used friends' addresses to illegally collect tax returns. And, in 2002, he was caught with heroin in prison.

Still, he was paroled in 2008 and was sent to live in a halfway house in South Carolina. He liked that state and, upon his release, founded the God's Few motorcycle club, which later became the Rock Hill Nomads chapter of the Hells Angels.

Before long, Bifield was "Diamond Dan" again. He earned his nickname for wearing garish amounts of gold and jewels as a way to show off his wealth, despite never having held a legitimate job as an adult, aside from placing small ads in *Chrome*—a defunct magazine for motorcycle customizers—that offered to buy and sell jewelry through the mail.

After the chapter had some violent run-ins with other area bikers, law enforcement started an operation to investigate what they were up to. Through the use of paid informants and other methods, the feds gathered enough evidence that the Rock Hill Nomads were selling cocaine, methamphetamine, "bath salts," prescription opioids and firearms, including those illegally adjusted to allow automatic fire, that they could charge them all. They also discovered that a series of mysterious arsons had been set by members of the club, including Bifield. The targets were all businesses or residences owned or rented by people who had crossed the chapter.

In all, twenty people—including Bifield, his wife, Lisa, and the entire chapter—were arrested and variously charged with trafficking drugs, trafficking firearms, money laundering, extortion, arson and racketeering. Bifield was charged with all of those offenses, while Lisa was charged with trafficking, money laundering, racketeering and firearms offenses.

The weight of the evidence was so heavy that fifteen of the original twenty pleaded guilty before Bifield and his wife were tried. Facing thirty years to life, Bifield agreed to plead guilty to just one charge—racketeering—and received a seventeen-and-a-half-year sentence.

It's significant that Bifield pleaded guilty to racketeering because that means he is legally and publicly admitting that at least some members of the chapter acted as a crime organization. In effect, he was breaking the one cardinal biker rule by throwing his "brothers" under the bus for his own gain. In his statement, though, Bifield claimed the opposite of what he had signed under oath in court—that the Hells Angels were "not a criminal enterprise," and characterized them as "Americans, proud of our country, and we will fight and die for our country." Not only does that ring a bit hollow—Bifield never served in the military or any other branch of service, cheated the federal government out of tax returns he did not deserve, broke many federal statutes and fled to another country when the feds were looking for him—but it has absolutely nothing to do with the fact that he was guilty of racketeering.

Lisa Bifield also pleaded guilty to weapons charges and received seven years. She had made a deal with prosecutors to provide testimony against other Hells Angels, but it was withdrawn after they pleaded guilty, and her testimony was no longer of any use.

In the end, they all went to jail, and the feds had the right to call the chapter a criminal enterprise in a large part because of Bifield's plea. But since the chapter ceased to exist after the convictions, so did the criminal organization. So you might be tempted to think that Bifield is loathed by the biker community, especially supporters of the Hells Angels, because of his guilty plea.

You'd be wrong. There's a petition on Change.org to free Bifield and a Facebook page dedicated to supporting him in prison and exploring ways to get him freed. Parties are thrown in his honor and T-shirts are sold with his name, and a portion of the proceeds goes to him and his defense fund.

The logic behind the Free Diamond Dan movement—and thousands of people have shown their support online—is that they believe he never did anything wrong. The arrests, the convictions, the drugs and weapons found in his possession, the recorded deals he made with defendants, the burned-down buildings—it's all a lie, his supporters say. The feds made it up simply, the thinking goes, because they don't like bikers. I have even been told that since the Hells Angels had moved into the area, crime had dropped so precipitously that the police had time on their hands and were jealous of the Hells Angels. The informants were only in it for the money (even though the highest-paid of them received just $6,000 a month—hardly a huge payday for risking your life).

As Bifield himself put it: "From the first day I moved to South Carolina the law and police have made it known that they hate me and hate the Hells Angels and that they were out to get us. I couldn't understand why. We never really bother anybody!"

That's the mantra of bikers. Even if caught red-handed or after you've signed your confession, deny, deny, deny. It's always the other guy's fault.

But the practical reality is, certainly by weight of evidence, that many clubs—or at least individual chapters—are effectively criminal enterprises. Certainly the fact that so many members of such clubs have pleaded guilty to racketeering, which is defined as operating a criminal organization, should be a key indicator. However, these rackets have been limited to groups of members and not an existing chapter or club. In the case of the Bifields, every single member of the chapter pleaded guilty or was convicted of a felony, although not all of acting in concert with other members.

Of course, there was always some small-time crime associated with 1-percenter gangs, but for the past few decades, it has taken on an almost industrial level.

There are reasons for that, and the most obvious one is the changes that have taken place in our economy and demographics.

In 2015, Princeton economists Anne Case and Angus Deaton, a Nobel Prize winner, released the results of a landmark study that showed that white adults in the United States who do not possess a higher-education degree, especially men, are the only major demographic group for whom life expectancy is getting shorter. Case and Deaton point out that most of the increase in early mortality can be linked to what they call "deaths of despair"— suicides, drug overdoses and conditions brought about by alcoholism and obesity.

Several others studying the problems facing uneducated whites in contemporary society, like University of Michigan psychologist Richard E. Nisbett, attribute that rise in deaths, and the types of deaths, to stress and frustration caused by changes in the economy. "When I moved to Ann Arbor a few decades ago, a high school educated worker on the line at Ford made enough money to support a family of four, own a three-bedroom home in the suburbs, have two cars and a boat, and buy a cottage in northern Michigan," he wrote in his essay "The Disillusionment Hypothesis and the Decline and Disaffection for Poor White Americans." "The poorly educated man today can expect to be an assistant manager at a chain store, a security guard, or a jack of all trades—occupations that barely support a single individual in modest fashion, let alone a family of four in comfort."

Men who grew up believing they would have the same jobs that their fathers and grandfathers had left high school to find those jobs no longer existed. The jobs that hadn't been lost to technology or cheap overseas labor often required more education than they had or were prepared to get. Instead of walking out of school and into a factory and leaving at age sixty-five, they found themselves competing for fewer and fewer less-steady, lower-paying jobs with women, people of color and immigrants.

The stress and frustration of that can clearly lead many affected by those changes to alcohol, drugs and, yes, each other. For many, the fraternal atmosphere of motorcycle clubs can be a safe haven from the harsh realities of today's world. The clubhouse is an atavistic place, where men are men and make all the decisions, women are tolerated only if they keep their mouths shut and know their place, and people of other ethnicities are unseen and unheard. It is, as Sean, whose club patched over to the Hells Angels, told me, a place where "a white man can still be a white man."

Of course, that's not to say that all bikers are uneducated. I know of a handful with degrees, but they are far outweighed by the thousands I've encountered who have put on their Facebook pages (yes, bikers have Facebook pages) that they were educated at "The School of Hard Knocks, University of Life."

There's nothing wrong with diverse pathways in education. Plenty of people without degrees have been very successful in many different ways. But the statistics don't lie. People who don't undergo higher education are far more likely to face economic hardship and not have the ability to emerge from it.

For many of them, that's where biker clubs come in. In her exhaustive study on the psychology of bikers, Danielle Shields of the Rutgers University School of Criminal Justice points out that there are essentially two types of club members.

The first are what she calls the conservatives, those content to ride and party with their friends and less likely to be engaged in large-scale or continuing criminal activity. They are generally older, have some type of successful business or other steady income away from the club and have dedicated much of their lives to motorcycling.

The others, whom she calls the radicals, are drawn to the clubs because of the opportunity to engage in criminal activity with some degree of protection. They are typically younger, have no other income sources and picked up motorcycling more recently.

Older bikers I've spoken with tend to look down on these so-called radicals in no small part because of their fashion sense. They complain about how they have stylized their cuts, moving away from plain black leather or blue denim to bright colors and even armor plating. They complain about "designer" jeans and the expensive, illustrated T-shirts from companies like Ed Hardy and Afflicted, which, it could be argued, borrowed their design sense from the biker clubs. One older biker told me, with disgust, that he's seen plenty of these new-style bikers riding with running shoes on.

Their point is not lost on me; many young bikers join their clubs not for a love of bikes or a quest for brotherhood, but as a way to make money. As Sons of Silence member Big Larry said, "It's the clean-cut one you have to look out for—they're hiding something."

Clubs and chapters can be a mix of the two types of biker, Shields writes, but will be guided by either conservatives or radicals. And the higher one goes up the biker food chain—from small clubs (like the Heathens) to support clubs (like the Black Pistons) to regional powers (like the Breed) to multinationals (like the Hells Angels)—the more likely it is that the radicals will be in charge.

And, as pressures to earn a living mount on the very people 1-percenter clubs recruit, more and more of them are radicals, looking for a way to make a good living, turning clubs into gangs.

It's not completely without irony that the original bikers, so the clubs say, were men who couldn't live the humdrum existence of a comfortable life and a house in the suburbs, while now an increasing number of them have joined so that they can afford a comfortable life and a house in the suburbs.

"You could tell who was in it for the money," Mitch, the former Bandido told me. "But even the old guys, after all the talk about bikes was done, were like, fuck you, pay me."

If outlaw motorcycle clubs were ever about freedom, brotherhood and the open road, they are far less so now. Sure, they still ride, but the concept of freedom within a club is absurd. Members, and especially prospects, live intensely regulated lives with a number of rules that would shock an army drill sergeant. Hierarchy is made abundantly clear and strictly enforced. The selling point and rallying call of the clubs is that they don't follow mainstream society's rules, which is in essence true, but they replace them with their own far more draconian ones.

As far as brotherhood is concerned, for the most part, it has vanished. Although bikers party together and say and do all the required things, the mood inside clubhouses these days is anything but jovial and fraternal. The clubs have been betrayed so many times by snitches, often within the club, that trust is in extremely short supply. Claims of brotherhood, like so much else the bikers say, is just that—talk.

I put it to Pete, who is an ex–Hells Angels prospect but still holds the club in some regard, asking him how he could feel as though the other guys in his chapter were his brothers when so many Hells Angels had turned informant over the years.

"Well," he told me, after a long pause, "those snitches weren't true Hells Angels."

Well, they passed their prospecting period and wore their patch. That's true enough for me.

# Glossary of Biker Slang

The following is a list of slang terms used by biker clubs. I've tried not to include those that are obvious, archaic or in common usage outside of clubs.

### 1-percenter.
Member of a club that considers itself to be outlaws.

### 13.
The 13th letter of the alphabet, which, in biker culture, can represent marijuana, methamphetamines, Mongols or mother chapter (although many bikers say it stands for motorcycle).

### 22.
Prison.

## 81.

Hells Angels, from the eighth letter of the alphabet and the first. Other clubs have their own variations on the same scheme.

## 99-percenter.

A motorcyclist who does not claim to be a 1-percenter.

## AFFA.

Angels Forever, Forever Angels, a motto of the Hells Angels. Other clubs use the same phrase, substituting their own club's name, like Mongols Forever, Forever Mongols (MFFM).

## Air condition.

Shoot as many bullets into as possible as a message; usually said of buildings (like clubhouses) but can apply to cars and even people.

## Ape hangers.

High handlebars popular with customizers that can even rise above the rider's head. Riders of bikes equipped with such handlebars are said to resemble apes hanging from branches.

## Associate.

Someone who deals with a motorcycle club but is not a member, prospect or hangaround. Originally used by law enforcement and media, it's been adopted by many clubs, some of which sell "Known Associate" T-shirts.

## Backpack.

A tattoo of the club's logo on a member's back.

**Back warmer.**
A passenger on a motorcycle.

**Bagger.**
A large touring motorcycle with saddlebags.

**Bark-o-lounger.**
A comfortable touring motorcycle, usually Japanese or German. Often looked down upon by 1-percenters as being a compromise between a motorcycle and a car.

**Big Four.**
The four most established 1-percenter clubs—the Hells Angels, Pagan's, Outlaws and Bandidos—that the U.S. Federal Bureau of Investigation and the Criminal Intelligence Service Canada originally designated as "outlaw motorcycle gangs." The number has since grown to seven, but the concept of the Big Four remains.

**Big House Crew.**
Hells Angels term for imprisoned members. Other clubs have other names for the same concept.

**Big slab.**
Long stretch of highway.

**Biker-friendly.**
An adjective used to describe bars, restaurants and other places of business that welcome 1-percenters.

**Brain bucket.**
A helmet.

**Brother.**
A fellow member of a club (not used lightly).

**Cage.**
Car or truck.

**Cager.**
Someone driving a car or a truck.

**Chaps.**
Protective riding gear, usually leather, worn over the legs. Bikers rarely wear them anymore.

**Chapter.**
A group of members of a larger club that share the same clubhouse, name and bylaws, sometimes called a charter.

**Chase vehicle.**
Truck that follows a procession of bikers that carries supplies.

**Chopper.**
Customized motorcycle, especially one that has been stripped to its essentials to lose weight.

**Church.**
A regularly scheduled club meeting.

**Citizen.**
Anyone who is not a member, prospect, hangaround or associate of the club. It's not a compliment.

**Code 55.**

An order to hide all club affiliation in public, often during times of war.

**Colors.**

The patches on a member's vest that identify his club.

**Coupon.**

A speeding ticket.

**Cut.**

A leather or denim jacket fashioned into a vest by cutting off the sleeves. It's on the cut that a biker wears his colors.

**Dome.**

Helmet.

**Donor.**

A motorcycle used to supply parts to repair or customize another motorcycle.

**Dresser.**

A fully equipped touring motorcycle. See *bark-o-lounger*.

**Earned or bought.**

A question 1-percenters frequently ask about other bikers' patches. Earned means that the person in question had to perform some kind of act to receive the patch.

**Flash patch.**

A patch worn by posers with no affiliation to any club.

**Flying colors.**
Wearing the club's insignia (colors).

**Flying low.**
Riding well over the speed limit.

**GBNF.**
Gone but not forgotten; usually applies to deceased members or friends.

**Goof.**
An untrustworthy or otherwise contemptible person.

**Grocery getter.**
A car or truck owned by a biker.

**Hangaround.**
Someone who associates with the club and could be considered for membership.

**Harness bull.**
A uniformed police officer.

**Hog.**
A Harley-Davidson motorcycle; the nickname began in the 1920s when a group of racers called the Farm Boys were successful riding Harleys and had a pig as a mascot. The name was later adopted by the Harley Owners Group, and the Harley-Davidson company changed its stock symbol from HD to HOG in 1983.

**Independent.**
Someone who adopts a biker lifestyle or look but has no club affiliation.

**Ink.**
Tattoos.

**Ink slinger.**
A tattoo artist.

**Keep the dirty side down or keep the shiny side up.**
A common parting phrase for bikers, wishing one another a safe riding experience.

**Kill light.**
Large flashlight carried by many bikers that can be used as a weapon.

**LH & R, L & R or ML & R.**
Love, honor and respect; love and respect; or much love and respect; how bikers and their associates are expected to address one another, especially in writing.

**LE or LEO.**
A law enforcement officer.

**Lid.**
A helmet.

### Mamma.
A woman who is expected to be sexually available to all members of the club (also called honey, cuties and several other terms, depending on club and location).

### MC, M/C or MMC.
A motorcycle club.

### Monkey butt.
Soreness associated with a long ride.

### Mother chapter.
The headquarters of a motorcycle club with multiple chapters. Traditionally, but not always, the club's founding chapter.

### Mud check.
A test, usually an assault, to see if a prospect can act fearlessly under pressure. Mud checks can also apply to members of other clubs by threat of violence. It's an allusion to losing bowel control.

### *Ne conjuge nobiscum.*
Don't screw with us.

### Nomad.
Originally, Nomads were members of a chapter that had no clubhouse, but the term has now evolved to mean a chapter with some distinction.

### Old lady or ol' lady.
A woman whom a biker claims exclusive sexual rights to.

**OMG.**

Outlaw Motorcycle Gang, a law enforcement term clubs never use.

**OTB (over the bars).**

A collision that sends a motorcyclist flying over the handlebars.

**P.**

A chapter president.

**Participate.**

The act of joining a fight on behalf of the club.

**Patch holder.**

A member of a motorcycle club, also called a full patch.

**Patching in.**

The ceremonial presentation of a patch to a prospect elevated to member.

**Patching over.**

When a club gives up its patch in exchange for another, converting to the other club.

**Poker run.**

A game common among bikers in which several contribute money to a pot, then ride to five predetermined spots. At each stop, they receive a playing card. The biker with the best poker hand at the end of the run wins the pot.

## Poser.

Someone who attempts to look like a biker but does not adopt the lifestyle.

## Property of.

A slogan put on jackets, T-shirts or belt buckles provided to an old lady to signify that she is off limits to others sexually.

## Prospect.

A candidate for membership in a motorcycle club, also known as a striker.

## Rat packing.

A gang beating of an individual or greatly outnumbered group.

## Raw.

An adjective used to denote some association with the Hells Angels, derived from their color scheme of red and white.

## RC (riding club).

A motorcycle club with no outlaw pretense.

## Rice, rice burner or rice rocket.

A Japanese motorcycle; considered a derisive term.

## Riding 66.

Riding without colors to prevent provoking other bikers in their territory.

## Riding bitch.

Riding on the back seat of a motorcycle driven by someone else.

**Roader or road name.**

The nickname used within the club (as opposed to legal or government name).

**Rocker.**

Upper and lower, usually arced patches with text and no logos on the backs of cuts.

**RUB (rich urban biker).**

Someone who owns an expensive Harley but rides it rarely.

**RW (red and white).**

The Hells Angels, because of their colors.

**Sit-down.**

A one-on-one meeting, usually over serious business or punishment.

**Six-bends.**

An older type of handlebar, favored by customizers.

**Squid.**

An unskilled or inexperienced motorcyclist.

**Static.**

Perceived harassment from law enforcement.

**Suck to the bulls.**

Act cordially to police.

**Support club.**

A motorcycle club that takes orders from a more established club (law enforcement calls these puppet clubs).

**Supporter.**

A non-member who helps the club, usually financially.

**Three-piece patch.**

The patches on the back of a club member's vest that identifies his club and the territory it claims.

**Trailer queen.**

A customized motorcycle that is frequently shown and rarely ridden.

**Trainable.**

Said of a woman who bikers think could adapt to their lifestyle.

**Trike.**

A three-wheeled motorcycle, often used by older members.

**Turn out.**

Send a woman out to be a prostitute.

**Wings.**

Wing-shaped patches earned, usually through sexual escapades.

**Wrench.**

A mechanic.

# Acknowledgments

All of my books are collaborative efforts, and I would like, of course, to thank the bikers who took the time and risk to actually speak with me. Along with them, I'd like to thank the members of law enforcement, in particular Steve Cook, who helped me understand this other world. I also am grateful for the contributions of reporters around the globe who are in places (and times) I can't be. Of course, I absolutely have to thank the crew at HarperCollins in Canada, including (but not limited to) Jim Gifford, Natalie Meditsky, Kelly Hope, Lesley Fraser, Alan Jones, Zeena Baybayan and Lola Landekic. And finally, I'd like to thank my family—to whom I owe everything.